PRINCIPLE AND
POLICY IN CONTRACT LAW

Principles in contract law, though always presented as derived from the past, have been subject to constant reformulation, thereby, paradoxically, facilitating legal change while simultaneously seeming to preclude it.

Stephen Waddams argues that principle and policy have been mutually interdependent, propositions not usually being called principles unless they have been perceived to lead to just results in particular cases, and as likely to produce results in future cases that accord with common sense, commercial convenience and sound public policy. The influence of policy has been frequent in contract law, but an unmediated appeal to non-legal sources of policy has been constrained by the need to formulate generalizable propositions recognized as legal principles. This interrelation of principle and policy has played an important role in enabling an uncodified system to hold a middle course between a rigid formalism on the one hand and an unconstrained instrumentalism on the other.

STEPHEN WADDAMS is University Professor and the holder of the Goodman/Schipper chair at the Faculty of Law, University of Toronto.

PRINCIPLE AND POLICY IN CONTRACT LAW

Competing or Complementary Concepts?

STEPHEN WADDAMS

CAMBRIDGE
UNIVERSITY PRESS

CAMBRIDGE UNIVERSITY PRESS
Cambridge, New York, Melbourne, Madrid, Cape Town,
Singapore, São Paulo, Delhi, Tokyo, Mexico City

Cambridge University Press
The Edinburgh Building, Cambridge CB2 8RU, UK

Published in the United States of America by Cambridge University Press, New York

www.cambridge.org
Information on this title: www.cambridge.org/9780521196147

First published 2011

Printed in the United Kingdom at the University Press, Cambridge

A catalogue record for this publication is available from the British Library

Library of Congress Cataloguing in Publication data
Waddams, S. M.
Principle and policy in contract law : competing or complementary
concepts? / Stephen Waddams.
p.   cm.
Includes bibliographical references and index.
ISBN 978-0-521-19614-7 (hardback)
1. Contracts – Great Britain.   2. Contracts – Great Britain – Cases.   3. Contracts.   I. Title.
KD1559.W33   2011
346.4202 – dc23   2011023030

ISBN 978-0-521-19614-7 Hardback

CONTENTS

TABLE OF CASES

PREFACE

The words 'principle' and 'policy' have been very common in legal discourse but their meaning is far from self-evident. Principle, in relation to judicial decision-making, has been, almost invariably, a term of approbation; policy has sometimes been used with approval in this context, but has sometimes been contrasted with principle and has carried the implication that policy should be excluded from judicial consideration. Abstract debate conducted in terms of 'what is the true nature of contract law?' has often seemed to run into an impasse, with, on the one side, insistence on rigorous exclusion of all considerations of utility, convenience or policy, and assertion, on the other side, that such are the *only* relevant considerations. A historical perspective suggests that the dichotomy thereby implied is over-simplified. Principle and policy have not been contradictory, in the sense that one must be chosen to the exclusion of the other. On the contrary, they have been mutually interdependent. A proposition has rarely been accorded the name 'principle' unless it has been perceived to lead to a just result in the particular case under consideration, and to be likely to produce results in the future judged to be acceptable: the concept of principle, at the point in time when it has been invoked, has implicitly looked not only to the past, but also to the present and the future, incorporating residual considerations of justice in the individual case as well as what may broadly be called prudential considerations. On the other side, the influence of policy has been very frequent in contract law, but has generally been found appropriate only where a governing proposition can be formulated that is perceived as stable, workable in practice, appropriate for judicial application, that explains past decisions thought to have been rightly decided and that supplies an appropriate guide for the disposition of future instances. When such propositions have been formulated they have been called principles, but they are not thereby emptied of policy. A consequence of this interrelationship is that, from a historical perspective, contract law cannot be reduced to any single explanatory principle, internal or external.

This study seeks to demonstrate these interrelationships by examining the operation of the main features of English contract law (and of systems closely allied to it) as reflected in judicial decisions and in treatises since the eighteenth century: first, the requisites of contractual obligation (intention, agreement and consideration), then the most prominent reasons for non-enforcement of apparent contracts (inequality, mistake and public policy), and then the meaning and scope of the concept of enforcement itself. The perspective is historical, but the recent past is not excluded.

Reference is made at various points to *Principles, Definitions and Model Rules of European Private Law: Draft Common Frame of Reference* published in six volumes with commentary and notes in 2009. This document, in looking towards a harmonization of European legal rules, explores both the common ground and the differences between the common law and civilian legal systems, and among civilian systems. Whatever may turn out to be the official uses that may or may not be made in the future of the *Draft Common Frame of Reference*, it is relevant and useful to one seeking an understanding of what has been meant by principle and policy in English contract law, and the relation between the two concepts. The document shows that, when all aspects of each legal system are taken into account, different conceptual starting points have often led not only to similar results in practice, but to similar legal rules, and that general propositions can often be framed that capture both the underlying principles and the underlying policies of apparently diverse systems.

There is another reason why the *Draft Common Frame of Reference* is of particular relevance. It has been common since the eighteenth century, and earlier, for writers seeking order, simplicity, logic and elegance in English law to look, often somewhat enviously, towards civil law systems. It is necessary therefore, in exploring the meaning that principle has had in English law, to pay some attention to the civil law – or, perhaps it should be said rather, to the *idea* of the civil law entertained by English observers from time to time. A modern, detailed and reliable commentary, comparing European civilian systems with each other and with English and Irish law in respect of specific rules of contract law, and taking into account the practical working of each system, is a very valuable resource. It shows that, on many points, there has been no single 'civilian' principle that resolves all difficulties, and that all European systems, though using different tools, have had to struggle with conflicts and tensions similar to those that have demanded resolution in English law. Though the *Draft Common Frame of Reference* cannot give a full picture of every legal system it refers to, it serves to correct a simple contrast between the common law on the one hand and a supposed monolithic civil law on the other.

I am greatly indebted to past and present students, and to many friends and colleagues who have kindly read drafts and made helpful comments. I am grateful also to the University of Toronto and to the Social Sciences and Humanities Research Council of Canada for research leave and financial support, and to Brendan Donovan, Kevin Dorgan, Adam Hirsh, Julian House and Geoff Read for research assistance.

Stephen Waddams

Introduction: empire of reason, or republic of common sense?

'[I]f LAW be a *science*', said Sir William Jones in 1781, 'and really deserve so sublime a name, it must be founded on principle, and claim an exalted rank in the empire of *reason*'.[1] In *Goodisson* v. *Nunn* (1792), Lord Kenyon, in dealing with the then very controversial question of when contractual covenants were to be considered independent of each other, was faced with old cases apparently requiring a result that he thought was unjust. He was able to find that the old cases had impliedly been overruled by more recent cases:

> The old cases . . . have been accurately stated, but the determinations in them outrage common sense . . . I am glad to find that the old cases have been over-ruled; and that we are now warranted by precedent as well as by principle to say this action cannot be maintained.[2]

These two statements, eleven years apart, invite comparison. Both appeal to 'principle', but the word is used with different connotations. Jones spoke of principle as an essential component of the claim of the law – a claim of which Jones evidently approved – to be a rational science. There is no explicit place in this concept for individual judgment on the part of judges or of writers of what legal rules would, on general considerations, be beneficial or desirable in the interests of justice to the parties to a particular dispute or in the interests of society at large in the future. Lord Kenyon, on the other hand, though he also concludes his statement with an appeal to 'principle', was evidently motivated by a desire to avoid injustice to the defendant in the particular case, and to establish a rule that

---

1 Jones, *An Essay on the Law of Bailments*, 123 (emphasis in original). Every coherent subject of intellectual enquiry was supposed to have principles. See William Paley's very influential *The Principles of Moral and Political Philosophy* (1785), Lord Kames, *Principles of Equity* (1760), and many titles of eighteenth-century books on scientific and religious subjects.
2 *Goodisson* v. *Nunn* (1792) 4 TR 761, 764–5. The old cases cited by counsel were *Carton* v. *Dixon* (1640) Rol Abr 415, *Pordage* v. *Cole* (1669) 1 Wms Saund 319 and *Blackwell* v. *Nash* (1722) 1 Str 535.

would, in his judgment, be beneficial in future cases. Personal opinion was engaged, as is shown by the use of the very strong phrase in reference to the old cases, that they 'outrage common sense', and in the next words, 'I am glad to find that the old cases have been over-ruled'.

The two statements of Jones and Kenyon correspond to a long-lasting and continuing tension in contract law.[3] Jones's concept of law as a rational science planted a seed that found itself in very fertile ground during the succeeding century, and though, in the twentieth century, the claim of law to be a science faded, the claim that it was founded on principle did not. On the other hand, the ideas that the law must give attention to the particular circumstances of cases, and to what rules would be beneficial to society at large have also been prominent and persistent.

The statements of Jones and Kenyon both make implicit reference to the past. The word 'principle' means beginning (*principium*), but the tenor of Jones's statement is that principles are to be discovered by recourse to reason rather than to actual historical research.[4] The statement implies some degree of uncertainty about whether English law, as it stood in 1781, could successfully vindicate its claim to be a science ('*if* it really deserve so sublime a name'). The history of English law was not, on this view, determinative. Principles might be deduced from other sources, and, if they proved inconsistent with the law, it would follow that the law ought to be brought into conformity with principle.

Lord Kenyon also made reference to the past, indeed to several conceptually distinct past periods. 'The old cases', he says, referring to cases decided between 1640 and 1722, 'have been accurately stated'. These were the cases holding that a contracting party was bound to perform his or her side of a contract even if the other party had not performed. This was a perfectly logical position, and could well be said to be founded on reason, and, indeed, on principle. The defendant had made a promise; there was consideration for the promise; therefore the promise was binding, and the defendant was liable for damages for not performing it; if the defendant had any complaint of non-performance against the plaintiff (it might be urged), let him bring a separate counter-action. But the objection to this line of reasoning in Lord Kenyon's mind was that it might lead, and had led, to absurd and unjust consequences, particularly where the claimant

---

3 See *The Golden Victory*, discussed in Chapter 7, p. 188, and Chapter 8, pp. 228–9, below.
4 See D. Ibbetson, 'Sir William Jones and the Nature of Law', in Burrows and Lord Rodger of Earlsferry (eds.), *Mapping the Law*, 619.

was insolvent:[5] the defendant would be compelled to perform in full and would be left without any real prospect of obtaining either the counter-performance, or compensation for its failure. So Lord Kenyon asserted that 'the old cases' (i.e. those of which he disapproved) had been impliedly overruled by more recent decisions, particularly that of Lord Mansfield in *Kingston* v. *Preston* (1773, but not immediately reported).[6] Thus Lord Kenyon rejected the remote past by appealing to the more recent past.

In doing so, he said of the old cases: 'I admit the principle on which they profess to go; but I think that the judges misapplied that principle.' This reference to principle apparently denotes an even earlier time, before the old cases, in which a principle existed that later came to be 'misapplied'. Three past periods seem to be envisaged: a period before the old cases, the era of the old cases, and the era of the more recent cases. But the actual existence or operation of the principle in the first of these periods was not tested and could not be tested by historical evidence, because any contrary evidence would automatically fall under the same condemnation as the old cases. In other words, the principle assigned to the first temporal period, and the first temporal period itself, were notional.

On the face of his reasoning, Lord Kenyon might seem simply to have been applying unchanging principle (i.e. the principle notionally pre-vailing before the old cases and recognized in *Kingston* v. *Preston*). But what purported to be a recognition that the law *had changed* (old cases 'over-ruled', and 'we are *now* warranted') itself constituted a significant contribution to establishing the change in question, and the very power-ful condemnation of the old cases (the determinations in them 'outrage common sense') shows that general considerations of justice (as assessed in 1792), and judgment as to what rule was desirable for the future (also as assessed in 1792) were highly influential. Lord Kenyon himself recog-nized the significance of his own decision, saying, with reference to one of the older cases, 'to the latter part of that judgment I cannot accede. It is our duty, when we see that principles of law have been misapplied in any case, to over-rule it'. His appeal to the past was very different from that of Jones, but the two were alike in one respect: neither was primarily conducting a historical enquiry.

---

5 Lord Kenyon makes express reference to bankruptcy on page 764, and to insolvency on page 765.
6 *Kingston* v. *Preston* (1773), reported as part of counsel's argument in *Jones* v. *Barkley* (1781) 2 Doug 684. The date of publication of the first edition of Douglas's reports was 1783–84 (BL catalogue).

From the perspective of a subsequent observer, the decision in *Goodisson* v. *Nunn* was another significant event, and its date (1792) also significant in every subsequent account of the development of this branch of contract law. *Kingston* v. *Preston*, though decided in 1773, had not been immediately reported. It was reported anonymously in 1776 with Lord Mansfield's opinion given in very forceful and somewhat incoherent, ungrammatical and colloquial terms.[7] In this form it was not easily usable as a precedent. The judgment was reported five years later by a different reporter, who included the names of the parties, and who gave the judgment at greater length and with much greater coherence and elegance, all reported as part of counsel's argument in a different case (1781). This suggests that the change in the law did not occur immediately when *Kingston* v. *Preston* was decided in 1773, but only when it gained general acceptance in the profession, something to which the second reporter both responded and contributed by adopting the artificial device of including Lord Mansfield's judgment, in a form much more usable as a precedent, as part of the report of counsel's argument in the case of 1781.[8]

Corbin, though he approved of the result in *Goodisson* v. *Nunn*, commented at considerable length and with some asperity on Lord Kenyon's reasoning:

> Lord Kenyon, who is not suspected of being a radical judge, recognized that his decision was contra to many decisions of the past, decisions which he said 'outrage common sense'. At the same time he appeared not to believe that the law itself had changed. He said, 'I admit the principle on which they profess to go; but I think that the judges misapplied that principle'. This 'principle' he stated thus: 'Where they are dependent covenants, no action will lie by one party unless he have performed, or offered to perform his covenant'. To state a principle thus, in order to make the law appear to be static, is a mere unconscious juggling with words. It is no better than to say 'when covenants are dependent they are dependent'. The old judges did not misapply that principle, because it is not a principle and cannot be applied. The old rule was that the mutual covenants in a bilateral contract are independent and unconditional unless the parties, by some expression

---

7 As can be seen from the passage quoted in Chapter 4, p. 90, below, Lofft, 194, at 198. The first edition of Lofft was published in 1776. The case was indexed by Lofft not under 'contract' but under 'covenant' in the Table of the Principal Matters (n.p., following p. 814).

8 The background of *Kingston* v. *Preston* is discussed by James Oldham, 'Detecting Non-Fiction: Sleuthing among the Manuscript Case Reports for What was *Really* Said', in Stebbings (ed.), *Law Reporting in Britain*, 133, pointing out the often-overlooked report in Lofft, and giving a manuscript report from the Lincoln's Inn Library of the facts alleged and the arguments on both sides.

of intention, make them otherwise. The new rule, one which Lord Kenyon
was applying but did not state, is that when two performances, mutually
promised in a bilateral contract, are the agreed equivalents of each other,
and by custom or agreement are to be performed simultaneously, the
promises are concurrently conditional and dependent.[9]

Corbin's observations on the use and misuse of principle are of interest in
the context of the present study. It is true that the proposition quoted by
Corbin ('Where they are dependent covenants, no action will lie by one
party unless he have performed') cannot be the principle on which the old
cases were decided. But, on a fair reading of the report, Lord Kenyon did
not say that it was. He said that it was a proposition *conceded even by* the
old cases ('it is admitted in them all'). The principle accepted by Kenyon
on which the old cases 'profess to go' and to which (taking into account
the instant decision) Lord Kenyon could assent, would be a generalized
corollary of the proposition quoted, for example, that mutual covenants
may be dependent or independent according to circumstances. With the
principle so formulated, it would have been very appropriate to say that,
from Kenyon's point of view, it had been misapplied. But Kenyon did not
spell this out, and, later in his judgment, he did refer to the proposition
quoted by Corbin as a principle. By this technique, as Corbin implied,
he tended to smooth over the extent to which the law was changing. As
Corbin also said, Kenyon in fact applied a different proposition ('the new
rule'), which he did not precisely formulate.

As observations on Lord Kenyon in particular, Corbin's comments
might seem harsh, especially as Corbin approved whole-heartedly of the
result. In minimizing the extent of legal change, Kenyon was conforming
to a common judicial convention, and, as we have seen, Kenyon went
further than many judges have done in openly acknowledging that the
law had changed and was changing. But this response does not answer
the question why the claim to continuity with the past should have been
thought so important as to have become conventional. Looking at the
matter more broadly, Corbin's comment draws attention to an important
and continuing feature of legal reasoning in the common law system. Legal
change has been frequent, but has usually been accommodated by the
formulation of a proposition (a 'principle'), presented as already existing,
that can explain past decided cases, that justifies the instant decision and
that is thought to set a beneficial rule for the future. Kenyon's reference
to principle made it easier for his fellow judges to concur. Both, as it

9 *Corbin on Contracts*, s. 656 (1960 edition, vol. 3A, 147–8).

happens, had been counsel, on opposite sides, in *Kingston* v. *Preston*. Buller J (losing counsel in *Kingston*) said 'in truth if there had been no case in opposition to the antient cases, I should not have been afraid of making a precedent, the principle on which our decision is founded being universally admitted in all the cases'.[10] Grose J said that 'there is so much good sense in the later decisions, that it is too much to say that they are not law. There being several precedents in support of our decision, and those being founded in good sense and justice, I think we ought to take advantage of them'.[11] These comments demonstrate the close interrelation of principle, precedent, good sense, justice and policy.

Principle looked not only to the past, but also to the future. The judges in the late-eighteenth century were very conscious of their role in establishing appropriate legal rules for the future. Lord Mansfield is the judge best known as a reformer, but he was not alone in looking to the future: Buller J had, five years before *Goodisson* v. *Nunn*, associated the concept of principle with judicial rule-making, linking both with newly prevailing opinions:

> From that time [i.e. in the past thirty years] we all know that the great study has been to find some certain general principles, which shall be known to all mankind, not only to rule the particular case then under consideration, but to serve as a guide for the future.[12]

Selection of 'a guide for the future' necessarily imports an element of personal judgment, but this cannot be reduced to any single perspective. It would be true to say that one of the effects of the new rule in *Goodisson* v. *Nunn* was to facilitate commercial transactions by making it safer (less costly) for persons to enter into executory agreements. It would not be wholly implausible to suppose that the court was influenced by this consideration, though not expressed in these terms. Lord Kenyon was partly looking to potential future transactions when he said: 'Suppose the purchase money of an estate was £40,000, it would be absurd to say that the purchaser might enforce a conveyance without payment, and compel the seller to have recourse to him, who might be an insolvent person.'[13] But it would not be true to say that the facilitation of future commerce was the sole reason, or the sole justification, for the decision, nor, standing alone, could it have been sufficient to constitute a legal principle. The judges were influenced also by the desire to do justice to

---

10 *Goodisson* v. *Nunn*, note 2, above, at 765.   11 *Ibid.*, at 766.
12 *Lickbarrow* v. *Mason* (1787) 2 TR 63, 73.   13 *Goodisson* v. *Nunn*, note 2, above, at 765.

the particular parties before the court, and to persons who, before the decision, had entered into executory contracts that might subsequently result in disputes. Contract law has continually influenced commercial practice but has also been influenced by it, opposite effects that have been simultaneously contained in and confined by the concept of principle. Simon Deakin has made a similar point in saying that 'the relationship between norms and behaviour is one of mutual interaction, that is to say, of coevolution'.[14]

It became common, from the perspective of the twentieth century, to visualize the nineteenth century as an era in which principles of contract law were established and achieved unchallenged dominance,[15] followed by an era of scepticism, especially in American legal thinking, that, in its extreme forms, rejected all claims to principle in favour of various kinds of policy. In turn these views provoked a reaction in the late-twentieth century with a reassertion of principle, and, in some cases, a complete rejection of the concept of policy as a legitimate judicial consideration. Each of these opposing opinions and counter-opinions, while containing valuable insights, has tended to over-simplify the past, as successful intellectual movements often do in order to persuade readers of the weakness of the view they oppose and of the novelty and merits of the opinions newly offered. But the danger of this process is that, in seeking to correct what are perceived – often rightly – to be the errors of the past, the understanding of the past is itself distorted. It would be ironic if, under the influence of an over-simplified view of twentieth-century American legal realism, we should suppose that earlier legal reasoning really had been governed solely by formalistic considerations, for this would be to ignore the chief insight of the realists, namely, that legal results had, in the past, *not* been solely determined by formal considerations.[16] As we have seen already, elements both of principle and of policy pre-dated the nineteenth century, and, as subsequent chapters will show, both concepts continued to be influential during the nineteenth and twentieth centuries, in tension with each other, but at the same time complementary and mutually interdependent.

---

14 S. Deakin, 'Contracts and Capabilities: an Evolutionary Perspective on the Autonomy-Paternalism Debate' (2010) 3 *Erasmus Law Review* 141, 145.

15 A.W.B. Simpson, 'Innovation in Nineteenth Century Contract Law' (1975) 91 LQR 247, 250, reprinted in Simpson, *Legal Theory and Legal History* (1987) 171, 174.

16 See Tamanaha, *Beyond the Formalist-Realist Divide*, arguing that the history of American law has been severely over-simplified in this regard.

There has been a complex interaction between precedent and principle. Very commonly the two concepts have been invoked together, as in Lord Kenyon's statement 'that we are now warranted by precedent as well as by principle to say this action cannot be maintained'. When invoked together the two concepts almost always point in the same direction, and this is not by chance. On the face of it principle and precedent operate as independent reasons in support of a conclusion (not only is the conclusion supported by principle, but *also* by precedent, or 'authority'). But the concepts have been interrelated: rarely has a proposition been described as a 'principle' unless it could be supported by an appeal to the past; and rarely has a past decision been recognized as an 'authority' unless it has been perceived (at the time of recognition) to be supported by principle. Lord Mansfield said that 'the law of England would be a strange science indeed if it were decided upon precedents only. Precedents serve to illustrate principles ... and these principles run through all the cases',[17] that is, a glossator might fairly add, all the cases that a subsequent court is prepared to recognize as authoritative.

Lord Mansfield said that precedents served to illustrate principles, but he did not say that precedents could be dispensed with as mere surplusage. Precedents may illustrate principles, but the interrelation of the ideas runs in both directions: the principles of English contract law cannot themselves be formulated, or articulated, without reference, express or implicit, to decided cases. Past law ('properly understood', it may be added) has been used both as a source of principle and as evidence of it. Any advocate, addressing Lord Mansfield or his successors on a point of contract law, would have been ill-advised to dispense entirely with reference to past cases, and the same may be said of students seeking to satisfy examiners, and of writers purporting to offer accurate accounts of the law at any point in its history.

This last proposition was put to the test by Henry Colebrooke, who published in 1818 a remarkable book entitled *Treatise on Obligations and Contracts*. Colebrooke, like Sir William Jones, had spent much of his life in India. He was an eminent Sanskrit scholar, had written a digest of Hindu law, and had held office as a judge in India.[18] His book on contract law contains no preface, but it was evidently founded on the assumption that the law of contracts depended on and manifested universal principles, and that a satisfactory account could be offered of

---

17 *Jones v. Randall* (1774) Cowp 37, 39.   18 *Dictionary of National Biography*.

English contract law without reference to English cases. A note stated that 'the preface, with other preliminary and introductory matter, will be published with the second part of the volume', but the second part never appeared. The book is replete with references to Roman law, to the French Civil Code, to Hindu law and to civilian writers, including Barbeyrac, Pufendorf, Godefroy, Grotius, Domat, Pothier and Erskine. Marginal notes refer also to English writers, including Blackstone, Powell, Comyn and Newland, but there is scarcely a reference to any decided English case.

The book was not a success. It was privately printed, and the projected second part never appeared. 'The second portion', his son wrote in his biography, 'was considerably advanced; but he received little encouragement to pursue his task'.[19] His son offered an explanation for the failure, which probably reflected comments made to him and to his father by English lawyers and judges – or rather, the Colebrookes' *perception* of the significance of those comments – that 'the work is perhaps too succinct, and it is wanting in practical examples and illustrations';[20] probably a courteous way of suggesting that a useful account of English law requires reference to decided cases. Colebrooke's approach had the effect of abstracting, or detaching his account from the English law of contracts as a real social phenomenon, and his book, interesting as it is from several perspectives, offered little usable guidance to the actual content of English law in 1818. That such a book was unlikely to succeed in the legal marketplace may seem obvious in retrospect, but to Colebrooke himself it was evidently a severe disappointment. In 1823 he wrote in a private letter:

Nothing has been published by me on the law of Contracts, nor any other topic of jurisprudence, since the treatise on Obligations, which I published a few years ago, as the first part of a larger work. Shortly afterward, while I was preparing the sequel of it for the press, I became involved in [a troublesome lawsuit] ... I have neither health nor spirits for the undertaking, and cannot bring myself to make the effort of setting about it ... I have it in contemplation to prepare a preface and introduction to the Treatise on Obligations, as a single work, and give it with the notice of my final relinquishment of the greater work. The treatise is complete in itself, wanting nothing but a preface.[21]

19 Colebrooke, *Miscellaneous Essays*, 279.   20 *Ibid.*
21 *Ibid.*, 345–6 (letter to Sir Thomas Strange).

Colebrooke's son wrote, of the *Treatise*:

> Testimonies to its value have been repeatedly given by those who have
> followed the same path, and I think it was a matter of some disappointment
> to its author that it was not more generally appreciated. He had devoted to
> the subject much time and attention, and had compressed into the space
> of 250 closely printed pages an elaborate compendium of legal principles
> derived chiefly from the Roman jurisprudence, and had made considerable
> progress in a second volume.[22]

The fate of Colebrooke's book must have been known to every subsequent
nineteenth-century writer on English contract law. Chitty (1826), though
he referred at several points to the civil law, gave priority to English cases.
Addison wrote in his preface (1847) that English contract law was founded
'upon the broad and general principles of universal law' and that 'the law
of contracts may justly indeed be said to be a universal law adapted to all
times and races, and all places and circumstances, being founded upon
those great and fundamental principles of right and wrong deduced from
natural reason which are immutable and eternal'. He went on to compare
English writings on contract law, to their disadvantage, with 'the elaborate
and elegant works of Pothier'.[23] Following such a preface, the reader might
have expected a book like Colebrooke's, but the text of Addison's treatise
turned out to consist almost entirely of discussion of decided English
cases, reflecting in part, no doubt, commercial considerations, but also
the genuine impossibility of attempting to formulate principles of English
contract law without regard to their formulation and reformulation in
past judicial decisions.

   The power of every court to formulate the proper, or true principle
on which earlier cases were decided has often been used to accommodate
changes in the law, as strikingly illustrated a century after *Goodisson* v.
Nunn, by an assertion of Sir George Jessel, one of the most influential
judges of the nineteenth century:

> Now, I have often said, and I repeat it, that the only thing in a Judge's
> decision binding as an authority upon a subsequent Judge is the principle
> upon which the case was decided: but it is not sufficient that the case
> should have been decided on a principle if that principle is not itself a
> right principle, or one not applicable to the case; and it is for a subsequent
> Judge to say whether or not it is a right principle, and, if not, he may
> himself lay down the true principle. In that case the prior decision ceases

---

22 *Ibid.*, 315.   23 Addison, *A Treatise on the Law of Contracts*, preface, iv–v, vii.

to be an authority or guide for any subsequent Judge, for the second Judge who lays down the true principle in effect reverses the decision.[24]

This comment is not compatible with a static view of principle, because it applies also to the second judge who lays down what that judge considers to be the 'true principle', and whose opinion will be, in turn, liable to be 'in effect reversed' by a later judge. Jessel's opinion on this question did not escape contemporary criticism. One commentator wrote that:

> His acute and self-reliant genius when he was on the Bench chafed at the authority of cases decided by other judges, and he had an ingenious plan of eluding them by saying that he was not bound by the similarity of the case but only by the principle, and that there was no principle in them – a practice not conducive to the certainty of the law.[25]

Nevertheless, it is true, as Jessel's comment suggests, that many judges and commentators, in assessing what are the 'true' principles of past cases, have had recourse to general considerations, including fairness, common sense, and considerations of convenience.

The formulation by a court of the true principle underlying prior cases has enabled the subsequent court, without openly rejecting the past, to take into account very general considerations of justice between the parties to the instant dispute, as well as exercising a judgment as to what rule would be desirable for the future. In this way, general considerations of justice and convenience, so far from being opposed to the concept of principle, have been inextricably linked with it. This alignment has been widespread among judges. Lord Kenyon, as Corbin observed, is not suspected of being a radical judge; nor are the two judges who concurred with him.

These tensions were noticed by Henry Maine, who, in his influential and very widely read *Ancient Law* (1861) described them as the source of 'legal fictions', adding that:

> we habitually employ a double language, and entertain, as it would appear, a double and inconsistent set of ideas. When a group of facts come before an English Court for adjudication, the whole course of the discussion between the judge and the advocates assumes that no question is, or can be, raised which will call for the application of any principles but old ones, or of any distinctions but such as have long since been allowed . . . Yet the moment the judgment had been rendered and reported, we slide unconsciously

24 *Osborne to Rowlett* (1880) 13 Ch D 774, 785–6.
25 Foulkes, *A Generation of Judges*, 181.

or unavowedly into a new language and a new train of thought. We now
admit that the new decision *has* modified the law . . . We do not admit that
our tribunals legislate; we imply that they have never legislated; and yet we
maintain that the rules of the English common law, with some assistance
from Chancery and from Parliament, are coextensive with the complicated
interests of modern society.[26]

This line of thinking was absorbed into nineteenth-century English legal
thought. In 1880 a book was published by W.E. Ball, entitled *Principles
of Torts and Contracts*. The book itself has not been influential, but the
opening words of the preface indicate that Maine's general point had been
quite widely assimilated:

In theory, the Common Law of England consists of a system of immemorial
rules, of which the cases decided in her Majesty's Courts are only the
exemplification. Practically, however, it is very well known that to a very
large extent judicial decisions originate that which they profess only to
apply.[27]

Frederick Pollock, in the first edition of his treatise on contracts (1876) did
not doubt that the principles of contract law were to be 'tested by common
sense and convenience'.[28] In 1905 Pollock published an article consisting
of notes on Maine's book, subsequently republished with Maine's text,
and as a separate volume.[29] In commenting on the passage just quoted,
Pollock, while not conceding that the courts 'legislated', showed that
he accepted Maine's principal points, though with some nuances and
modifications of language. Pollock wrote:

No intelligent lawyer would at this day pretend that the decisions of the
Courts do not add to and alter the law. The Courts themselves, in the course
of the reasons given for those decisions, constantly and freely use language admitting that they do so . . . English judges are bound to give
their decisions in conformity with the settled general principles of English
law . . . At the same time . . . it is part of their duty to lay down new rules
if required . . . It is true that at many times the Courts have been over-
anxious to avoid the appearance of novelty; and the shifts to which they
resorted to avoid it have encumbered the Common Law with several of the
fictions which Maine denounces . . . It would be rash to suppose that the
age of legal fictions is wholly past. When 'Ancient Law' was written one

26 Maine, *Ancient Law*, 29–32 (emphasis in original).
27 Ball, *Principles of Torts and Contracts*, preface.   28 See Chapter 2, p. 24, below.
29 Maine, *Ancient Law*, with introduction and notes by Frederick Pollock, 46–7; Pollock,
Introduction and Notes to Sir Henry Maine's "Ancient Law", 8–9. See Duxbury, *Frederick
Pollock and the English Juristic Tradition*, 48–9.

example was quite recent in our Courts, the rule that a man who professes to contract as an agent is deemed to warrant that he has authority from his alleged principal. This is a fiction, but beneficent and elegant, and it is now fully accepted.[30]

Maine's observations appear to anticipate the writings of the twentieth-century American legal realists. His *Ancient Law* was well known to Holmes,[31] who has been called one of 'the great forerunners' of legal realism.[32] One of the reasons why American legal realism had little impact in England may have been that those insights of the realists that were likely to strike an English reader as plausible had, by the end of the nineteenth century, already been absorbed into the mainstream of English legal thinking.[33] Pollock was well aware of the tensions identified by Maine, but he did not feel called upon to resolve them by demanding either the unfettered dominance of considerations of common sense and convenience, or, on the other hand, their eradication.[34]

The mutability of principles was recognized by a twentieth-century judge who commented that 'the common law evolves not merely by breeding new principles but also, when they are fully grown, by burying their progenitors'.[35] Sir John Baker has said that the study of legal history is the study of legal change,[36] and no one doubts that the law has changed, sometimes radically, often in response to perceived social changes. Yet such changes are not easily reconcilable with the idea of eternal and immutable principles, unless expressed in the most general terms. The development of legal principles, it has sometimes been suggested, is for the courts, while their abrogation or radical alteration is for the legislature. But no infallible, or even workable, criterion has emerged for distinguishing in this context

---

30 F. Pollock, 'Notes on Maine's "Ancient Law"' (1905) 21 LQR 165, 172–3, under the heading 'English case-law and fiction'.

31 See *Holmes-Pollock Letters*, 31, 120–1.

32 Duxbury, *Patterns of American Jurisprudence*, 64, though pointing out that Holmes was not a committed anti-formalist. See also 70 ('proto-realist').

33 See also Chapter 2, p. 32, below (Lord Herschell, 1892). Brian Tamanaha, *Beyond the Formalist-Realist Divide*, has shown that views like those of Maine and Pollock were widely held also in nineteenth-century America.

34 On Pollock's relation to jurisprudence, see Duxbury, *Frederick Pollock and the English Juristic Tradition*.

35 Lord Diplock in *Hongkong Fir Shipping Co. Ltd* v. *Kawasaki Kisen Kaisha Ltd* [1962] 2 QB 26, 71.

36 J. Baker, 'Why the History of English Law Has Not Been Finished' (2000) 59 *Cambridge Law Journal* 62, 63.

between development and abrogation, or between incremental and radical change.

On its face, the doctrine of precedent looks to the past, but, when combined with the power of the court to discern a previously unformulated and unrecognized principle, an element of regard to the future is necessarily incorporated. Judges have often made explicit reference to the fact that their decision will lay down a rule for the future,[37] an enterprise that necessitates an evaluation of whether or not the contemplated rule is likely to conform to justice, good sense, convenience and the general benefit.

Such considerations have often been called considerations of policy, but usage has not been precise. Peter Cane has written that 'the word "policy" is one of the most under-analysed terms in the modern legal lexicon'.[38] Neil MacCormick wrote, similarly, that:

> 'Policy' has become a hideously inexact word in legal discourse, but if we wish to use it with any exactitude at all, we had better use it as denoting those courses of action adopted by Courts as securing or tending to secure states of affairs conceived to be desirable.[39]

This definition is wide enough to include general considerations of justice between the parties to a particular dispute,[40] as well as considerations of social welfare in the future. The phrases 'common sense' and 'good sense', and the words 'convenience', 'fairness', 'equity' and 'justice' have often, expressly or by implication, been used to include both kinds of consideration.

'It is somewhat curious', Pollock told his readers in 1876, 'that no such thing as a satisfactory definition of Contract is to be found in any of our books.'[41] Similar statements have been made in the twentieth century, and in the twenty-first. James Gordley wrote (1991) that 'today we have no generally recognized theory of contract',[42] and Stephen Smith has said (2004) 'there is no single theory of contract that is universally accepted; rather there exists a variety of mutually exclusive theories, with few elements in common'.[43] Despite much writing on contract theory no consensus has

37 E.g. *Earl of Macclesfield* v. *Fitton* (1683) 1 Vern 168, 169, where the judge 'declared his opinion in this case, and also as a rule in all other cases of this nature, for the future'.
38 P. Cane, 'Another Failed Sterilisation' (2004) 120 *Law Quarterly Review* 189, 191.
39 MacCormick, *Legal Reasoning and Legal Theory*, 263.
40 See A. Robertson, 'Constraints on Policy-based Reasoning', in Robertson and Tang Hang Wu (eds.), *The Goals of Private Law*, 261, 265.
41 Pollock, *Principles of Contract*, 1st edn., 1 (opening words of text).
42 Gordley, *The Philosophical Origins of Modern Contract Doctrine*, 230.
43 Smith, *Contract Theory*, viii.

emerged on a single explanation or justification for contractual liability, nor is there any agreed definition. A number of ideas have been in play, including those of will, autonomy, mutual consent, agreement, promise, bargain, reliance, expectation, entitlement, utility, efficiency, convenience, common sense, good faith and public policy. Abstract debate in terms of 'what is the true nature of contract law?' has failed to reach a resolution, with insistence on one side on rigorous exclusion of all considerations of utility, convenience or policy, and assertion on the other side that such are the *only* relevant considerations. A historical enquiry tends to show that the truth has been both more complex and more interesting than what is suggested by this sharp dichotomy.

An unpublished work entitled *Of Contracts*, written early in the eighteenth century by Jeffrey Gilbert, later Chief Baron of the Exchequer, though not offering a comprehensive account of the subject, discussed particular aspects of contract law, notably the doctrine of consideration, at length.[44] In 1737 the anonymously published *A Treatise of Equity*, attributed to Henry Ballow, pointed out that equity, in contrast to the common law, implicitly recognized, by its jurisdiction to decree specific performance, that contracts were a source of obligations.[45] The fact that this point was made in a treatise on *equity*, and that it was contrasted with the common law, is revealing of prevailing contemporary legal attitudes to the subject.

Blackstone's *Commentaries on the Laws of England* (1765–9) allowed no explicit place to contracts as a distinct part of English law.[46] Blackstone likened his work to a map, writing that 'an academical expounder of the laws... should consider his course as a general map of the law, marking out the shape of the country, its connexions and boundaries, its greater divisions and principal cities'.[47] Blackstone's map gave no definite place to contract law, though he mentioned contracts in several places. A definition of contract was offered in book 2 (rights of things) as part of a chapter (entitled 'Of title by gift, grant, and contract') dealing with methods of acquiring rights to property.[48] In book 1 (rights of persons) contracts were mentioned as part of the law of master and servant, and of husband and wife, and in book 3 (private wrongs) assumpsit was mentioned as providing a remedy for breaches of promises, considered as wrongs. In respect of husband and wife, Blackstone wrote that 'our

44 Written about 1710, British Library, Hargrave, 265.
45 Ballow, *A Treatise of Equity*, 4–5.
46 Blackstone, *Commentaries on the Laws of England*.   47 *Ibid.*, vol. 1, 35.
48 *Ibid.*, vol. 2, c. 30. Hale had also, about a century earlier, listed contract as a means of acquiring property, *The Analysis of the Law*, 79.

law considers marriage in no other light than as a civil contract'.[49] This assertion is startling at first sight – so much so that, when quoted, it has usually been to jocular or facetious effect – for the differences, in Blackstone's time, between marriage and contracts were so many and so obvious that they scarcely require enumeration. But the question, for present purposes, is not what the assertion reveals about Blackstone's view of marriage, but what it reveals about his view of contracts. The comment shows that Blackstone did not visualize contracts as a body of controlling principles from which legal obligations were derived: if he had thought in those terms he would have given contract law a place on his map, and a different place from matrimonial law. It was not that Blackstone thought contracts unimportant – he refers to marriage as 'the most important contract of any'[50] – and contracts were an important means of transferring property rights, and an important aspect of the law of private wrongs. But he did not think of legal issues as 'part of' an independently existing contract law. It would be more accurate to say that he thought of contracts as 'part of' several different areas of the law – a means of effecting various different legal consequences (marriage, employment, transfer of property) – and hence to be found in several different places on his map.

Blackstone's treatment of contracts was noted as a serious deficiency (as it came to be seen in the nineteenth century) by Joseph Chitty, who published an edition of the *Commentaries* in 1826:

> It will be remarked that the observations of the learned Commentator in the text, contain but a small part of the law of contracts, which has so greatly increased since his work was published. The more ancient books and present abridgements are very defective in information upon this subject, and the student must therefore resort to the modern elementary works.[51]

On Blackstone's treatment of assumpsit in book 3, Chitty wrote even more forcefully:

> This subject is not so well arranged or considered, as most parts of this work. Indeed it is observable, that contracts and the remedies for the infraction of them, are by no means, in any part of this work, well discussed. In the second volume, contracts are cursorily considered, as one of the means by which a title to personal property may be acquired. In the

49 Blackstone, *Commentaries on the Laws of England*, vol. 1, 433.   50 *Ibid.*, 436.
51 Joseph Chitty (the elder) (ed.), *Commentaries on the Laws of England by the late Sir W. Blackstone*, 442 note.

present volume [book 3], which professes to describe injuries and their remedies in general, it is inexpedient to consider the nature of contracts more particularly.[52]

The first published treatise on English contract law (Powell, 1790 – one of the 'modern elementary' works mentioned by Chitty) had given conceptual unity to the subject,[53] and this was extended by the appearance in English translation (1806) of Pothier's treatise on obligations,[54] and by at least twelve nineteenth-century English books.[55] The demarcation of contract law had far-reaching implications, including a division between property and obligations, and divisions among various classes of obligations. Some writers also implied, like Colebrooke, and Addison in his preface, that English contract law was a manifestation of a universal order.

By far the most influential of the later nineteenth-century English contract books were those of Frederick Pollock (1876)[56] and William Anson (1879).[57] The titles of both books commenced with the word 'Principles'. Neither Pollock nor Anson spoke in such strong terms as Addison, but they nevertheless implied, both by the titles to their books and by remarks addressed to their readers, that there were certain propositions about English contract law, deserving of the name 'principles', that had some sort of special status as primary, fundamental or indisputable, or that constituted a source from which rules used to determine particular cases were derived, and that those propositions could be identified and formulated.

But if we ask precisely what *were* these principles, the answer proves surprisingly elusive.[58] The word has been used in many different senses, the meaning varying according to what is implicitly contrasted with it (principle and rule, principle and policy, principle and precedent, principle and authority, principle and pragmatism, principle and practice, principle and convenience, principle and utility, general principle and particular rule, general principle and particular case); on a controversial

---

52 *Ibid.*, vol. 3, 154 note. The first edition of his son's treatise on contracts (Joseph Chitty, the younger) appeared in the same year.
53 Powell, *Essay Upon the Law of Contracts and Agreements.*
54 Pothier, *A Treatise on the Law of Obligations, or* Contracts, translated W.D. Evans. The words 'treatise' and 'contracts' are in (contrasting) italics on the title page, showing that Evans regarded the work as primarily a treatise on the law of contracts.
55 See Simpson, 'Innovation in Nineteenth Century Contract Law', note 15, above.
56 Pollock, *Principles of Contract*, 1st edn.   57 Anson, *Principles*, 1st edn.
58 See S. Waddams, 'What *Were* the Principles of Nineteenth-century Contract Law?', in Lewis, Brand and Mitchell (eds.), *Law in the City*, 305, on which parts of this and the next chapter are based.

legal question two or more conflicting principles can usually – perhaps always – be identified; principles may be stated and restated at an infinite number of levels of generality, and commonly the word has been used to mean no more than a reason or rule framed at a higher level of generality than another; sometimes a principle has meant more than a rule – a rule that is absolutely stringent, but at other times the word has signified something less than a rule – an objective desirable in general terms but liable to be outweighed by countervailing considerations; whenever it is said, as it often is, that two principles come into conflict, one or both of them are liable to be outweighed by countervailing considerations. Often the meaning of the word merges with the idea of 'maxim'.[59] The word has a rhetorical component, and very commonly it has signified a reasoned, or a well-reasoned legal argument; often it has meant little more than a legal rule, or a reason in support of a rule, that the writer or speaker considers persuasive, legitimate, or satisfactory – and this partly explains why unprincipled reasons are never recognized as having permanently prevailed, and why those reasons that have prevailed have tended to be called principles.

Principle has been a conveniently ambiguous concept, signifying, on the one hand, a proposition to be *derived from* past decisions and, on the other hand, a proposition to be *applied to* past decisions as a criterion of their validity and authenticity. Thus, the concept of principle has succeeded in combining elements of inductive with deductive logic, elements of 'bottom-up' with 'top-down' reasoning,[60] and elements of formalism with consequentialism.

Principle cannot be fully distinguished from legal rules.[61] Every principle, when applied to a particular case, generates a proposition that can be formulated as a legal rule. But this rule, when in its turn applied to a more particular instance, is itself apt to be called a principle. Rules have constantly been revised as new instances have arisen that cannot be accommodated by the rule as previously formulated. What is supposed to be the underlying reason for the rule, often called 'the principle', or 'the true principle', is then formulated in such a way as to produce a

59 Early uses of the concepts of principle and maxim are discussed by A.W.B. Simpson, 'The Rise and Fall of the Legal Treatise' (1981) 48 *University of Chicago Law Review* 632, reprinted in *Legal Theory and Legal History*, 273, at 282–5.
60 K. Mason, 'Do Top-down and Bottom-up Reasoning Ever Meet?' in Bant and Harding (eds.), *Exploring Private Law*, 19.
61 See Hart, *The Concept of Law*, 2nd edn, 261; Duxbury, *Frederick Pollock and the English Juristic Tradition*, 249.

satisfactory result in the instant case, and so as to produce satisfactory results in future cases, and the rule is reformulated accordingly. There is flexibility in this process, but, provided it does not reverse itself too often, it has proved to be compatible with a considerable degree of stability.

Principles are often – perhaps usually – themselves exceptions to other principles. Consider the following series of propositions: contracts should be enforced; however, the normal remedy for breach of contract is only money damages; however, if damages are inadequate specific performance may be decreed; however, specific performance will never be ordered for the performance of personal services; however, an injunction may be issued to restrain a person from breaking a negative covenant; however, such an injunction will never be issued if its practical effect is to compel specific performance. Or, to take another series, agreements should be enforced; however, not unless there is consideration, and performance of a pre-existing duty is not consideration; however, performance of a pre-existing duty may be consideration if it confers a practical benefit on the promisor; however if the promise has been obtained by duress it is not enforceable. Each of these propositions has been called a principle, but they are not parallel with each other, and each shows the preceding proposition, or set of propositions, to have been incomplete.

Principles, when approved, have often been called 'first principles', general principles', 'elementary principles', 'fundamental principles', 'true principles', 'ruling principles', 'basic principles', 'governing principles', 'controlling principles', 'established principles', 'underlying principles' or 'overriding principles'. But it is by no means clear how these adjectives differ, if at all, from each other, or how they qualify or add to the meaning, if they do, of 'principles'.

In *Principles, Definitions and Model Rules of European Private Law: Draft Common Frame of Reference*, an international document published in 2009 designed to foster the harmonization of European private law, the authors identify four principles that 'underlie' the whole project. These are said to be freedom, security, justice and efficiency.[62] The authors go on to say that 'it is characteristic of principles such as those discussed that they conflict with each other'.[63] They also point out that 'the principles overlap', adding that 'many of the rules which are designed to ensure genuine freedom of contract can also be explained in terms of contractual justice'.[64] The

---

62 *Principles, Definitions and Model Rules of European Private Law: Draft Common Frame of Reference*, vol. 1, 37; Outline Edition, 60.
63 *Ibid.*   64 *Ibid.*, Outline Edition, 61; Full Edition, vol. 1, 38.

authors further seek to distinguish between 'underlying' principles (the four just mentioned) and 'overriding' principles 'of a high political nature', adding that 'the two categories overlap'.[65] These comments illustrate the continuing difficulty in modern times of attaching a single or simple meaning to the concept of principle, and of distinguishing it from policy. Any of the many objectives identified by the *Draft Common Frame of Reference* as principles might well be called policies. Principles, as well as policies, are apt to conflict with each other.

Twentieth-century legal theorists have expressed differing views on the relation between policy and principle. Ronald Dworkin contrasted the two concepts, suggesting that principle only, and not policy, belonged properly to the judicial sphere.[66] On the other hand Neil MacCormick wrote that 'the spheres of principle and policy are not distinct and mutually opposed, but irretrievably interlocking'.[67] These assertions, though apparently to opposite effect, might well be reconciled by a full examination of the meaning that each writer gave to the words principle and policy, in the light of the context and of their other writings. This is not a task that can be undertaken here. Dworkin's usage was, no doubt, effective and appropriate for his purpose, but it is evident from his writings that he did not intend to exclude from the concept of principle, as he understood it, general considerations of morality, the long-term good of society, and right judgment[68] – considerations which others, including MacCormick, would have called policy. Few writers could claim to have been rigorously consistent in their uses of these two words.

A historical study cannot show which linguistic usage is superior, or which approach would be preferable in an ideal legal system. But it can show that, over a considerable period of time in English contract law

---

65 *Ibid.*, Outline Edition, Introduction, para. 16, at 14; Full Edition, vol. 1, 8.

66 Dworkin, *Taking Rights Seriously*.

67 MacCormick, *Legal Reasoning and Legal Theory*, 263. See also, to similar effect, Bell, *Policy Arguments in Judicial Decisions*, 6, 213, 247.

68 The New York case of *Riggs* v. *Palmer* 115 NY 506 (1889), refusing to apply a statute that on its face entitled a murderer to inherit from his victim, was given as a prime example of the application of principle (Dworkin, *Taking Rights Seriously*, 23), but the principle applied by the court (that no one should profit by his or her own wrong) was clearly influenced by considerations of morality and the public interest. In *Justice in Robes*, at 270, Dworkin showed that he was well aware of the changes over time in contract law reflecting, as he said, 'different emphases on the relative importance of freedom of contract, efficiency in commerce, imposing fairness on commercial practice, and protecting people with inadequate bargaining power'. See also Duxbury, *Frederick Pollock and the English Juristic Tradition*, 165, contrasting the uses of 'principle' by Pollock and Dworkin.

and in the law of related jurisdictions, the formulation of principles, in the sense of generalized justifying propositions, has very commonly been influenced by considerations of convenience, common sense, a general sense of what is just in the particular case and a judgment of what is desirable for the future. Looking at the matter from the other side, the concept of principle has also imposed restraint. The freedom of judges to do what seems just in a particular case or to pursue objectives that they consider socially desirable has been constrained by the need to formulate generalized justifying propositions, capable of sufficient precision to be appropriate for judicial application, and likely to ensure a measure of regularity, predictability and stability. When a principle has been perceived to have consequences that are unjust or inconvenient, the countervailing considerations have often been cast in the form of a proposition that itself has been called a principle, but these considerations are not thereby emptied of policy. In these senses, principle and policy have been mutually interdependent. This interdependence goes far to show why the history of contract law has not been reducible to any single explanatory concept or principle, internal or external: considerations in opposition to any proposed principle, dependent in part on the general exercise of judgment, can themselves be formulated as countervailing principles. The questions raised here will be explored in the following chapters, first in relation to the requisites of contractual obligation (intention, agreement and consideration), secondly in relation to the main reasons, or sets of reasons, for withholding enforcement of contracts (inequality, mistake and public policy), and finally in relation to the meaning and scope of the concept of enforcement itself.

2

Intention, will and agreement

Almost all the nineteenth-century writers on contract law took, as their conceptual point of departure, the idea of agreement, or mutual assent. This idea, often dignified by the Latin phrase *consensus ad idem* (agreement to the same thing), was usually called a principle. But even a cursory examination of English law, as it actually worked in practice, shows that proof of mutual assent, in the ordinary sense of those words, was not a requirement for the imposition of contractual obligation. One eminent legal historian has gone so far, indeed, as to suggest that the 'mysterious phenomenon of agreement' was an 'organizing myth' that encouraged 'the suspension of disbelief'.[1]

Let us consider, as an illustrative example, the simple question of whether an offer could be effectively withdrawn without communication to the offeree. If there were a stringent principle that contractual obligation depended on intention, or on mutual consent, or concurrence of wills, it would follow that there ought to be no liability where the offeror had demonstrably intended to withdraw the offer before acceptance. A much-discussed test case was that of an offer sent by mail, with a subsequent retraction also sent by mail; the legal issue was whether the offeror was bound if the offeree purported to accept the offer without notice of the offeror's change of mind. On this issue Pothier, the great French jurist, had expressly said that there could be no contractual liability because 'there is not that consent, or concurrence of . . . wills, which is necessary to constitute the contract of sale'. This was a legal conclusion derived from a principle, and one at a very high level, namely mutual consent. But Pothier, aware of the inconvenient and potentially unjust consequences of this conclusion, added that, although there could be no *contractual* liability, an equivalent liability could be imposed on the offeror on a non-contractual basis: 'this obligation results from that rule

---

1 A.W.B. Simpson, 'Raffles v. Wichelhaus and Busch' in Simpson, *Leading Cases in the Common Law*, 156–7.

of equity (*équité*) that no person <u>should suffer</u> for the act of another: *nemo ex alterius facto praegravari debet*.[2] By these means Pothier preserved the principle (no *contractual* liability without consent), while suggesting a solution that protected the expectation of the offeree and answered to his and his readers' instinctive sense of fairness.

Whatever the merits of Pothier's approach as a matter of French law, it could not, despite Pothier's very high reputation in England, appeal to the nineteenth-century English mind. English equity could not have imposed such a liability as Pothier contemplated, and there was no tort known to the common law that fitted the facts. Moreover the Latin maxim relied on by Pothier (no one shall suffer by the act of another) would have struck a nineteenth-century English lawyer as far too wide. The refusal to impose contractual liability, followed by the imposition of a non-contractual liability equivalent to – or even more extensive than – what the contractual liability would have been had it existed, appeared to the English legal mind to be fictitious, convoluted, and potentially unjust.

Pothier's approach to this question was accepted by Chitty (1834) but Chitty omitted altogether any discussion of Pothier's suggestion of non-contractual liability.[3] Leake (1867) expressly differed from Pothier and Chitty:

> The passage from Pothier [quoted above] has been cited by some writers as in accordance with English law [referring to Chitty] but it is here submitted that it is inconsistent with the decisions above cited and contrary to principle in regarding as the test of agreement abstract intentions of the parties instead of the <u>expression of intention communicated between</u> them.[4]

It is notable that Leake rejected Pothier's view, based on the actual intention of the parties, as 'abstract', invoking the concept of 'principle' in support of his own contrary opinion. Benjamin in his second edition (1873) followed Leake's opinion and subjected Pothier's reasoning to severe criticism, writing that 'it is impossible to read the reasoning of this eminent jurist in the passages just cited, without feeling that it fails to meet the difficulties of the case. He places the proposer in the instances suggested under all, and more than all, the obligations of a purchaser, while insisting that he has made no purchase'.[5] Pollock (1876) also rejected

2 Pothier, *Treatise on the Contract of Sale*, 18.
3 Chitty, *A Treatise on the Law of Contracts*, 2nd edn, 12–13.
4 Leake, *The Elements of the Law of Contracts*, 20 note.
5 Benjamin, *A Treatise on the Law of Sale*, 2nd edn, 58.

Pothier's approach. Pollock commented on 'the manifestly unjust consequences' of permitting the offeror to retract after reliance by the offeree,
and rejected Pothier's non-contractual solution, calling it 'cumbrous and
inelegant'. Pollock then asserted that 'the declaration of an *animus con-
trahendi* [intention of contracting] . . . when once made must be regarded
as continuing so long as no revocation of it is communicated to the other
party. A revocation not communicated is in point of law no revocation
at all'. Pollock then added: 'These principles, it seems to us, are entirely
right if tested by common sense and convenience, and are in accordance
with the authorities of the common law when rightly understood.'[6]

This last sentence deserves a little attention. Pollock, having set out
two rather specific propositions ('an offeror's declaration of intention
must be regarded as continuing', and 'a revocation not communicated
is no revocation') evidently newly formulated by himself to support the
conclusion he favoured on the point in issue, then called these propositions principles ('these principles'), while Pothier's idea of concurrence
of wills, which might more naturally be considered a general or fundamental principle, but the apparent consequences of which Pollock was in
the process of rejecting, was not, in this particular passage, called a 'principle'. Writers have rarely designated lines of reasoning that they are in
the course of rejecting as 'principles'. Pollock was conscious of expressing
a personal opinion, and was somewhat embarrassed by this, as is shown
by his awkward use of the editorial plural ('it seems to us'). His opinion,
moreover, was plainly based primarily on general considerations of justice
and policy ('common sense and convenience', and avoidance of 'manifest
injustice'). It is significant that principles were to be 'tested' by common
sense and convenience: in case of conflict, it would seem, it was the principles (or apparent principles) that must give way. These considerations
were then made to conform to the convention within which Pollock was
writing, that of a barrister indirectly addressing an English judge on the
actual state of English law ('in accordance with the authorities of the
common law'). This last phrase sounds impressive but, since no directly
relevant authorities were mentioned, it can claim little independent substance. Moreover, it is evident from the next three words ('when rightly
understood') that the search for authorities was neither a technical nor
primarily a historical enquiry. 'Right understanding' impliedly imported
the author's own opinion, primarily informed, as the context shows, by
considerations of common sense, convenience and avoidance of injustice.

6 Pollock, *Principles of Contract*, 1st edn, 11.

It is tempting to suppose that a choice must be made between two views: either Pollock reached his conclusion on the basis of pure principle, or, on the other hand, he must have reached it on the basis of common sense, convenience and justice, the appeal to principle being mere form. But this dichotomy tends to over-simplification. To call form in legal reasoning 'mere form' is to underestimate its historical significance, and is to overlook the possibility that Pollock was influenced *both* by the argument of principle *and* by the argument of convenience, common sense and justice. That Pollock, like most other legal writers, including judges, found it necessary to cast his argument in the form of deduction of results from previously existing principles may not by any means be a trivial or accidental aspect of legal reasoning.

Pollock's approach to this question was rewarded with almost immediate success, for, in 1880, in *Byrne* v. *van Tienhoven*, Mr Justice Lindley, to whom, incidentally, Pollock's book had been dedicated, expressly rejected Pothier's view and adopted Pollock's, calling his book the 'excellent work on *Principles of Contract*', and showing none of the later reluctance of English judges to cite modern authors (he referred also to Leake and Benjamin).[7] Lindley J went on 'to point out the extreme injustice and inconvenience which any other conclusion would produce', adding that 'both legal principles and practical convenience require that a person who has accepted an offer not known to him to have been revoked shall be in a position safely to act upon the footing that the offer and acceptance constitute a contract binding on both parties'. Shortly afterwards, in *Stevenson* v. *McLean*,[8] Lindley J was expressly followed on this point by another judge.

'Principle' has often been contrasted with 'policy' and in some contexts the contrast is apt, but in this instance it is evident that principle and policy were not opposed, either in Pollock's mind or in Lindley's. Indeed, it was the flexibility of the concept of principle that enabled Pollock to give expression to his views on justice, protection of reliance, convenience and common sense – considerations often summarized as 'policy' – while adhering to the conventional framework within which he was writing. Lindley J also perceived harmony, not opposition, in the concepts of legal principles, practical convenience and protection of the promisee's reasonable expectation.

---

7 *Byrne & Co.* v. *Leon van Tienhoven & Co.* (1880) 5 CPD 344 (March 6).
8 (1880) 5 QBD 357 (Lush J, May 25).

In his third edition (1881), Pollock was able to cite the two judicial decisions of 1880 as authoritatively settling the question, omitting the awkward phrasing of his first edition, and substituting this much smoother
formulation: 'In the earlier editions of this book the question was treated
as practically settled, but only in 1880 was it actually decided ... [citing
the two cases].'[9] Thus the mutual interaction between writer and judge
enabled each to disclaim an unmediated appeal to such very general considerations as common sense, convenience and justice. Pollock, though
influenced, as we have seen, by these considerations, relied also, in his first
edition, on the assertion that his proposed principles were 'in accordance
with the authorities of the common law when rightly understood'. Pollock's conclusion, together with Leake's and Benjamin's, in turn enabled
the judges to rest their decisions not simply on their own opinion of what
was just and convenient, but on a previously recognized principle, and,
from the third edition, Pollock, in turn again, was able to omit his own
opinion with the supporting arguments and inform his readers that the
law on the point had now been satisfactorily settled.

A contrast often made is between contract law as giving effect to the
will of the promisor and contract law as protecting the reliance, or the
expectation of the promisee. It will be seen from this example that both
ideas were present in Pollock's treatment of the question in issue, and that
they were interrelated. Pollock spoke of the promisor's *animus contra-
hendi* (intention of contracting), suggesting the primary importance of
intention, but he said that intention 'must be regarded as continuing' until
notice of revocation had been given. This is a fictitious reason, because, on
the assumed facts, it is known with certainty that the promisor's intention
does *not* continue. Pollock evidently thought the fiction to be necessary,
and his principal reason was the 'manifest injustice' that would otherwise
ensue if the offeree had acted on the offer without notice of its retraction, that is to say, the need to protect the offeree's reasonable reliance, or
expectation of what promise had been made.

Meanwhile Anson, in his first edition (1879) had taken a different view
of revocation of offers. Anson, while conceding that a rule protecting
the offeree was needed in cases of correspondence between parties at a
distance, asserted that 'when the parties are in immediate communication a proposal may be revoked without notice to the person to whom
it is made', and added a footnote expressly critical of Pollock's view:
'Mr Pollock, in his work on Contract, p. 10, lays it down that "a proposal

9 Pollock, *Principles of Contract*, 3rd edn, 25–6.

is revoked only when the intention to revoke it is communicated to the other party". We venture however to think that this rule must be received with the limitations suggested by the cases cited in the text.'[10]

Pollock's reply (included in his third edition) pointed out that the headnote to one of these cases, *Dickinson* v. *Dodds*, was misleading insofar as it implied that the court decided that an offer could be effectively withdrawn without communication to the offeree. Pollock gave similarly short shrift to Anson's treatment of the other case cited, *Cooke* v. *Oxley*, being enabled, by the decisions of 1880, summarily to foreclose further discussion: 'It is right to add that *Cooke* v. *Oxley* may be so read as to support the opinion that a tacit revocation need not be communicated at all. But the apparent inference to this effect is expressly rejected in *Stevenson* v. *McLean*, and therefore need not be discussed here.' He added a footnote (omitted in later editions), emphasizing, perhaps rather unkindly, Anson's evident reliance on the erroneous headnote: 'Sir W. R. Anson, writing in 1879, and troubled by this construction of *Cooke* v. *Oxley*, and apparently accepting the head-note in *Dickinson* v. *Dodds*, makes a distinction between cases "where the parties are in immediate communication" and where they "communicate by correspondence". In the light of the latest authorities no such expedient seems necessary.'[11] For Anson, *Cooke* v. *Oxley* was a useful illustration of a simple and fundamental principle (contracts require mutual assent), but Pollock, while conceding that the case could be read to support that view, thought that it must yield to another proposition, itself now elevated to the status of principle (revocation requires communication). For Anson, fidelity to principle lay in maintaining a general rule that actual concurrent intention was needed, and confining the admitted exception (where parties corresponded at a distance) to its minimum scope. The price of this approach was an awkward and anomalous distinction between parties in immediate communication and parties corresponding at a distance. Pollock was able to cut this Gordian knot by formulating and asserting as the dominant principle the proposition that revocation requires communication. This produced a convenient result but the price here was to undercut the principle that contractual obligation depended on mutual

---

10 Anson, *Principles*, 1st edn, 17 note. The cases referred to were *Cooke* v. *Oxley* (1790) 3 TR 653, which had generally been read to support Anson's view, and *Dickinson* v. *Dodds* (1876) 2 Ch Div 463, which might be, but need not be, so read. The reasoning in *Cooke* v. *Oxley* was very brief, and both cases were complicated by the issue of whether a promise made, without consideration, to keep an offer open was binding.

11 Pollock, *Principles of Contract*, 3rd edn, 29.

assent, and to demonstrate the malleability of the concept of principle itself. Anson was still arguing the point in his fifth edition (1888),[12] but substantially conceded to Pollock in the sixth (1891).[13]

Thus it came to be established as a matter of English law, and not subsequently doubted, that the 'true principle' applicable in these circumstances was that retraction of an offer requires communication to the offeree. But what kind of enquiry established this truth and this principle? It is evident in the particular instance that this was not a principle discoverable by logic, or by historical research, or by anything analogous to enquiries engaged in by natural scientists. It required argument based, in part, on personal judgment, guided by very general considerations of convenience, justice and common sense, and accurate prediction by academic writers of what would be acceptable to English judges.

The resolution of this issue might naturally be summarized by saying that the principle (concurrent intention required for contractual obligation) was subject to an exception. But this way of putting the matter raises further questions. Is the exception to be framed narrowly (retraction of offers requires communication), or broadly (the reasonable expectation of the offeree is to be protected)? Is the exception itself based on a competing principle, and is the number of potential exceptions and competing principles indeterminate? Is the resolution of conflicts between competing principles itself based on any principle that can be articulated? These questions are partly conceptual, partly logical and partly linguistic. They are not questions about the past, and they cannot be answered by historical evidence.

Did English contract law in 1880 depend on concurrence of intention? This *is* a question about the past, and it can be answered by historical evidence. The answer is, no. The issue of retraction of offers is only one example of imposition of liability contrary to the intention of the promisor. It was also the law at this date that a promisor might be bound by a contractual term he or she never intended to agree to, if the promisee reasonably thought that he or she had agreed to it; that words in documents were to be construed according to the meaning reasonably ascribed to them by the promisee, not the meaning intended by the promisor; and contracts made by an agent acting within his apparent authority were binding on the principal even though the agent had acted in plain defiance of explicit instructions.[14] All these rules tended to protect the reasonable

---

12 Anson, *Principles*, 5th edn, 33.   13 Anson, *Principles*, 6th edn, 34.
14 *Summers* v. *Solomon* (1857) 7 E & B 879, 884–5 (Coleridge J).

expectation of the promisee – that is, the reasonable expectation of what had been promised – where it conflicted with the actual intention of the other party.

Where contractual negotiations were conducted by correspondence, protection of the offeree's interest required not only a rule that revocation of offers was ineffective unless communicated, but the further rule that an acceptance, when dispatched, was effective immediately, for, without such a rule, the offeree would run the risk of receiving notice of revocation while the message of acceptance was in transit. In a case of 1818 the defendant had offered to sell wool, but, having misdirected the offer and not receiving an answer when expected, had sold the wool to a third party. It was argued that the defendant could not be bound by a contract until he knew of its existence. But to this principled argument the court gave a pragmatic answer:

> If that were so, no contract could ever be completed by post. For if the defendants were not bound by their offer when accepted by the plaintiffs till the answer was received, then the plaintiffs ought not to be bound till after they had received the notification that the defendants had received their answer and assented to it. And so it might go on *ad infinitum*. The defendants must be considered in law as making, during every instant of the time their letter was travelling, the same identical offer to the plaintiffs; and then the contract is completed by the acceptance of it by the latter.[15]

The result in *Adams* v. *Lindsell* might have been supported by adopting the proposition, discussed above, that revocation requires communication.[16] But the case has been taken to establish the rule that acceptances sent by post are effective on mailing. The rule was confirmed by the House of Lords in a Scottish case of 1848, where Lord Cottenham LC, also approving the pragmatic approach, said that '[c]ommon sense tells us that transactions cannot go on without such a rule'.[17] Later cases made it clear that the chief reason for the rule was to protect the reliance of the offeree, even where it did not correspond with the intention of the offeror, enabling the offeree, as one case put it, to go 'that instant into the market' to make subcontracts in firm reliance on the effectiveness of

---

15 *Adams* v. *Lindsell* (1818) 1 B & Ald 681.
16 The court held that the answer was received 'in course of post' because the defendants were responsible for the misdirection of the offer. This aspect of the decision might be disputed if the offeree had reason to know, as he probably would have done, that the offer had been misdirected and that the defendant expected an earlier reply.
17 *Dunlop* v. *Higgins* (1848) 1 HLC 381, 400.

the mailed acceptance.[18] The reason for the rule ('an exception to the general principle') was 'commercial expediency'.[19] In *Byrne* v. *van Tienhoven*, mentioned above in connection with the rule that revocations were ineffective until communicated, Lindley J made it clear that protection of the offeree's reliance lay behind both that rule and the rule that acceptances were effective on mailing:

> Before leaving this part of the case it may be as well to point out the extreme injustice and inconvenience which any other conclusion would produce. If the defendants' contention were to prevail no person who had received an offer by post and had accepted it would know his position until he had waited such a time as to be quite sure that a letter withdrawing the offer had not been posted before his acceptance of it.

He added, in a sentence quoted earlier:

> It appears to me that both legal principles, and practical convenience require that a person who has accepted an offer not known to him to have been revoked, shall be in a position safely to act upon the footing that the offer and acceptance constitute a contract binding on both parties.[20]

The references to 'extreme injustice and inconvenience', and the conjunction of 'legal principles and practical convenience' show that principle was, in Lindley's mind, inseparable both from general considerations of justice between the parties and from considerations of public interest.

Pollock thought that the postal acceptance rule was contrary to what he called 'the main principle . . . that a contract is constituted by the acceptance of a proposal'.[21] In his first edition he said that the rule had consequences that were 'against all reason and convenience'.[22] In his third edition, after the rule had been confirmed by a decision of the Court of Appeal,[23] Pollock retreated, reluctantly accepting the decision ('the result must be taken, we think, as final'),[24] though not without a parting shot praising the dissenting judgment in the Court of Appeal ('It is perhaps not too presumptuous to regret that the Lord Justice Bramwell's view did not prevail').[25] But Pollock's mind was still not at rest on this question when he wrote the preface to his ninth edition forty years later:

---

18 *Re Imperial Land Co. of Marseilles; Harris's Case* (1872) LR Ch App 587, 594 (Mellish LJ).
19 Lord Brandon in *Brinkibon Ltd v. Stahag Stahl GmbH* [1983] 2 AC 34, 48 (HL).
20 *Byrne* v. *van Tienhoven*, note 7, above, at 348.
21 Pollock, *Principles of Contract*, 1st edn, 8. 22 *Ibid.*, at 11.
23 *Household Fire and Accident Insurance Co.* v. *Grant* (1879) 4 Ex D 216.
24 Pollock, *Principles of Contract*, 3rd edn, 36. 25 *Ibid.*, at 35.

> The remarks on the formation of contracts by correspondence . . . are
> recast. I have come to regard this formerly vexed question as belong-
> ing to the class where, in the presence of conflicting and indecisive views
> of convenience (for I do not now think there is any decisive one), it is
> best to follow out elementary principles and not be alarmed if some of the
> minor consequences have a look of paradox.[26]

The invocation of 'elementary principles' might seem to suggest a return
to the 'main principle' of Pollock's first edition, i.e. that acceptance must
be communicated. However, he continued, as though answering this
implicit suggestion, but without indicating a change of direction:

> A certain and fairly simple rule with known consequences, leaving it free
> to the parties to make other provision if they see fit, is better than an
> elaborate scheme which aims at a complete solution for all possible events,
> but, as experience has shewn, may well fail to exhaust them. In the case in
> hand the law settled by the Court of Appeal has been in force these forty
> years, and does not appear to have been found inconvenient.[27]

The 'elementary' principle that Pollock here follows out is not that of his
first edition (that acceptance must be communicated), but the proposition
that a settled and convenient legal rule should be adhered to, and the conflict with what was earlier called 'the main principle' is now characterized
as an odd, but evidently tolerable, 'look of paradox'.

Some cases suggested that the basis for the rule was that the offeror, in
sending an offer by mail, impliedly authorized the offeree to give a message
of acceptance to the Post Office, which then received the acceptance, at
the time of mailing, as the offeror's agent.[28] The attraction of this line
of thinking was that it appeared to supply a principle that reconciled the
postal acceptance rule with the proposition that contractual obligations
depended on intention. However, the principle proved inadequate when
tested by a case in which the offer had not been sent by mail, but had
been handed over in person, and the acceptance had been sent by mail.
The offeror, who had attempted to revoke the offer, argued that, since the
offer had not been mailed, no implied authority had been given to accept
by mail, and therefore that the rule did not apply. Lord Herschell rejected
this argument, saying that the notion of implied authority was fictitious:

---

26 Pollock, *Principles of Contract*, 9th edn, vii.   27 *Ibid.*, at vii–viii.
28 *Re National Savings Bank Association (Hebb's Case)* (1867) LR 4 Eq 9, 12 (Lord Romilly
   MR), *Household Fire Ins. Co.* v. *Grant*, note 23, above, at 218 (Thesiger LJ), 227 (Bagallay
   LJ).

> I am not sure that I should myself have regarded the doctrine that an acceptance is complete as soon as the letter containing it is posted as resting upon an implied authority by the person making the offer to the person receiving it to accept by those means. It strikes me as somewhat artificial to speak of the person to whom the offer is made as having the implied authority of the other party to send his acceptance by post. He needs no authority to transmit the acceptance through any particular channel; he may select what means he pleases, the Post Office no less than any other. The only effect of the supposed authority is to make the acceptance complete so soon as it is posted, and authority will obviously be implied only when the tribunal considers that it is a case in which this result ought to be reached. I should prefer to state the rule thus: Where the circumstances are such that it must have been within the contemplation of the parties that, according to the ordinary usages of mankind, the post might be used as a means of communicating the acceptance of an offer, the acceptance is complete as soon as it is posted.[29]

The frank recognition here that legal fictions were in play, and that the courts employed them selectively in order to reach results thought to be desirable, anticipates insights more generally associated with the twentieth-century school of thought known as American legal realism.[30]

The assertion that nineteenth-century contract law rested on a 'will theory' has been so often repeated as almost to attain the status of received wisdom. It is true that the phrase 'consensus ad idem' was in frequent use, and that some judicial statements do support a theory of subjective consent.[31] But, taken as a whole, the historical evidence shows that the will of the promisor was, in practice, neither necessary nor sufficient. The rules mentioned earlier show that, in many important respects, the will of the promisor was not necessary for contractual obligation. The requirements of consideration and of conformity with public policy show that neither was the will of the promisor sufficient. A clear, simple, elegant, orderly, coherent and logical explanation of contract law would, no doubt, be desirable, if attainable, but it cannot be a virtue to misdescribe the past, or to impose upon it an order that was not there.

A reason commonly given for the enforcement of promises was that it tended to protect the reliance and expectation of the promisee.[32] William

---

29 *Henthorn* v. *Fraser* [1892] 2 Ch 27 (CA), at 33.
30 See notes 111–12, below, and Chapter 1, p. 7, above.
31 Kindersley VC in *Haynes* v. *Haynes* (1861) 1 Dr. & Sim. 426, 433, *Dickinson* v. *Dodds*, note 10, above.
32 See J.H. Baker, 'From Sanctity of Contract to Reasonable Expectation?' [1979] *Current Legal Problems* 17, 22–3, citing Adam Smith, Paley, Austin, Holland and others.

Paley, in his *Principles of Moral and Political Philosophy* (1785) gave this as the primary reason for enforcing promises:

> They who argue from innate moral principles suppose a sense of the obli-
> gation of promises to be one of them; but, without assuming this, or
> anything else, without proof, the obligation to perform promises may be
> deduced from the necessity of such a conduct to the well-being, or the
> existence, indeed, of human society. Men act from expectation. Expec-
> tation is in most cases determined by the assurances and engagements
> which we receive from others. If no dependence could be placed upon
> those assurances, it would be impossible to know what judgment to form
> of many future events, or how to regulate our conduct with respect to
> them. Confidence, therefore, in promises, is essential to the intercourse of
> human life ... But there would be no confidence in promises, if men were
> not obliged to perform them: the obligation therefore to perform promises
> is essential to the same ends, and in the same degree.[33]

Paley was not a lawyer, and is not now very highly regarded as a philosopher, but he had a strong influence on nineteenth-century English thought, including legal thought, or, perhaps, it might be more accurate to say that his writings reflected attitudes that were found to be very congenial in the nineteenth century. His *Principles* was for many years included in the severely select reading list of the Cambridge Board of Moral Sciences Studies.[34] His chapter on promises included an elaborate example designed to show that promises were to be interpreted in the sense understood by the promisee, if known to the promisor, and not in the sense subjectively intended by the promisor. The example given was of the conqueror Tambourlaine, who, having induced the surrender of a besieged city by promising that no blood would be shed, proceeded to bury the defenders alive. Paley's conclusion was that Tambourlaine was (morally) bound by the sense in which he knew that his promise would be understood, even though he never himself actually intended it. This rather bizarre example was included at length in Joseph Chitty's much-used treatise on the law of contracts (second edition, 1834), maintained in successive editions until nearly the end of the century,[35] and must have been known to every student of English contract law. Paley was expressly

---

33 Paley, *The Principles of Moral and Political Philosophy*, 106. Hume had earlier argued that
    the will of the promisor could not create obligations and that 'the obligation of promises
    is an invention for the interests of society', D. Hume, *A Treatise of Human Nature*, vol. 3,
    114, 116.
34 Whewell, *Lectures on the History of Moral Philosophy in England*, 279.
35 Chitty, *A Treatise on the Law of Contracts*, 2nd edn, 62, 12th edn., 127–8. Not found in 1st
    edn. (1826) or in 13th edn (1896).

relied on in argument in the very important case of *Smith* v. *Hughes*,[36] and seems to have influenced the court's formulation in that case of the objective principle of contractual obligations.[37] Blackburn J said, in a passage that has been quoted and relied on throughout the common law world, directly and indirectly, perhaps more than any other single passage in contract law: 'If, whatever a man's real intention may be, he so conducts himself that a reasonable man would believe that he was assenting to the terms proposed by the other party, and that other party upon that belief enters into the contract with him, the man thus conducting himself would be equally bound as if he had intended to agree to the other party's terms.'[38]

The underlying basis of this line of thinking was not intention, or mutual agreement, but protection of the promisee's expectations. It followed that a promisor might be bound by the promisee's reasonable understanding of what promise had been made, even though contrary to the actual intention of the promisor. The corollary was that if the promisee actually knew of the promisor's real intention, the promisee would have no reasonable expectation of holding the promisor to a different meaning. Paley was expressly mentioned by Hannen J in support of the important proposition, for which *Smith* v. *Hughes* is sometimes cited, that a promisor cannot be held to a meaning known by the promisee *not* to have been intended.[39] This conclusion rests not on any subjective theory of contract formation, but on the limits of a theory based on protection of reasonable expectations (i.e. expectations of what promise had been made are protected, but only insofar as really held).

Judah Benjamin, in his treatise on sale (1868) mentioned in his discussion of contract formation, and again in his discussion of mistake, that if a person manifested an intention, so as to induce another to act upon it, he would be estopped from denying that the intention as manifested was his real intention.[40] This suggestion appears to have been influential in some cases. Benjamin was cited in *Smith* v. *Hughes*,[41] though on another point, and in a later case of 1876 Blackburn J said that the taker of a railway baggage ticket was 'precluded' from denying assent to the terms printed on it, and Mellor J said that the plaintiff was 'precluded ... from setting up any defence that she did not deposit the luggage on the terms which the ticket ... contained, or assent

---

36 (1871) 6 QB 597.   37 *Ibid.*, at 607.   38 *Ibid.*, at 607.   39 *Ibid.*, at 610.
40 Benjamin, *A Treatise on the Law of Sale*, 1st edn, 39, 306; 2nd edn, 326.
41 See note 36, above, at 599.

thereto'.[42] Later editors of Benjamin's book transferred the relevant passage from the mistake chapter to the earlier chapter on contract formation, and went so far as to suggest that cases where there was no subjective assent were not cases of contract at all, but were to be explained by the non-contractual principle of estoppel:

> Cases arise in which, although there is in fact no mutual assent, *and accordingly no contract*, one of the parties may be estopped by his statements or conduct from setting this up. In such cases there may be said to be a quasi-mutual assent . . . [quoting the statement of Blackburn J from *Smith v. Hughes*, above].[43]

'Quasi-mutual assent' has not endured as a concept.[44] The concept springs from an attempt to exclude from contract law all instances of liability that are not compatible with the principle that contractual liability rests on mutual assent. But the distinction between persons liable because there is a contract, and persons liable because they are estopped from denying that there is a contract would in most cases, as between the contracting parties, be a distinction without a difference: if a person is estopped from denying contractual liability, it could truly be said that, as between the parties, to most legal intents and purposes, there is a contract.[45] To put the point another way, if there is a general rule that persons taking a ticket are precluded from denying their assent to the terms printed on it, that rule must be of central concern to every student of contract law, and could not plausibly be marginalized as part of the law of estoppel, or of procedure. Lord Devlin, in 1964, referring to a dictum of Lord Blackburn in the case of 1876[46] doubted that 'the ordinary law of estoppel applies to such cases'.[47] The earlier discussion will be recalled of the intended revocation of an offer accepted by the offeree in ignorance of the offeror's change of mind. Pothier thought that the offeror should be liable, but he could not reconcile the imposition of contractual liability with the principle of concurrence of intention. The explanation proposed, that liability should be imposed *as though there were a contract* but explained

---

42 *Harris* v. *Great Western Railway Co* (1876) 1 QB 515, at 524 and 530.
43 Benjamin, *A Treatise on the Law of Sale*, 5th edn, 106 (emphasis added).
44 But it was repeated in the 6th edn., 131–2.
45 But, as the Australian High Court pointed out in *Taylor* v. *Johnson* (1983) 151 CLR 422, the difference in legal technique may be significant where a distinction between void and voidable contracts is crucial.
46 *Harris* v. *Great Western Railway Co.*, note 42, above.
47 *McCutcheon* v. *David MacBrayne Ltd* [1964] 1 WLR 125, 133. See also the discussion of estoppel in Chapter 3, below, at pp. 70–3.

on non-contractual grounds, is closely parallel to the estoppel explanation proposed by Benjamin (who himself had a civilian background) and his later editors, and it springs from the same attempt to preserve at any cost the principle of mutual assent. Both are vulnerable to Pollock's criticism that the explanations are 'cumbrous and inelegant'.

An important aspect of the concept of agreement is its relation to that of mistake. As Professor George Palmer pointed out, there is a distinction between, on the one hand, a misunderstanding between the parties as to what the terms of the contract are, and, on the other hand, a mistake as to an underlying fact or circumstance that induces a party to enter into a contract.[48] The latter kind of mistake is discussed in a later chapter, where it will be suggested that the conflation of the two kinds of mistake, though apparently offering an attractive simplification, has led to intractable difficulties.[49]

The dominance, by the time of the decision in *Smith* v. *Hughes*, of the objective rules of contract formation and interpretation left very little scope for admitting difference in understanding between the parties as a defence to contractual obligation. If the defendant's words or conduct led the claimant reasonably to understand that the promisor was agreeing to something, the promisor was normally bound by that understanding even though it differed from his or her actual intention. This result followed from the finding that the understanding of the claimant was reasonable: if the promisee's understanding was reasonable, the promisor, as a reasonable person, was taken to know of it, and was, therefore, bound to accept responsibility for it.

The prevalence of this way of thinking was manifested in the important case of *Parker* v. *South Eastern Railway Co.*, decided a few years after *Smith* v. *Hughes*. The question in issue was whether customers depositing baggage at a railway station were bound by a limitation of liability printed on the ticket given to them at the time of the deposit, even if they had not read the ticket and did not know of the limitation. Two cases, in both of which there had been verdicts for the customers, were heard together by the newly established Court of Appeal, with the intention of settling what was regarded as an important and controversial question. Counsel on opposite sides, both with more than a passing interest in the relevant principles, happened to be Judah Benjamin and Frederick Pollock, the latter making one of his very rare appearances in

---

48 Palmer, *Mistake and Unjust Enrichment.*   49 See Chapter 5, below.

court.[50] Benjamin, for the railway, argued first, somewhat surprisingly, that there was no contract at all between the parties: 'the plaintiffs sue on an alleged contract to keep the goods safely, but there is no contract if one party means one thing and the other party means something else; there must be a consensus ad idem'. It is significant that this proposition was immediately contradicted by Bramwell LJ, who (possibly having read Benjamin's book) interrupted the argument to say: 'Not so; one of the parties may so conduct himself as to lead the other to believe that there was a contract.'[51] Benjamin then argued, switching from a subjective to an objective principle, that, if there was a contract, the customer was bound by the terms on the ticket, adding that the acceptance of luggage was for the convenience of passengers, and making the telling point that 'it is absurd to hold that for a charge of 2d a company ought to become liable to make good a loss of perhaps hundreds of pounds'. It should be noted here that the terms on the ticket were not oppressive or unreasonable: the limitation was to the sum of £10, a very large amount in relation to the probable value of the baggage of an ordinary traveller. Pollock argued presciently, though unsuccessfully, that if the railway's argument succeeded, wholly unreasonable terms might be effectively inserted on printed tickets.[52]

The Court of Appeal held that the customers were bound by the printed terms if it was reasonable in the circumstances for the railway to assume that customers generally would know that the ticket contained contractual terms, even if they did not know what they were. Mellish LJ relied heavily on an analogy with bills of lading, another instance where contractual documents were binding on customers even though not signed by them:

> If a person who ships goods to be carried on a voyage by sea receives a bill of lading signed by the master, he would plainly be bound by it, although afterwards in an action against the shipowner for the loss of the goods, he might swear that he had never read the bill of lading, and that he did not know that it contained the terms of the contract of carriage, and that the shipowner was protected by the exceptions contained in it. Now the reason why the person receiving the bill of lading would be bound seems to me to be that in the great majority of cases persons shipping goods do know that the bill of lading contains the terms of the contract of carriage; and the shipowner, or the master delivering the bill of lading, is entitled to assume that the person shipping goods has that knowledge. It is, however,

50 Neil Duxbury says of Pollock that 'only twice is he recorded as appearing in court'. Duxbury, *Frederick Pollock and the English Juristic Tradition*, 29.
51 *Parker* v. *South Eastern Railway Co.* (1877) 2 CPD 416 (CA), at 418.   52 *Ibid.*, at 419.

> quite possible to suppose that a person who is neither a man of business nor a lawyer might on some particular occasion ship goods without the least knowledge of what a bill of lading was, but in my opinion such a person must bear the consequences of his own exceptional ignorance, it being plainly impossible that business could be carried on if every person who delivers a bill of lading had to stop to explain what a bill of lading was.[53]

This reasoning depends not at all on the concept of actual assent by the particular customer, but rather on the idea that it is reasonable for the shipowner to expect that 'in the great majority of cases' customers will know that they are accepting contractual terms, and that it is reasonable for shipowners to carry on business in this manner.

Applying this line of reasoning to the case at hand, Mellish LJ continued:

> Now the question we have to consider is whether the railway company were entitled to assume that a person depositing luggage, and receiving a ticket in such a way that he could see that some writing was printed on it, would understand that the writing contained the conditions of contract, and this seems to me to depend upon whether people in general would in fact and naturally, draw that inference.[54]

Mellish LJ concluded that a new trial was necessary, and Bagallay LJ agreed, saying that the customer would be bound if he 'had good reason to believe that there were upon the ticket statements intended to affect the relative rights of himself and the company'.[55] This is again an objective test that does not depend on actual assent by the particular customer.

Bramwell LJ, in a very vigorous judgment, would have gone further in the railway's favour and would have entered judgment for the defendant without a new trial. He showed a marked lack of sympathy with the claimants:

> The plaintiffs have sworn that they did not know that the printing was the contract, and we must act as though that was true and we believed it, at least as far as entering the verdict for the defendants is concerned. Does this make any difference? The plaintiffs knew of the printed matter. Both admit they knew it concerned them in some way, though they said they did not know what it was; yet neither pretends that he knew or believed it was not the contract. Neither pretends he thought it had nothing to do with the business in hand; that he thought it was an advertisement or other matter unconnected with his deposit of a parcel at the defendants' cloak-room.

53 *Ibid.*, at 422.   54 *Ibid.*, at 422–3.   55 *Ibid.*, at 425.

They admit that, for anything they knew or believed, it might be, only they did not know or believe it was, the contract. Their evidence is very much that they did not think, or, thinking, did not care about it. Now they claim to charge the company, and to have the benefit of their own indifference. Is this just? Is it reasonable? Is it the way in which any other business is allowed to be conducted? Is it even allowed to a man to 'think', 'judge', 'guess', 'chance' a matter, without informing himself when he can, and then when his 'thought', 'judgment', 'guess', or 'chance' turns out wrong or unsuccessful, claim to impose a burthen or duty on another which he could not have done had he informed himself as he might? Suppose the clerk or porter at the cloak-room had said to the plaintiffs, 'Read that, it concerns you', and they had not read it, would they be at liberty to set up that though told to read they did not, because they thought something or other? But what is the difference between that case and the present? Why is there printing on the paper, except that it may be read? The putting of it into their hands was equivalent to saying, 'Read that'. Could the defendants practically do more than they did? Had they not a right to suppose either that the plaintiffs knew the conditions, or that they were content to take on trust whatever is printed?[56]

The emphasis here is entirely on the reasonableness of the railway's conduct of its business and on the unreasonableness of the customers' claims; there is no concession whatever to the notion that they could only be bound by their actual consent. The difference of opinion in the court shows that this was a step too far for the majority, who, by ordering a new trial, sought to maintain the principle that individual assent (albeit on an objective test) was theoretically necessary.[57] Bramwell responded to Pollock's argument about unreasonable terms by saying that 'there is an implied understanding that there is no condition unreasonable to the knowledge of the party tendering the document and not insisting on its being read – no condition not relevant to the matter in hand'.[58]

Pollock, in the second edition of his treatise, had considerable difficulty with the *Parker* case. The result could scarcely be reconciled with the principle of mutual assent. Neither could the use made by Bramwell of Pollock's own argument: Pollock had argued that unreasonable terms might be printed on tickets and therefore the law should be that no customer should be bound unless he had actually assented to the terms.

56 *Ibid.*, at 427.
57 The decision to order a new trial was evidently a compromise since the third judge, Bagallay J, indicated that his initial inclination had been to dismiss the appeals: *Parker*, note 51, above, at 429.
58 *Ibid.*, at 428.

But Bramwell's answer was that unreasonable terms on tickets could be invalidated for unreasonableness, a concept equally incompatible with the principle of consent of the parties.

Clearly Pollock was very uncomfortable with the decision:

> The result, as it stands at present, appears to be that it is a question of fact in each case whether the notice given by the company was reasonably sufficient to inform the depositor at the time of making the contract that the company intended to contract only on the special terms. A person who, knowing this (or having reasonable means of knowing?), enters into the contract, is then deemed to assent to the special terms; but this, again, is probably subject to an implied condition that the terms are relevant and reasonable. The whole subject, however, remains by no means free from uncertainty.[59]

On the crucial question awkwardly posed in parentheses '(or having reasonable means of knowing?)', Pollock added a footnote:

> It seems very difficult to reconcile this with principle. Actual knowledge may of course be inferred as a fact from reasonable means of knowledge.[60]

This last comment did little to assist, because actual knowledge was clearly not the basis of the decision in the *Parker* case.

In the third edition (1881) the corresponding footnote was greatly expanded to express Pollock's reservations about the *Parker* case, and its relation to principle:

> Are reasonable means of knowledge equivalent to actual knowledge? It seems better on principle to say that actual knowledge may be inferred as a fact from reasonable means of knowledge, and inferred against the bare denial of the party whose interest it was not to know. This is one of the rules of evidence which are apt in particular departments to harden into rules of law. But 'constructive notice', after being fostered to a monstrous growth by the Court of Chancery, is now in deserved discredit.[61]

The long footnote then continued with quotations (in Latin) from the Digest, and a concluding comment to the effect that 'one cannot help observing that before the recent cases on the subject the conditions printed by railway companies on their tickets, and the corresponding notices exhibited by them, were far from being "claris literis, unde de plano recte legi possit" (in clear letters and plainly legible), or "in loco evidenti" (in

---

59 Pollock, *Principles of Contract*, 2nd edn, 31.   60 *Ibid.*, note.
61 Pollock, *Principles of Contract*, 3rd edn, 46 note.

an obvious place)'. This rambling footnote points up the conflicting lines of thought in Pollock's mind, and is of interest in the present context for that reason. The train of Pollock's thought seems to have been as follows: perhaps the *Parker* decision could be reconciled with the principle of assent by saying that actual assent is needed and it is a question of evidence in each particular case as to whether the customer had in fact assented to the terms; but, unfortunately, this is just the approach that the *Parker* case rejected; perhaps, then, there could be a presumption that customers always in fact assent to terms on tickets; but, if the presumption is to be practically irrebuttable, it would be reminiscent of artificial and fictitious rules elsewhere in the law and hardly something that I would wish to commend; still, it would be very desirable to induce the railways to make their terms clearer to their customers; but then again it is hard to see how that result can be made to flow from a contractual principle of mutual assent. The fact that Pollock thought it necessary to include this rather complex and obscure train of thought, but yet confined it to a footnote, indicates an unresolved conflict in his mind.

Where a contractual document had been signed, or jointly adopted by the parties as containing their agreement, there was even less scope for difference of understanding to operate as a defence to contractual obligation. In almost all cases of such difference the court could find that one party's understanding was more reasonable than the other's, and in such a case the other party would be bound by the more reasonable interpretation even though it might be clear that it differed from that party's actual intention.[62]

This approach was reinforced by the parol evidence rule, which, where a contract had been reduced to writing, purported to exclude evidence tending to modify or contradict the writing. The parol evidence rule is, on its face, in tension with the principle of mutual assent, for the rule specifically excludes the evidence that would show the actual intention of the parties. Addison nevertheless called the parol evidence rule a principle of law, and offered this reason in support of it:

> This general rule or principle of law has been established on the ground that the writing stands higher in the scale of evidence than the oral testimony, and that the stronger evidence ought not, therefore, to be controlled by the weaker.[63]

---

62 E.g. *Hobbs* v. *Esquimault and Nanaimo Railway* (1899) 29 SCR 450.
63 Addison, *A Treatise on the Law of Contracts*, 159.

This is not a satisfactory reason because the comparative cogency of written and oral evidence necessarily varies according to the question in issue and the surrounding circumstances, and because the parol evidence rule purports to exclude all extrinsic evidence, written as well as oral. Pollock in his first edition postponed his discussion of the parol evidence rule to the chapter on mistake. Like Addison, he considered the parol evidence rule to be a principle – indeed an obvious principle:

> The principle from which the law sets out is one almost too obvious to be worth stating, being that on which we daily act in all the transactions of life: namely that men are to be taken to mean what they say.[64]

Though this proposition is said to rest on principle, it is a quite different principle from Addison's and quite different also from the principle of mutual assent; indeed, it is bound sometimes to conflict with the latter principle. A principle 'too obvious to be worth stating' invites scrutiny, and the sentence just quoted has certain weaknesses, logically, empirically, ethically and historically. The reason given by Pollock for acceptance of the 'principle' is that it is an assumption on which 'we daily act in all the transactions of life'. The truth of this proposition might be disputed, but, supposing it to be true, it does not follow that we *always* act on that assumption, still less that we *ought* always to act on it. Pollock says that people 'are to be taken' to mean what they say, but this is ambiguous: if he means that, as a matter of fact, people always mean what they say, the assertion is palpably false; it must be very well known, and especially to a student of contract law, that people do *not* always mean what they say. But if the phrase means 'adopted as a rule of law', then this is to assume the answer to the question in issue, which is, when ought the law to hold that a contractual document is conclusive? Moreover, Pollock's principle does not support the parol evidence rule as actually developed in English law, and might in many cases well be deployed in direct opposition to it, for what parties 'say' is not confined to what they put into writing.

Pollock maintained this sentence in the next three editions, but in the fifth edition (1889) there was a significant change. He removed the subject to a chapter entitled 'Duties under contract' which he described as 'a new chapter on the more general rules of interpretation'.[65] The reason now offered in support of the parol evidence rule was that:

---

64 Pollock, *Principles of Contract*, 1st edn, 410.
65 Pollock, *Principles of Contract*, advertisement to 5th edn.

> It would be contrary to general convenience, and in the great majority of
> the cases to the actual intention of the parties at the time, if oral evidence
> were admitted to contradict the terms of a contract as expressed in writing
> by the parties.[66]

This is entirely different from the reason given in the earlier editions. It
is strange that a principle thought for ten years to be so elementary as to
be 'almost too obvious to be worth stating' should be displaced so readily
by 'general convenience'. By using the phrase 'in the great majority of
the cases', Pollock recognizes that in a minority of cases (but they might
not be a minority of *disputed* cases) the effect of the parol evidence rule
has been and must be to contradict the actual intention of at least one
of the parties. But the interests of such a party, as well as the operation of
any principle of mutual assent were outweighed by considerations of
'general convenience', that is to say by considerations of what Pollock
regarded as good policy. This reason also has its weaknesses in the absence
of a satisfactory explanation of why it is 'generally convenient' to force
upon a person an obligation that has not been agreed to. Is it because
of considerations of justice that weigh in favour of the party seeking
enforcement (if so, what are they?), or is Pollock really suggesting that
there is an independent public interest in maintaining the sanctity of
documents that overrides considerations of justice between the parties?

The parol evidence rule, with its many and complex exceptions cannot
be explained on the principle of mutual assent standing alone, but it
does not follow that the concept of assent has been irrelevant, nor does
it follow that a principle related to considerations of justice between the
parties cannot be formulated in support of the rule. Stephen Leake, in
The Elements of the Law of Contracts (1867) had suggested that 'the reason
of this rule is, that it would be contrary to the agreement of the parties to
admit any other evidence of the contract than the writing agreed upon by
them as containing it'. Leake went on to suggest that this principle could
offer an explanation of the many exceptions to the rule, saying that 'if the
parties have drawn up a writing without intending that it should constitute
an agreement between them, or without intending that it should contain
the whole agreement between them, the reason of the rule, and therefore
the rule itself, does not apply to such writing'.[67] This offers a much
more plausible explanation both of the rule and of its exceptions than
Addison's, and than either of Pollock's two approaches. The rule and its

66 Pollock, *Principles of Contract*, 5th edn, 236.
67 Leake, *The Elements of the Law of Contracts*, 103.

exceptions could largely be accounted for by the proposition that a party is conclusively bound by the terms of a document when, but *only* when, the party seeking to enforce the document reasonably understands that the former party has agreed that it should be conclusive. This line of thinking, though not adopted by English writers, and omitted by Leake from his second edition,[68] was taken up by Corbin, who wrote, in discussing the related question of interpretation of documents:

> If there is in fact a 'plain, ordinary, and popular' meaning of words used by the parties, that fact is evidential that the parties used them with that meaning. It is fully overcome, however, as soon as the court is convinced that one of the parties used and understood the words in a different sense and that the other party had reason to know it.[69]

This line of thinking is consistent also with Pollock's later opinions on reasonable expectation as the basis of contractual obligation,[70] but he did not develop this view in relation to the parol evidence rule. The proposition in the early editions that 'men are to be taken to mean what they say' might plausibly have qualified as a principle if Pollock had added 'when they lead another reasonably to rely on that meaning'.

The proposition will be recalled from *Smith* v. *Hughes* that a person might be bound contrary to his actual intention 'if he so conducts himself that a reasonable man would believe that he was assenting to the terms proposed by the other party'. This formulation implies that a mere difference of understanding as to the terms of a contract is not a defence to contractual obligation, but it does require some sort of link between the conduct of the promisor and the understanding of the promisee. Thus a defendant could not be made liable by an outright forgery, no matter how reasonable the claimant's supposition that the document was genuine. Nor is the defendant liable for the effect of a message accidentally garbled in transmission.[71] Where the defendant's signature to a contractual document is induced by the fraud of a third party the signer has sometimes been excused, but the tendency of many twentieth-century cases has been to make this exception very narrow, in order to protect the reasonable expectation of persons relying on the signature.[72] The effect has been that

---

68 Leake, *An Elementary Digest of the Law of Contracts*.
69 *Corbin on Contracts*, 1963 edn., vol. 3, 108, and to similar effect on other aspects of the parol evidence rule.
70 See pp. 52–3, below.   71 *Henkel* v. *Pape* (1870) LR 6 Ex 7.
72 *Saunders* v. *Anglia Building Society* [1971] AC 1004 (HL), *Marvco Color Research Ltd* v. *Harris* [1982] 2 SCR 774.

signers have sometimes been held to be bound by documents that are wholly contrary to their actual intentions.

It is possible to envisage a case in which the ambiguity of language prevents a court from preferring one party's meaning to the other's. Illustrations are extremely rare, because in most cases one party's understanding will be found to be the more reasonable and will prevail. The rarity of instances goes far to explain the prominence in this context of the case of *Raffles* v. *Wichelhaus*, where the parties had entered into a written agreement for the sale and purchase of a quantity of cotton 'to arrive ex *Peerless*, Bombay'. There were two ships of that name both sailing from Bombay, one in October and the other in December. The seller intended the December ship, but when this arrived in Liverpool, the buyers refused to accept or pay for the cotton, and, in response to the seller's action, pleaded that they thought the contract referred to the October ship. On demurrer to this plea the buyers argued that 'there was no consensus ad idem and therefore no binding contract'.[73] Judgment was given for the defendants without hearing further argument and without reasons. As Professor Simpson pointed out in his study of the case, it is odd that a decision without any judicial reasons whatever should attain the status of a leading case.[74]

The prominence of the case has been due partly to Leake, who offered it as an instance of a case where 'there is no real agreement . . . and consequently no contract',[75] and to Benjamin, who discussed it in the context of mutual assent, and again in his chapter on mistake. The attraction of the case from the point of view of a treatise writer was that it supplied an illustration of the failure of an apparently valid contract that had been reduced to writing on the sole ground of difference in understanding, or lack of *consensus ad idem*, the phrase used effectively by successful counsel. Such illustrations were extremely rare – practically non-existent – for the reasons discussed above. The conceptual purity of the decision, from the treatise writer's point of view, depended on the fact that the case was decided on a demurrer: had it gone to trial there very probably would have been a finding that one party's understanding was more reasonable than the other's. But, since it was decided on the pleadings, there was no opportunity for such a finding. The court's decision, though no reasons were given, may fairly be taken to stand for this proposition: if an ambiguity is of such a kind that neither party's understanding can be

---

73 *Raffles* v. *Wichelhaus* (1864) 2 H & C 906, 908.   74 Simpson, note 1, above.
75 Leake, *The Elements of the Law of Contracts* 178.

preferred, there is no contract. In these circumstances it would be true to say that neither party 'has so conducted himself' as to create a reasonable understanding that he was assenting to the other's terms; because of the ambiguity neither party can be held responsible for the other's expectation. This conclusion is necessary in order to avoid the difficulty that, if each party were responsible for the other's understanding, each could successfully sue the other on a different contract.

The attraction of *Raffles* v. *Wichelhaus* for the illustration of principle is understandable. Benjamin used the case to illustrate 'the general principle that contracts can only be effected by mutual assent',[76] and 'for Pollock', Professor Simpson wrote, '*Raffles* v. *Wichelhaus* was a godsend, for it was very difficult to find any cases which could be used to illustrate and support his true consent theory'.[77] From a historical perspective it is the very rarity of the case that is its significant feature. It was convenient – perhaps even necessary in the prevailing intellectual climate – to take mutual assent as a conceptual starting point for the study of contract law, but the very rarity of such cases as *Raffles* v. *Wichelhaus*, like the exception that proves the rule, only goes to emphasize that, in practice, actual consent was not normally a requirement of contractual obligation.

The phrase 'implied term' has been used in contract law with several different meanings.[78] Sometimes it means what the parties actually agreed; sometimes what they would probably have agreed if they had contemplated the issue that has arisen; very often it means what reasonable persons would have agreed if they had contemplated the issue in question. The meanings have overlapped in application because it is easy to presume that contracting parties intend what is reasonable, and this presumption creates a convenient correspondence between the intention of the parties and the justice of the result.

The last meaning (what reasonable persons would have agreed) necessarily imports the court's own sense of justice, for a writer (court or commentator) naturally attributes to hypothetical reasonable persons an agreement that leads to a fair, just and reasonable result. This approach has been used to avoid unfair results, by introducing implied terms to the effect that, despite appearances, the parties cannot truly have intended to agree to anything that would lead to a very unequal exchange.[79] The

---

76 Benjamin, *A Treatise on the Law of Sale*, 1st edn, 36. See MacMillan, *Mistakes in Contract Law*, 189, pointing out that Leake preceded Benjamin in giving prominence to the case.
77 Simpson, note 1, above, at 160.
78 Leaving aside, in the present discussion, terms 'implied by law'.
79 See Chapter 4, below.

approach has also been employed in order to relieve against the effects of mistake and of unexpected changes in circumstances.[80] The attraction of this approach is that both kinds of problem (unfairness and mistake) can be resolved without apparently departing from an application of the parties' intention. But the appearance is, in the end, illusory, because the court necessarily imports its own view of what is fair and just in the circumstances. Implied terms thus incorporate a residual sense of justice between the parties, the attainment of which is itself a policy. Lord Wright wrote, extrajudicially, in 1939 that:

> the judge finds in himself the criterion of what is reasonable. The Court is in this sense making a contract for the parties – though it is almost blasphemy to say so. But the power of the Court to do this is most beneficial.[81]

In the twenty-first century an English judge, recognizing that the court's power to imply terms goes beyond what is strictly 'necessary', said that 'questions of reasonableness, fairness and the balancing of competing policy consideration are more important than the elusive standard of necessity'.[82]

It is true to say that English law has, by implying terms and by other techniques of interpretation, often reached the same results as would, in other systems, be reached by application of concepts of good faith, or of 'good faith and fair dealing'.[83] Implied terms, however, are in one sense wider, and in another sense narrower than what is suggested by the phrase 'good faith'. Absence of good faith, in any ordinary sense of the words, is not a requirement for implication of a term, and the presence of good faith is not a defence to an action for breach of an implied term. A party's belief, no matter how honest and reasonable, that he or she is not bound by a particular obligation is wholly irrelevant if the court finds that the obligation has, as a matter of law, been incurred. The Supreme Court of Canada made this point in a case in which a term had been implied into an invitation for tenders for a construction project, with the result that the defendant was held liable to an unsuccessful tenderer for accepting a non-compliant bid. The defendant claimed that it had acted in perfect good faith, honestly believing that it had no such obligation to unsuccessful tenderers, and there is no need to doubt this claim, since

---

80 See Chapter 5, below. 81 Wright, *Legal Essays and Addresses*, 259.
82 Dyson LJ in *Crossley* v. *Faithful & Gould Holdings Ltd* [2004] EWCA Civ 293.
83 The phrase 'good faith and fair dealing' appears in the Second Restatement of Contracts (1979), s. 205, referring to the Uniform Commercial Code, 1–201(19) and 2–103(1)(b), and in the *Draft Common Frame of Reference*, III–1:103. See Chapter 8, pp. 213–15, below.

it was quite reasonable as the law had formerly stood. But the claim was rejected:

> The respondent's argument of good faith in considering the . . . bid to be compliant is no defence to a claim for breach of contract: it amounts to an argument that because it thought it had interpreted the contract properly it cannot be in breach. Acting in good faith or thinking that one has interpreted the contract correctly are not valid defences to an action for breach of contract.[84]

It is only by giving a very special meaning to the phrase that the result in this case, or the results in many other cases of implied terms, could be said to depend on 'good faith'.

Terms have often been implied into contracts in order to avoid what would otherwise be an unjust enrichment. Like many other legal expressions, 'unjust enrichment' has had both a general meaning (undue advantage) and a specific meaning (that branch of private law, sometimes called restitution, concerned with reversing enrichments). Considerations of unjust enrichment (in its general sense) have influenced many aspects of the law of property, torts and contracts, including implied terms. Lord Goff said, in a case of advance hire paid under a charterparty for periods in which the hire was not due, that 'even in the absence of [an] express contractual provision advance hire which proves to have been paid in respect of a period during which the vessel was rendered off hire under a term of the contract must ordinarily be repaid, and *if necessary a term will be implied into the contract to that effect*'.[85] Lord Goff went on to say that 'the existence of the agreed [contractual] regime renders the imposition by the law of a remedy in restitution both unnecessary and inappropriate'.[86] His conclusion, therefore, was that restitution and contract were to be kept distinct in this case, but his reasoning demonstrates their mutual interdependence: a remedy in restitution is *unnecessary* precisely because contract law resolves the question in accordance with all relevant considerations of justice, but, where the parties have not dealt with the matter expressly, the court will imply a contractual term for repayment *if necessary*, and what makes such an implication 'necessary' is evidently closely related to the avoidance of unjust enrichment.

---

84 *MJB Enterprises Ltd* v. *Defence Construction (1951) Ltd* (1999) 170 DLR (4th) 577, at para 54.
85 *Pan Ocean Shipping Ltd* v. *Creditcorp Ltd* [1994] 1 WLR 161 (HL), 164 (emphasis added).
86 *Ibid.* Crucial aspects of the *Pan Ocean Shipping* case were the insolvency of the shipowner and the assignment of the disputed payment to a third party. See Lord Goff at 166.

It will be seen from this discussion that there is a complex interrelation between implied terms in contracts, unjust enrichment and policy. In an era when unjust enrichment was not recognized as an independent cause of action, the technique of implied terms was often used to avoid an unjust enrichment. The more recent recognition of an autonomous cause of action for unjust enrichment does not invalidate these cases. Courts in interpreting contracts continue to imply terms for several reasons, one of which continues to be the avoidance of unjust enrichment, itself an important policy. It would be ironic if recognition of unjust enrichment as an autonomous cause of action should lead to a failure to recognize its importance as a pervasive and immanent general concept elsewhere in private law.

A prominent feature of the English law of agency was, and is, that a contractual obligation may be imposed on a person, even directly contrary to that person's actual intention, if an agent, having the person's apparent authority, purports to contract on that person's behalf. The effect of this rule is parallel to and to some extent combines the rules discussed earlier in this chapter regarding the attempted revocation of an offer not notified to the other party, and, more generally, the objective rule of contractual liability formulated in *Smith* v. *Hughes*. In all of these instances the effect of the law has been to protect the reasonable expectation of a claimant even where it has conflicted with the actual intention of the defendant.

Anson, in his first edition, summarized the relevant aspect of agency law as follows:

> A principal cannot, by instructions addressed to the agent, restrict his authority in reference to third parties. If he places a man in such a position as invests him with an apparent authority to do certain acts, and then instructs him privately not to do them, he will nevertheless be bound if the agent disobeys the instructions in contracting with a third party who is ignorant of them.[87]

Anson evidently felt some difficulty in reconciling agency law with the principles set out elsewhere in his book, for he relegated agency to an appendix, and said in the introduction that he regarded agency as 'a matter alien to a general discussion of the principles of contract'.[88] But the law of agency cannot be marginalized as an irrelevant, accidental or exceptional feature of contract law. It is scarcely necessary to emphasize that, at the time that Anson was writing, and subsequently, almost all

---

87 Anson, *Principles*, 1st edn, 334.   88 *Ibid.*, vi.

commercially significant contracts were made, on one side or on both, by agents. The mutual assent of individual minds had become, even in the 1870s, something of a rarity in actual legal practice.

Pollock, in his first edition, had put agency into an appendix to the chapter on mistake. In the third edition he incorporated the subject into the chapter on capacity of parties, explaining in the introduction that 'I have adopted Savigny's view of agency as an extension of the natural man's capacity by an institution of positive law'.[89] This proposition would certainly have struck his readers as highly artificial, abstract and fictitious, and Pollock himself does not seem to have been thoroughly convinced by it, for he added immediately: 'Theoretical objections may certainly be found to this view, but I believe that there are at least as grave ones to any other.' This suggests that Pollock found difficulty in reconciling some aspects of agency law with his general theme. He offered no further explanation of how the imposition of liability on a person contrary to his or her actual intention was compatible with a principle of mutual assent, but this aspect of agency law was consistent with Pollock's later views, which, beginning with the third edition, gradually moved away from reliance on Savigny and the concept of mutual assent towards a preference for the concept of protection of reasonable expectations as the basis of contract law.

Pollock's third edition (1881) introduced many important changes. The introduction to that edition included the following remarkable passage:

> The first chapter, which deals with the fundamental definitions, and the first conditions of the formation of a contract, has been *almost entirely re-written*, partly because some of the questions there discussed have been put on a new footing by recent decisions, partly because the treatment of first principles appeared on revision to be in sundry respects inadequate.'[90]

An acknowledged change of opinion is usually – perhaps always – to be counted to the credit of an author, but the rewriting, within five years, of the most fundamental part of a book entitled 'Principles', and on the grounds here stated (new judicial decisions, and appearance of inadequacy, on revision, of the author's treatment of *first principles*), must engender doubt about the eternal and immutable nature of the principles – those asserted in 1881 as well as those asserted in 1876.

In the third edition the preface was replaced by a lengthy and discursive 'Introduction' which included, at its sixteenth page, the following passage:

---

89 Pollock, *Principles of Contract*, 3rd edn, vi.   90 *Ibid.* Emphasis added.

The law of contract is in truth nothing else than the endeavour of the sovereign power, a more or less imperfect one by the nature of the case, to establish a positive sanction for the expectation of good faith which has grown up in the mutual dealings of men of average right-mindedness... The most popular description of a contract that can be given is also the most exact one, namely that it is a promise or set of promises which the law will enforce... The primary questions... of the law of contract are first, what is a promise? and next, what promises are enforceable? To examine these questions is the object of the present book. The importance and difficulty of the first of them depends on the fact that men can justly rely on one another's intentions, and courts of justice hold them bound to their fulfilment, only when they have been expressed in a manner that would convey to an indifferent person, reasonable and reasonably competent in the matter in hand, the sense in which the expression is relied on by the party claiming satisfaction.[91]

In the fourth edition this passage was sharpened, and made much more conspicuous by being promoted to the opening words of the preface. The concept of reliance and expectation and their relation with intention was elaborated by this sentence: 'He who has given the promise is bound to him who accepts it, not merely because he had or expressed a certain intention, but because he so expressed himself as to entitle the other party to rely on his acting in a certain way.'[92] In the fifth edition (1889) these passages (slightly revised) were moved from the preface, and promoted to still greater prominence as the opening words of the first chapter of the text itself.[93]

Connected with these changes was the development of the concept of 'promise'. The tentative opening note of the text of the first edition ('it is somewhat curious that no satisfactory definition of contract is to be found') was replaced by 'a series of statements in the form of definitions, though necessarily imperfect may help clear the way'. The first of these was that 'every agreement and promise enforceable by law is a contract', and a definition of 'promise' followed.[94] In the fifth edition the concept of promise was given further prominence, and the description of a contract as 'a promise or set of promises which the law will enforce' appeared in the second sentence of the main text.[95]

In a letter to Holmes in 1920, Pollock, commenting on recent American writings, said: 'It is rather amusing to see your new lights trumpeting reasonable expectation as the real fundamental conception in contract. I

91 *Ibid.*, at xx.   92 Pollock, *Principles of Contract*, 4th edn, Preface.
93 Pollock, *Principles of Contract*, 5th edn, 1.
94 Pollock, *Principles of Contract*, 4th edn, 1.
95 Pollock, *Principles of Contract*, 5th edn, 1.

agree, of course, having put it in my 3rd edition, <u>ad init.</u>, nearly forty years ago, only without a trumpet obligato.'[96] This comment reveals that Pollock was conscious that his views of 'the real fundamental conception in contract' had altered in the five-year period between the dates of the first and third editions (1876 and 1881). It also shows that reasonable expectation was, in Pollock's mind, an aspect of reliance, and that protection of the one was the natural corollary of protection of the other.[97]

The fact that a concept seen five years later as 'the real fundamental conception' should have eluded the author during the years of work he put into the first edition of a treatise on general principles is revealing. Also revealing is Pollock's reference to the absence of 'trumpet obligato'. It is certainly true that the passages in question were introduced without fanfare. Buried as they were in the long introduction (not exactly, therefore, '*ad init.*[at the beginning]'), they could hardly have been less conspicuous in the third edition, and they were only gradually promoted, first to the beginning of the preface in the fourth edition, and then to real prominence in the fifth, and subsequent, editions. This suggests that Pollock was by no means sure of his ground in 1881, and was not ready to commit himself fully to a rejection of the idea that contractual obligation depended on intention. It is doubtful whether Pollock would have used the phrase 'real fundamental conception' in this context in 1881, but it is significant that, when he looked back forty years later, he then thought that his insight on this point dated from that time.

The idea of reasonable expectation gained further ground in successive editions. In the fifth edition (1889), under the headings 'Interpretation generally', and 'Effect of promise', Pollock wrote:

> The nature of a promise is to create an expectation in the person to whom it is made. And, if the promise be a legally binding one, he is entitled to have that expectation fulfilled by the promisor. It has, therefore, to be considered what the promisor did entitle the promisee to expect from him. Every question which can arise on the interpretation of a contract may be brought, in the last resort, under this general form.[98]

96 *Holmes–Pollock Letters*, vol. ii, 48 (August 10, 1920), underlining in original. A later letter (vol. ii, 53–4) shows that the reference was to the Wigmore Celebration Volume (*Celebration Legal Essays* (1919)), and especially to Roscoe Pound.
97 See L. Fuller and W. Perdue, 'The Reliance Interest in Contract Damages' (1936) 46 Yale LJ 52, at 52.
98 Pollock, *Principles of Contract*, 5th edn, 234. The passage was maintained in subsequent editions. See also article by Pollock, 'Contract' in *Encyclopaedia Britannica* (1910), vol. 7, 38: 'the guiding principle is, or ought to be, the consideration of what either party has given the other reasonable cause to expect of him'.

The idea of reasonable expectation is given prominence, indeed ultimate precedence here, and associated also with the idea of entitlement. As we have seen, Pollock was anxious in 1920 to claim credit with Holmes for anticipating American scholars on this point, and Pollock's next published edition (ninth edition, 1921) gave very prominent approval to 'the modern tendency to look to "the realization of reasonable expectations" as the ground of just claims rather than an artificial equation of wills or intentions', with reference to Roscoe Pound, and the work mentioned in Pollock's letter to Holmes of 1920.[99] The express rejection here of 'an artificial equation of wills and intentions' indicates, as Neil Duxbury has pointed out, a marked departure from continental theorists, particularly Savigny,[100] and Pollock's open recognition that the concept of intention could not, on its own, supply a complete explanation of contractual obligation. The contrast with Pollock's first edition could scarcely have been more striking. There he had, in his second paragraph, assimilated 'agreement' with '*vertrag* as used by Savigny, whose analysis . . . we follow almost literally in this paragraph', quoting Savigny in German (which must have passed many of Pollock's readers by) because 'a perfectly literal translation is not practicable'.[101]

Pollock did not, however, reject the idea of intention as irrelevant. He did not see intention and expectation as exclusive alternatives, but as complementary. In his article on contract in the *Encyclopaedia Britannica* (1910) he wrote 'The obligation of contract is an obligation created by the will of the parties. Herein is the characteristic difference of contract from all other branches of law' – an endorsement, it would seem, of the 'will theory' – yet he added, a few lines later, that 'the guiding principle still is, or ought to be, the consideration of what either party has given the other reasonable cause to expect of him'. Intention, expectation, entitlement and good faith were not, in Pollock's mind, alternatives, of which one only was to be chosen to the exclusion of the others, but complementary aspects, all of which were necessary for an understanding of contract law. The concept of reasonable expectation implicitly incorporates a reference to intention, because the crucial question is not what the promisee reasonably expects the promisor to do, but what the promisee reasonably expects that the promisor has *undertaken* to do.

99 Pollock, *Principles of Contract*, 9th edn, 1921, footnote (a), on page 1 of the text.
100 Duxbury, *Frederick Pollock and the English Juristic Tradition*, 194.
101 Pollock, *Principles of Contract*, 1st edn, 1 and 2 (notes).

The demarcation of contractual liability from other sources of legal liability is, as Pollock's reference to 'the characteristic difference of contract from all other branches of legal obligation' indicates, closely related to these questions.[102] It will be recalled from the discussion, above, of the question of uncommunicated retraction of offers that Pothier suggested that, though contractual liability was (from his point of view) conceptually impossible in that case, an equivalent liability might be imposed on a non-contractual basis. Suggestions of this sort have quite often been made in respect of various aspects of English contract law, with liability proposed to be based on concepts of property, equity, estoppel, tort or unjust enrichment. This method appears to preserve principles of contract law, but the price is very high: the principles are only preserved by removing all inconvenient instances into other categories and foreclosing discussion of them. The method is weak as a historical account of the actual reasons for decisions, and tends to produce a simplification more apparent than real, for the non-conforming legal issues, though apparently removed from the writer's and from the reader's agenda, do not disappear, and continue to require adjudication and resolution. Moreover, there is the same difficulty in identifying unifying principles in the other categories to which the issue may be displaced.

Anson, in contrast to Pollock, thought that the demarcation of contracts from other sources of legal obligation was an essential first step to understanding the principles of contract. Anson opened his first edition with this: 'In commencing an inquiry into the principles of the law of contract it is well to consider what are the main objects of the inquiry and in what order they arise for discussion. It would seem that the first thing to be considered is the relation of contract to other legal conceptions: if this can be ascertained, we get some definite notion of the subject of our inquiries.'[103] Anson recognized distinct categories of contractual, delictual and quasi-contractual liability. But he also distinguished the liability to pay compensation for breach of contract from contractual liability itself, allocating the two kinds of obligation to entirely separate categories. He also recognized that the obligation to pay a judgment could not readily be accommodated under other headings, and that neither could matrimonial obligations nor obligations arising from trusts. He thus postulated six categories of obligation: contract, delict, quasi-contract, breach of contract, judgment and miscellaneous. Whatever the merits of this scheme from the points of view of logic and elegance, it did not appear to

102 See Waddams, *Dimensions of Private Law.*   103 Anson, *Principles,* 1st edn, 1.

correspond with the previous history of English contract law, nor, despite being carried through seventeen editions over a period of fifty years,[104] did this aspect of Anson's work attract any following from his contemporaries or successors.

Many of the English nineteenth-century writers, including Pollock and Anson, made reference to civilian writings, especially to Pothier (1699–1772) and to the German jurist, Savigny (1779–1861). But the invocation of the names of Pothier and Savigny does not establish that Pollock and Anson were actually influenced by what they had written. As we have seen, Pollock gradually distanced himself from Savigny's views on intention. On the influence of civil law more generally, he wrote in his fifth edition (1889), that 'for my own part I have found myself, as time goes on, rather less than more disposed to make Romanistic elements bear up any substantial part of the structure of the common law'.[105] There is a note of personal and nostalgic sense of loss in this comment, ('for my own part . . . found myself . . . as time goes on'), for the attraction of the civil law lay in its close connection with a search for order, elegance and a 'scientific' approach to the study of English law, ideas that could not be easily abandoned.

A different question is whether, and to what extent, Pollock and other English writers were in fact correct in their understanding of nineteenth-century civil law systems. It is possible that the difference between English and Continental law on the question of subjective intention was more apparent than real. Whatever may have been the actual law on this question in various systems in the nineteenth century, it appears from the *Draft Common Frame of Reference* that in the twenty-first century most European systems do not, on this point, differ greatly in practice from English law. The *Draft Common Frame of Reference* provides that: 'The intention of a party to enter into a binding legal relationship or bring about some other legal effect is to be determined from the party's statements or conduct as they were reasonably understood by the other party.'[106] In the comment the drafters say that 'this represents the law in many (probably the majority) of Member States',[107] with reference to the statement of Blackburn J from *Smith* v. *Hughes*, quoted above, as representing English law on the point.[108] The present writer is not in a position to assess the

104 Anson, *Principles*, J.C. Miles and L.J. Brierly (eds.), 17th edn, 7–8.
105 Pollock, *Principles of Contract*, 5th edn, 698.
106 *Draft Common Frame of Reference*, II – 4:102.
107 *Ibid.*, Comment B, and vol. 1, 274–6, notes 1–11.   108 *Ibid.*, vol. 1, 275–6, note 5.

accuracy of the *Draft Common Frame of Reference* comment in relation to
the many civilian jurisdictions referred to. The words 'many (probably the
majority)' indicate some uncertainty. Nevertheless, the fact that the comment was made is significant as showing, at the very least, that it would
be a mistake to suppose a monolithic adherence in civilian jurisdictions
to a principle of subjective intent.

The word 'principle' had a certain rhetorical component, indicating,
usually, propositions favoured by the writer. But the relation of principles, as understood by the nineteenth-century writers, to the actual prior
history of English law is by no means obvious. The assessment of the law
as it is at the time of assessment is itself a complex process, involving
elements of historical enquiry, of judgment, of synthesis, of aspiration,
and of prediction. The issue is further complicated by what may be called
the forensic convention, that is, the convention that the writers were indirectly addressing an English judge, as a barrister might do, and seeking to
persuade him of the actual state of contemporary English law. The writer's
view of what the law ought to be tended, therefore, to be expressed in
terms of what the law already was – 'in accordance with the authorities of
the common law when rightly understood', as Pollock put it.[109]

It will be seen from the discussion in this chapter that the principles of
contract formation, though often supposed to be simple and uncontrover-
sial, have been far from self-evident, and have sometimes been in conflict
with each other. In contract law certain 'bridging' concepts have enabled
conflicting principles to be accommodated. Thus the concept of 'promise'
has accommodated the ideas both of the promisor's intention, and of an
assurance given to the promisee: a promise is something intended by
the promisor, but it is also something received by the promisee. Somewhat analogously, the concept of 'reasonable expectations' incorporates
by implication a reference to the intention of the promisor, because the
expectation that has been protected is not simply an expectation of *receiving* the promised performance, but an expectation that the promisor has
intended to promise it. It would, therefore, from a historical perspective,
be a mistake to attempt to simplify or purify either of these ideas by
stripping away either of their dual aspects, that is, by seeking to explain
contract law solely in terms of intention, or, on the other hand, solely in
terms of protection of the promisee's interests. The success of the concepts has been founded in their very impurity, that is, in their ability
simultaneously to embrace more than one idea.

109 Pollock, *Principles of Contract*, 1st edn, 11.

Neil Duxbury, in an article written in 2005, recalls a question asked of him at a workshop he presented at an American law school: 'So, if you guys didn't have Langdell and legal realism, what *did* you have?' Duxbury recounts that his reply was that 'we just showed a profound dedication to underachievement and muddling along'.[110] The general tenor of Duxbury's article is, similarly, to compare English and American jurisprudence to the advantage of the latter. Without doubting this general assessment, however, it may be suggested that the lines of thought that animated Langdell[111] on the one hand and the American legal realists on the other were, in neither case, entirely original: they were both present in nineteenth-century English writing. Langdell himself did not go so far as Addison (1847) who spoke of contract law as 'a universal law adapted to all times and races, and all places and circumstances' and as 'immutable and eternal'. And few of the realists would have found it necessary to differ greatly from Pollock's testing and reformulation of principle (1876), by considerations of 'common sense and convenience' for the avoidance of 'manifest injustice', or Lord Herschell's comment (1892) that 'authority will obviously be implied only when the tribunal considers that it is a case in which this result ought to be reached'.[112]

110 Duxbury, 'English Jurisprudence between Austin and Hart' (2005) 91 *Virginia Law Review* 1, 90.
111 Langdell's views (usually assimilated with formalism) were more complex than suggested by some of the realists. See B.A. Kimball, 'The Langdell Problem: Historicizing the Century of Historiography, 1906–2000' (2004) 22 *Law and History Review* 277, especially at 302–11. See also Duxbury, *Patterns of American Jurisprudence*, 64, pointing out that Holmes and Pound were not committed anti-formalists.
112 See the comments on Maine in Chapter 1, at p. 12, above.

3

Promise, bargain and consideration

As we have seen, Addison asserted in 1847 that the principles of contract law were immutable, universal and eternal.[1] This kind of assertion rests on an assumption that contract law everywhere must be governed by the same principles, a proposition that might aptly be described as a 'syncretic and ahistorical supposition'.[2] An examination of the doctrine of consideration, before and after 1847, shows that the conceptual bases of the doctrine, often, but not always, called principles, have varied markedly from time to time, as has the substance of the law.

Often the idea of 'principle' has been used to denote the reason that is supposed to underlie a legal rule. One difficulty with this approach, from a historical perspective, is that it tends to dissolve the rule into the supposed principle. To take a simple example, the minimum age of contractual capacity at common law was 21 years. It may be supposed that the underlying reason for this rule was to ensure that contracting parties had sufficient understanding and maturity. But a legal rule exists independently of the reason for it, even when a single reason can be identified, and, of course, a rule that contracting parties must have attained the age of 21 years is not the same thing as a rule that contracting parties must be of sufficient understanding and maturity: there are many mature 20-year-olds, and many immature 21-year-olds. A more serious difficulty is that very often legal rules have been supported by several different reasons, which may be inconsistent with each other, and each insufficient,

---

1 Addison, *A Treatise on the Law of Contracts*, Preface, iv–v.
2 The phrase is David Ibbetson's: Jones, *An Essay on the Law of Bailments*, edited by and with introduction by David Ibbetson, 66. See also Ibbetson, 'Sir William Jones and the Nature of Law', in Burrows and Lord Rodger of Earlsferry (eds.), *Mapping the Law*, 619, at 629 and 634. Syncretism, in theology, is the claim that all religions are fundamentally similar. Addison's claim that the principles of contract law had been universal could be tested by a comparison of English law with other legal systems. It seems implausible that the claim could be sustained in respect of the doctrine of consideration, notably absent from many systems.

standing alone, to explain or support the rule. For example, two or more reasons might be given in support of a legal rule, none of which is sufficient in itself either as explanation or as justification, and which, though often coinciding in their legal result, tend to require opposite results in particular cases.

Nowhere is this phenomenon more apparent than in relation to the rule that a contractual promise must be supported by consideration. In an unpublished treatise written about sixty years earlier than Blackstone's *Commentaries*, Jeffrey Gilbert, like Blackstone in his second book, envisaged contract primarily as a means of transferring property. Gilbert commenced his work by saying:

> Contracts are two-fold: verbal and solemn. Now contract is the act of two or more persons concurring, the one in parting with, and the other in receiving some property right or benefitt. The most notorious way of transferring of right from one to the other is this by contract for all men by their labour and industry did first acquire to themselves a property so they may by other acts of their own transferr that property where they please, and all laws have allowed it as a settled maxim that the right of disposall must of necessity follow the rights of absolute dominium, for certainly as a man may be industrious for himself he may be so also for another and therefore the establishment of the propriety must be in his hands to whom the disposition is made and no doubt as the notion of propriety was begotten from humane necessity so was also this of contract.[3]

Gilbert then devoted many pages to the topic of consideration, with minute discussion of numerous hypothetical and decided cases, showing that consideration was regarded by him as an important, difficult, controversial and complex topic. Gilbert gave, as the first reason for the legal requirement of consideration, the need to protect potential defendants from liability for rash promises. Having said that some opinions favoured 'the punctuall performance of every verbal promise', he continued:

> Others held that no obligation arises from a naked promise and that the force of the engagement doth totally depend on the consideration and they take it to be a thing of great rigour that a man should dispose of the fruits and effects of a long and painfull industry and all the certain advantages and conveniences of life by the meer breath of a word and the turn of an unwary expression; they also think that the very laws of self-preservation will not permitt it for what reason of conscience can oblige a man to those words that tend to his own destruction, but if a valuable consideration had

---

3 Gilbert, *Of Contracts*, f. 39 (some punctuation added, abbreviations expanded, and capitalization removed).

been received the bargain is compleat for another man's industry comes
in the place of his own . . .

Gilbert continued by saying that English law 'hath held the middle
between these two extreames', in that formal contracts were enforceable,

> so that if a man will oblige himself under the solemnitys of law whereby his
> contract appears to be seriously intended, it shall ever be obligatory and
> the consideration shall be intended . . . but if the contract be verball only
> it binds in respect of the consideration, otherwise a man might be drawn
> into an obligation without any real intention by random words, ludicrous
> expressions, and from hence there would be a manifest inlet to perjury
> because nothing were more easy than to turn the kindness of expressions
> into the obligation of a real promise.[4]

Consideration is a conveniently flexible word, embracing three very different ideas: deliberation, reason for making the contract and reason for
enforcing it. Gilbert's reference to perjury adds a fourth idea: the requirement of consideration tends to supply reliable evidence that the promise
in question has actually been made.

This last idea was taken up by Lord Mansfield in *Pillans* v. *Van Mierop*.[5]
In that case a promise had been given in a commercial context by the
defendant, in a signed writing, to guarantee repayment of money already
advanced by the plaintiff. Lord Mansfield favoured enforcement. He said:

> I take it, that the ancient rule about the want of consideration was for the
> sake of evidence only; for when it is rendered into writing, as in covenants,
> specialties, bonds &c there was no objection to the want of considera-
> tion. And the Statute of Frauds proceeded upon the same principle. In
> commercial cases amongst merchants, the want of consideration is not an
> objection.[6]

Wilmot J, like Gilbert, thought that the requirement of consideration originally 'was intended as a guard against rash inconsiderate declarations'.[7]
This reason also would have been sufficient to justify enforcement in
the particular case, but he and the other judges managed, with some
difficulty, to find consideration (in the sense of value exchanged). Subsequent references to the case have tended to amalgamate the principle
favoured by Lord Mansfield (promises are enforceable if there is reliable
evidence that they were made) with that favoured by Wilmot J (promises
are enforceable if made with due deliberation). The proposition that
promises are enforceable if made with serious intent, for example, tends

4 *Ibid.*, at ff. 39–40.   5 (1765) 3 Burr 1663.   6 *Ibid.*, at 1669.   7 *Ibid.*, at 1670.

to fuse the two ideas, and a requirement of writing might satisfy both simultaneously,[8] but the ideas are distinct, as Lord Mansfield's reference to the Statute of Frauds reveals, for there might be very reliable evidence that a promise was in fact made, even though made rashly. Lord Mansfield, by appealing to a proposed principle, attempted to dissolve the rule that consideration was always required into some such rule as that promises in writing, or commercial promises in writing, were enforceable. Arguments can, of course, be made in favour of Mansfield's opinion, but it was not a historically accurate account of the previous law, and his view was decisively rejected by the House of Lords, on the advice of the judges, a few years later in *Rann* v. *Hughes.*[9] Standing alone, the need to protect the promisor from rash promises could not explain the English law of consideration. Neither, standing alone, could the need for reliable evidence. But, as Gilbert's writing shows, both these ideas had been influential.

Included in Gilbert's account of consideration, quoted above, is another reason for the doctrine of consideration, namely, that it tends to prevent the dissipation of wealth by assuring to the promisor an equivalent in exchange for the wealth he gives up ('what reason of conscience can oblige a man to those words that tend to his own destruction, but if a valuable consideration has been received the bargain is compleat for another man's industry comes in the place of his own'). Standing alone, this reason also is insufficient to explain or to justify the actual law, because there was no need in English law for consideration to be of equal value to the promise sought to be enforced. But this is not to deny that the reason was, as a matter of history, influential, or that, as a matter of fact, it did (in some cases, though not in all) tend to prevent the dissipation of wealth. A purely gratuitous promise was, and is, unenforceable, and this rule, though it can easily be circumvented, has, in some cases, prevented dissipation of wealth.

Another set of reasons for the doctrine of consideration relates to the ideas of reciprocity and entitlement. As Guenter Treitel wrote, the claims of a promisee who has given nothing for the promise 'are less compelling than those of a person who has given (or promised) some return for the promise'.[10] One who has paid for a promise has a stronger claim than one who has not paid for it to assert an entitlement to performance of the promise, and the promisor has a correspondingly greater obligation

8 See L. Fuller, 'Consideration and Form' (1941) 41 *Columbia Law Review* 799.
9 (1778) 7 TR 350 note. 10 Treitel, *The Law of Contract*, 11th edn, 67.

to perform the promise, and to perform it to its full extent. One of the reasons that tend to support specific performance and the expectation measure of damages is that the promisee has bought and paid for the right to performance. Peter Benson has demonstrated the links among the concept of entitlement, the doctrine of consideration, and the extent of the usual remedies for breach of contract.[11]

Pothier, whose work on obligations was published in English translation in 1806, defined contract in terms of agreement and consent,[12] and an aspect of consideration that made the doctrine attractive to nineteenth-century English writers was that it seemed to import into English law, by implication, a requirement of agreement, or mutual assent, something that the concepts of promise and *assumpsit*, standing alone, could not do. From the perspective of some civilian systems, it might be said that consideration had served to fill a gap left in English law by the under-development, until the nineteenth century, of the concept of mutual assent.[13] Comyn (1807), very early in his treatise, linked the concepts of bargain, consent, agreement and consideration, writing that 'a contract... is defined to be a bargain or agreement, voluntarily made... upon a good consideration'.[14] Chitty quoted Lord Loughborough to the effect that 'a bargain without a consideration is a contradiction in terms, and cannot exist'.[15] An incidental effect of this approach was to marginalize the law relating to formal contracts, or covenants. Whereas for Gilbert, a century earlier, the law relating to formal contracts had been an integral part of the conceptual starting point ('contracts are two-fold: verbal and solemn'),[16] Comyn's treatise was, by its title, expressly restricted to contracts not under seal, as was Chitty's treatise of 1826.[17]

Yet another reason given in support of the doctrine of consideration was that it tended to protect creditors in cases where the promisor was insolvent. Lord Denman said, in *Eastwood* v. *Kenyon*:

---

11 P. Benson, 'The Unity of Contract Law' in Benson (ed.), *The Theory of Contract Law*, 118.
12 Pothier, *A Treatise on the Law of Obligations, or* Contracts, 1, c. 1, s. 1, vol. 1, p. 3. There was an earlier American translation by F.-X. Martin (1802).
13 The degree to which mutual assent was part of earlier English law is discussed by P.A. Hamburger, 'The Development of Nineteenth-Century Consensus Theory of Contract' (1989) 7 *Law and History Review* 241.
14 S. Comyn, *A Treatise of the Law Relative to Contracts*, 2.
15 Chitty, *A Treatise on the Law of Contracts*, 2nd edn, 22 note, quoting from *Myddleton* v. *Lord Kenyon* (1794) 2 Ves Jun 391, 408.
16 See notes 3 and 4, above.   17 Chitty, *A Treatise on the Law of Contracts*, 1st edn.

The enforcement of such promises by law, however plausibly reconciled by the desire to effect all conscientious engagements, might be attended with mischievous consequences to society; one of which would be the frequent preference of voluntary undertakings to claims for just debts. Suits would thereby be multiplied, and voluntary undertakings would also be multiplied, to the prejudice of real creditors. The temptations of executors would be much increased by the prevalence of such a doctrine and the faithful discharge of their duty rendered more difficult.[18]

Where, as is common in cases of charitable pledges, the action is brought against the estate of the promisor after death, there is the added argument that enforcement of the promise will be at the expense of possibly needy dependants.[19]

One reason commonly given for the enforcement of promises has been that it tends to protect the reliance and expectation of the promisee. As we saw in Chapter 2, William Paley, in his *Principles of Moral and Political Philosophy* (1785) gave this as the primary reason for enforcing promises.[20] Paley was expressly relied on in argument in the very important case of *Smith* v. *Hughes*,[21] and was linked with the court's formulation in that case of the objective principle of contractual obligations.[22]

Paley continued his discussion of promises by considering and rejecting the argument that society could manage satisfactorily without enforceability of promises:

Some may imagine, that if this obligation were suspended, a general caution and distrust would ensue, which might do as well: but this is imagined, without considering how, every hour of our lives, we trust to and depend upon others; and how impossible it is to stir a step, or, what is worse, to sit still a moment, without such trust and dependence. I am now writing at my ease, not doubting (or rather never distrusting, and therefore never thinking about it) that the butcher will send in the joint of meat which I ordered; that his servant will bring it; that my cook will dress it; that my footman will serve it up; and that I shall find it upon my table at one o'clock. Yet have I nothing for all this but the promise of the butcher, and the implied promise of his servant and mine. And the same holds of the most important as well as the most familiar occurrences of social life.[23]

---

18 *Eastwood* v. *Kenyon* (1840) 11 A & E 438, 451.
19 In the leading Canadian case of *Dalhousie College* v. *Boutilier Estate* [1934] SCR 642 the promisor had suffered 'severe financial reverses which prevented him from honouring his pledge'. The action was brought against the estate after the death of the promisor.
20 See Chapter 2, p. 33, above. 21 (1871) 6 QB 597. 22 See Chapter 2, above.
23 Paley, *The Principles of Moral and Political Philosophy*, 107.

It is notable that all the examples given are of exchange transactions. If one thinks, as Paley did, of what promises are useful or necessary to an organized society, one thinks naturally of exchange transactions, not of gift promises. It is easy to imagine a well-organized society in which gift promises are not enforceable – eighteenth-century English society was a case in point – but it is more difficult to imagine an organized society without enforcement of exchange transactions. In this way, consideration has been linked with ideas of expectation and reliance, and, more generally, of social order.

Chitty, in his second edition (1834) gave as reasons in support of the doctrine first (like Gilbert) the protection of the promisor from improvidence, secondly, the improbability of reliance on gratuitous promises, and thirdly, the availablity of formal contracts:

> A gratuitous undertaking may form the subject of a moral obligation, – it may be binding in honour, – but does not create a legal responsibility. It is not unreasonable to assume that it was entered into improvidently: nor can the party who has received such a promise have sustained any serious injury from the neglect to observe it. The law cannot reasonably be expected to enforce an imperfect obligation of this nature. It has afforded to parties the means of rendering even a gratuitous engagement binding, viz. by the execution of a *deed* which imports deliberation.[24]

A rule supported by so many and by such various reasons has led inevitably to instances where the rule, as currently formulated, applies, but where the underlying reasons, or some of them, do not. English law has had much difficulty with the question of modification of contracts, where additional value is promised by one party in exchange for performance by the other of an obligation already due under an earlier contract. It has often occurred that during performance of a contract circumstances change so that one party finds himself or herself in a position to demand from the other a higher payment than that originally agreed. A number of nineteenth-century cases involved sailors, who, having agreed to serve for the whole of a voyage at a certain wage, subsequently demanded a higher wage when the ship was at a place where substitute services were not readily obtainable. The renegotiated contracts were generally set aside. According to Campbell's report of the leading case of *Stilk* v. *Myrick*,[25] the reason for this result was that performance of a

---

24 Chitty, *A Treatise on the Law of Contracts*, 2nd edn, 23 (emphasis in original).
25 (1809) 2 Camp 317, followed in *Harris* v. *Carter* (1854) 3 E & B 559, *Frazer* v. *Hatton* (1857) 2 CBNS 512.

pre-existing contractual duty could not constitute consideration. Thus, where a contract had been entered into at a fixed price, a subsequent rene-gotiation or variation consisting of an agreed increase in the price was unenforceable.

The rule in *Stilk* v. *Myrick* (as reported by Campbell, and as it was generally understood to be) was much criticized on the grounds that it did not correspond to commercial understanding, that it failed to recognize that actual performance was of greater real practical value than a legal right to performance, and that it was easily circumvented by the parties or by a court desirous of enforcing the variation.[26] But criticism was often tempered with the observation that the rule, though difficult to defend in terms of consideration, was yet serving a useful purpose in offering, albeit indirectly, some legal protection against taking undue advantage of economic pressure. *Stilk* v. *Myrick* itself was a case in point, where sailors, having agreed to serve on a voyage for certain wages, were promised higher wages in order to induce them not to desert during the course of the voyage. It is evident that one of the reasons for the decision was to protect the shipowner from a potentially extortionate threat by the crew to desert the ship in a distant place where there was no ready supply of substitute labour. An earlier case, *Harris* v. *Watson*[27] had also refused to enforce such a contract, but had given as the reason that 'if this action was to be supported, it would materially affect the navigation of this kingdom . . . for if sailors were in all events to have their wages, and in times of danger entitled to insist on an extra charge on such a promise as this, they would in many cases suffer a ship to sink, unless the captain would pay an extravagant demand they might think proper to make'. A different report ('Espinasse) of *Stilk* v. *Myrick*, running together the ideas of principle and policy, states that the judge (Lord Ellenborough) 'recognized the principle of the case of *Harris* v. *Watson* as founded on just and proper policy',[28] and in a subsequent decision in the Admiralty Court (*The Araminta*, 1854) where the sailors had secured payment in gold of the extra money in advance of performance (they were tempted to desert to gold diggings in Australia in 1852) and so the doctrine of consideration

---

26 B. Reiter, 'Courts, Consideration and Common Sense' (1977) 27 *University of Toronto Law Journal* 439.
27 (1791) Peake 102.
28 6 Esp 129, 130. 'Espinasse did not have a very high reputation as a reporter, but on the other hand he was one of the counsel in the case and had the means of knowledge. See Chapter 6, pp. 150–2, below.

was of no assistance, *Stilk* v. *Myrick* was interpreted as holding that the variation of the contract was 'illegal'.[29]

In *Williams* v. *Roffey Bros & Nicholls (Contractors) Ltd*[30] (1990) the English Court of Appeal held a renegotiation to be enforceable. In that case, a subcontractor had contracted to perform carpentry work at an agreed price. When the work was partly done it became clear that the subcontractor would not complete it at the contract price, and the head contractor, who was subject to a penalty clause in the main contract for delay in completion, agreed to pay a higher price for completion of the carpentry work. This latter agreement was held to be enforceable. The court held that performance of an existing obligation might constitute consideration. References to 'principle' were prominent. Glidewell LJ, who gave the leading judgment, rejected the argument that this conclusion was contrary to principle:

> If it be objected that the propositions above contravene the principle in *Stilk* v. *Myrick* I answer that in my view they do not: they refine and limit the application of that principle, but they leave the principle unscathed ... it is not in my view surprising that a principle enunciated in relation to the rigours of seafaring life during the Napoleonic wars should be subjected during the succeeding 180 years to a process of refinement and limitation in the present day.[31]

But Glidewell LJ added the very significant proviso that the renegotiation would be liable to be set aside if there were economic duress, which he called 'another legal concept of relatively recent development,[32] thereby suggesting that the result in *Stilk* v. *Myrick* might be supported, though not on the reasoning given in Campbell's report. Many have welcomed the demise of consideration in this context, but it is not easy to say precisely what has replaced it. What exactly, in the court's view, was the governing concept of enforceability and how did it apply in practice to contractual renegotiations? These questions are not very easily answered.[33] One approach has been to attempt to distinguish between a 'threat' and a mere 'offer to renegotiate', on the ground that there is something wrongful about a threat but not about an offer.[34] In *Williams* v. *Roffey* it was

---

29 *The Araminta* (1854) 1 Sp Ad & Ecc 224 (High Court of Admiralty).
30 [1991] 1 QB 1 (CA) at 10, 19.   31 *Ibid.,* at 16.   32 *Ibid.,* at 13.
33 For a fuller discussion see S.M. Waddams, 'Commentary on "The Renegotiation of Contracts"' (1998) 13 *Journal of Contract Law* 199 and 'Unconscionable Contracts: Competing Perspectives' (1999) 62 *Saskatchewan Law Review* 1.
34 See S. Smith, 'Contracting under Pressure: a Theory of Duress' (1997) 56 *Cambridge Law Journal* 343.

suggested that there was no duress because the proposal for renegotiation emanated from the head contractor. Purchas LJ thought this a conclusive point,[35] but it is evident that the subcontractor had indicated, by conduct if not by words, that he was not likely to complete the work on time at the contract price. It cannot be crucial that the threat not to complete was implicit rather than explicit. Indeed, it may be in the very cases where there is no real choice that it is unnecessary to spell out the threat, or even to make what could readily be called a 'threat' at all. In *The Araminta*, the case of the payment to the ship's crew at the Australian gold diggings in 1852, it was the master who, after several desertions, took the initiative and called together the rest of the crew, offering them increased wages if they would work the ship short-handed. Dr Lushington said, of the master's payment, that it was made voluntarily, adding:

> I have used the expression *voluntarily*, because I think the effect of the evidence is, that the crew exercised no compulsion towards him, though, perhaps, in another sense of the word, such payment was not voluntary, and the more apt expression may be, and the one nearest to the truth, that he was compelled by circumstances to make that payment.[36]

This is indeed very often an apt expression to describe such cases, and for this reason it is doubtful whether the conclusion can be resisted that in *Williams* v. *Roffey Bros*, as in most cases of this sort, there was a threatened breach of the first contract. The decision that the modified contract was nevertheless enforceable lends support to the view that, where the pressure on the other party is not excessive,[37] many courts have accepted that it is legitimate to gain an advantage in this way.

This leaves it very difficult to state what principles govern modification of contracts. Glidewell LJ said that the principle of *Stilk* v. *Myrick* was left 'unscathed',[38] but any formulation of that principle before 1990 would

---

35 [1991] 1 QB 1 at 21.   36 1 Sp Ad & Ecc 224 at 229 (emphasis in original).

37 The Second Restatement of Contracts, s. 89 provides that modifications are enforceable if 'fair and equitable' in view of unexpected circumstances. The Uniform Commercial Code, 2–209 makes modifications enforceable, explicitly subject however, by comment 2, to a test of good faith.

38 Purchas LJ said, at 21, that 'the rule in *Stilk* v. *Myrick* remains valid as a matter of principle, namely, that a contract not under seal must be supported by consideration', but the proposition that a contract must be supported by consideration is not the 'principle' or the 'rule' for which *Stilk* v. *Myrick* had been cited during the previous 180 years; it is that the performance of an obligation owing under a pre-existing contract cannot amount to consideration for a return promise, however valuable timely performance might be to the promisor in the actual circumstances (see following note). So stated, the rule (or principle) is not consistent with the reasoning or the result in *Williams* v. *Roffey*.

have plainly demanded the opposite result to that reached in *Williams* v. *Roffey Bros.*[39] Though 'unscathed' (which means undamaged or intact) the principle is said to be refined and limited, but it is not at all clear what these refinements and limitations amount to, if in truth they leave the principle of *Stilk* v. *Myrick* (as reported by Campbell) intact. Consideration is still necessary; however, performance of a pre-existing contractual duty may amount to consideration (but does not always do so); however, again, even if there is consideration the modification will not be enforceable if there is economic duress; however, yet again, it is not explained why the quite severe pressure on the head-contractor in *Williams* v. *Roffey* (the threat of the penalty clause) did not amount to duress. Breach of contract is a wrong, but apparently it is permissible to gain an advantage by threatening to break a contract. Economic duress was said, by Glidewell LJ, to 'provide another answer to the question of policy which has troubled the courts since before *Stilk* v. *Myrick* and no doubt led, at the date of that decision, to a rigid adherence to the doctrine of consideration'.[40] This sentence shows the complex interconnection between principle and policy. 'Rigid', in legal argument, is never a word of approbation, so Glidewell's suggestion seems to be that *Stilk* v. *Myrick* can be justified only on the basis of 'policy', but it is not very clear what the policy was or is (protection of the navigation of the kingdom, or avoidance of economic duress), or how it relates to the 'unscathed' principle.

The question of modification of contracts has been further complicated by a link with the concepts of reliance and estoppel.[41] Reliance has posed perhaps the greatest difficulties for the English doctrine of consideration. Subsequent reliance on a promise does not constitute consideration, but the consequence of denying all legal significance to the promise can be severe injustice. One of the simplest imaginable examples of reliance arises when a landowner promises to give the land to another person (commonly, a close relative) and the other person, relying on the promise, builds on the land. The promisor (or, as it has more usually been, his or her

---

39 E.g. Cheshire and Fifoot, *The Law of Contract*, 6th edn, 77, calling it 'the somewhat obvious rule that there is no consideration if all the plaintiff does is to perform or to promise the performance of an obligation already imposed upon him by a previous contract between him and the defendant'. Mocatta J in *North Ocean Shipping Co. Ltd* v. *Hyundai Construction Co. Ltd* [1979] QB 705, 712–13, called it 'the well-known principle', and 'the present rule'.

40 [1991] 1 QB 14.

41 In *Collier* v. *P. & M.J. Wright (Holdings) Ltd* [2008] 1 WLR 643 (CA) it was held that an agreement to accept part payment of a debt in full satisfaction might be enforceable by the concept of estoppel.

estate after death) then seeks to revoke the promise. These facts have presented a problem for Anglo-American law because the transaction, being gratuitous, is not enforceable as a contract. Property has not been legally transferred; neither has the promisor committed any tort. Nevertheless the courts of equity gave relief to the promisee.[42] These cases could not be reconciled with orthodox contract doctrine and have therefore been ignored or marginalized by many writers on contract law. They have usually been described by commentators as cases of proprietary estoppel but this phrase is scarcely explanatory. In some of the cases avoidance of unjust enrichment was evidently a crucial factor: in the leading case of *Dillwyn* v. *Llewelyn*,[43] for example, the plaintiff had expended the very large sum of £20,000 in improving land that was originally worth only £1,500. One of the considerations in the mind of a court faced with such facts has been the enrichment that would enure to the defendant if no measure of enforcement were available, and one of the reasons for favouring proprietary estoppel as a rule is that unjust enrichment is *very apt* to occur in such circumstances, and so the rule tends to prevent unjust enrichment. But unjust enrichment has not been present in every particular case,[44] and the remedy has not normally been measured by enrichment. As Peter Birks wrote, 'the doctrine has a *dimension* to it which has nothing to do with restitution/unjust enrichment'.[45] This is true, but it does not follow that considerations of unjust enrichment have been irrelevant. Many of the cases have had the effect of protecting reliance, but the measure of recovery is not, where the plaintiff becomes effectively the owner of the land, restricted to out of pocket loss. Non-contractual reliance has sometimes been protected by concepts of wrongdoing, but in these cases there is no wrongdoing in the ordinary sense. Though the phrase 'equitable fraud' has sometimes been employed, no actual proof of wrongdoing has been required: the defendant acts fraudulently, in the eyes of equity, by failing to do what is just. As expressed in *Wilmott* v. *Barber* (1880), 'the plaintiff must prove that he [the defendant] has acted fraudulently, *or*

42 *Dillwyn* v. *Llewelyn* (1862) 4 D F & J 517, 6 LT 878, *Ramsden* v. *Dyson* (1866) LR 1 HL 129, *Wilmott* v. *Barber* (1880) 15 Ch D 96, *Plimmer* v. *Wellington* (1884) 9 App Cas 699 (PC), *Inwards* v. *Baker* [1965] 2 QB 29 (CA), *Crabb* v. *Arun DC* [1976] Ch 179 (CA), *Greasley* v. *Cooke* [1980] 1 WLR 1306 (CA), *Stiles* v. *Tod Mountain Devt Ltd* (1992) 64 BCLR (2d) 366 (SC).
43 (1862) 6 LT 878 at 879.   44 See Beatson, *Anson's Law of Contract*, 27th edn, 119.
45 Birks, *An Introduction to the Law of Restitution*, 290 (emphasis added). Goff and Jones, *The Law of Restitution* and P. Maddaugh and J. McCamus, *The Law of Restitution* included discussion of these cases in their books, but Burrows, *The Law of Restitution* wrote definitely, at 404, that these cases 'have not been restitutionary'.

that there has been such an acquiescence on his part as would make it fraudulent for him *now* to assert his legal rights'.[46]

The word 'fraudulent' in the last clause of this passage means 'unjust', and cannot be explained except in terms of concepts other than wrongdoing. The defendant must, by action or inaction, induce the plaintiff's reliance, but no proof of intention to mislead or deceive is required.[47] The only 'fraud' required to be proved is an unwillingness to do what equity considers just. A similar comment may be made in relation to the concept of unconscionability.[48] If equity protects the plaintiff's reliance, it will be, by that very fact, against conscience for the defendant to defeat it. 'Inequitable', 'fraudulent', 'unconscionable' and 'unconscientious' have been, in this context, four ways of saying the same thing.[49]

Where a party to a contract indicates that strict rights will not be enforced, equity has in some cases prevented that party from resuming the strict rights where it would be inequitable to do so. In *Hughes* v. *Metropolitan Railway* a landlord who was entitled to demand repairs on six months' notice, gave the notice, but then indicated by his conduct that the running of the period of notice was suspended. The House of Lords held that the landlord could not enforce its strict rights without giving the tenant a reasonable opportunity of compliance. 'Principle' might be thought to permit the landlord to assert its strict rights, because there was no consideration for the implied promise to suspend them, but the court relied on another proposition, also called a principle – indeed actually called 'the first principle':

> [I]t is the first principle upon which all courts of equity proceed, that if parties who have entered into definite and distinct terms involving legal results – certain penalties or legal forfeiture – afterwards by their own act or with their own consent enter upon a course of negotiation which has the effect of leading one of the parties to suppose that the strict rights arising under the contract will not be enforced, or will be kept in suspense, or held in abeyance, the person who otherwise might have enforced those rights will not be allowed to enforce them where it would be inequitable

46 *Wilmott* v. *Barber* (1880) 15 Ch D 96, at 106 (emphasis added), *Gerrard* v. *O'Reilly* (1843) 3 D & War 414 (Ir Ch).
47 *Wilmott* v. *Barber*, note 46 above, at 105 (Fry J). This is a common usage in equity. See L.A. Sheridan, *Fraud in Equity* and Chapter 4, below.
48 See Spence, *Protecting Reliance: the Emergent Doctrine of Equitable Estoppel*, 55–66, *Giumelli* v. *Giumelli* (1999) 161 ALR 473 (Aust. HC).
49 See A. Robertson, 'Reasonable Reliance in Estoppel by Conduct' (2000) 23 *University of New South Wales Law Review* 87, at 96–7.

having regard to the dealings which have then taken place between the parties.[50]

For 'the first principle', this is not very compendiously stated, and the reader might wonder how many other such 'first principles' there might be, whether they are a closed number, and whether they can all be definitively formulated.

In *Central London Property Trust Ltd* v. *High Trees House Ltd*, a landlord had reduced the rent of an apartment building during wartime, and the question arose whether, after the war, the landlord could resume its right to the full rent. Although the landlord made no claim for arrears, the judge, Denning J, took the opportunity to say that arrears could not have been claimed. Denning J formulated the following proposition:

> I prefer to apply the principle that a promise intended to be binding, intended to be acted on and in fact acted on, is binding so far as its terms properly apply.[51]

This 'principle' had nowhere previously been formulated, and a few years later Denning himself (then a member of the Court of Appeal) was forced to retreat substantially from it.[52] The result of this advance and hasty retreat has been a very high degree of uncertainty about the scope of the alleged principle. Denning LJ used the word 'principle' five times in his fairly short judgment,[53] but it is not at all clear what principle the decision applied. Unanswered questions include whether a previous legal relationship between the parties is necessary, whether detrimental reliance is essential, whether estoppel can create new legal rights, whether the promisee's remedy is limited to protection of reliance, and whether strict rights can be resumed on reasonable notice. Lord Denning wrote, extrajudicially, in 1979, that the effect of the *High Trees* case and its extensions 'has been to do away with the doctrine of consideration in all but a handful of cases'. He suggested abandoning the 'archaic word "estoppel"' and proposed the following formulation, again invoking the elusive concept of principle:

> It is a principle of justice and of equity. It comes to this: when a man, by his words or conduct, has led another to believe that he may safely act on the faith of them – and the other does act on them – he will not be

---

50 (1877) 2 App Cas 439, 448 (HL).   51 [1947] 1 KB 130, 136.
52 *Combe* v. *Combe* [1951] 2 KB 215 (CA).   53 *Ibid.*, at 219–20.

allowed to go back on what he has said or done when it would be unjust
or inequitable for him to do so.[54]

This formulation would have struck most contemporary readers as too
vague and general, and Lord Denning tried yet again in 1982 to formulate
a 'general principle' that would account for all instances of estoppel:

> The doctrine of estoppel is one of the most flexible and useful in the
> armoury of the law. But it has become overloaded with cases... It has
> evolved during the last 150 years in a sequence of separate developments:
> proprietary estoppel, estoppel by representation of fact, estoppel by acqui-
> escence, and promissory estoppel. At the same time it has been sought
> to be limited by a series of maxims: estoppel is only a rule of evidence,
> estoppel cannot give rise to a cause of action, estoppel cannot do away
> with the need for consideration, and so forth. All these can now be seen to
> merge into one general principle shorn of limitations. When the parties to
> a transaction proceed on the basis of an underlying assumption – either
> of fact or of law – whether due to misrepresentation or mistake makes no
> difference – on which they have conducted the dealings between them –
> neither of them will be allowed to go back on that assumption when it
> would be unfair or unjust to allow him to do so. If one of them does go
> back on it, the courts will give the other such remedy as the equity of the
> case demands.[55]

But neither can this formulation be adjudged a success. In 1996 Millett LJ
said that 'the attempt to demonstrate that all estoppels . . . are governed by
the same principle has never won general acceptance'.[56] In 2001 Lord Goff
said, of the statement of Lord Denning's just quoted: 'This broad statement
of the law is most appealing. I yield to nobody in my admiration for Lord
Denning; but it has to be said that his attempt in this passage to identify
a common criterion for the existence of various forms of estoppel . . . is
characteristically bold.'[57] Lord Goff then, having quoted a statement from
a treatise to the effect that estoppel should not be permitted to undermine
the doctrine of consideration, added:

> I myself suspect that this statement may be too categorical; but we cannot
> ignore the fact that it embodies a fundamental principle of our law of
> contract. The doctrine of consideration may not be very popular nowa-
> days; but although its progeny, the doctrine of privity, has recently been

---

54 Denning, *The Discipline of Law*, 223.
55 *Amalgamated Investment and Property Co Ltd* v. *Texas Commerce International Bank Ltd*
   [1982] QB 84, 122 (CA).
56 *First National Bank* v. *Thomson* [1996] Ch 231, 236 (CA).
57 *Johnson* v. *Gore Wood & Co* [2002] 2 AC 1, 39–40 (HL).

abolished by statute, the doctrine of consideration still exists as part of our law.[58]

Lord Goff then said, of estoppel, 'in the end I am inclined to think that the many circumstances capable of giving rise to an estoppel cannot be accommodated within a single formula, and that it is unconscionability which provides the link between them'.[59] By this he meant that the underlying reason for estoppel is that it would be unfair for a person, having made an assertion that induces another to act to his or her detriment, to go back on the assertion. This approach also has its difficulties, and is also capable, in effect, of enforcing promises, as is illustrated by the Australian case of *Waltons Stores (Interstate) Ltd* v. *Maher*.[60] There, an owner of land demolished a building and commenced construction of a new one to the specifications of a prospective tenant. No binding lease was ever effected, but the prospective tenant was held to be estopped (in the view of the majority of the court) from retreating from an implied promise to complete the contract. The effect was that, although there was admittedly no contract, the prospective tenant was, paradoxically, bound by precisely those obligations that would have existed if there had been a contract, a consequence that, as a practical matter as between the parties, substantially qualifies the initial premiss that there was no contract.

Another aspect of the doctrine of consideration, referred to by Lord Goff in the passage just quoted, is its effect on contracts for the benefit of third parties, a topic that has given rise to much trouble in English law. In the old case of *Dutton* v. *Poole*,[61] a father, wishing to make a gift to his daughter and proposing to cut down trees to raise the necessary money, agreed with his son and heir that he would refrain from cutting down the trees if the son would pay the daughter £1,000. The son inherited the land with the timber intact, but refused to honour his promise. The promise was held to be enforceable in an action brought by the daughter and her husband.[62]

Until the mid-nineteenth century it was generally accepted by writers that this case was good law, though it was evidently an exception to the idea of privity of contract.[63] A variety of explanations was proposed.

---

58 *Ibid.*, at 40.   59 *Ibid.*, at 41.   60 (1987) 164 CLR 387.
61 (1689) 2 Lev 210, affd T Raym 302 (Ex Ch).
62 This was crucial, because the mother, who was the only witness to the agreement, would not have been competent to testify in an action brought by the father's estate, of which she was executrix. See 3 Keb 786, s.n. *Dutton* v. *Pool*.
63 Comyn, *The Law of Contracts*, vol. 1, 27, Addison, note 1, above, 247–8, quoting Lord Mansfield in *Martyn* v. *Hind* 1 Doug 142, 145, 'it is difficult to conceive . . . how a doubt

Gilbert, writing in the early-eighteenth century, approved of the result of the case, but encountered some difficulty in formulating a principle and defining its limits:

> So in consideration that the father of the defendant whose heir he is would not cut trees to pay the portion of the wife of the plaintiff sister of the defendant he assumed to pay to the wife of the plaintiff 1000*l*; the daughter and her husband may have an action on her father by reason of the nearness of relation and it is a debt to the daughter to make a provision [portion?] for her and so she is interested in the consideration and the son hath benefit by it; otherwise it is if the money had been paid to a stranger; the law therefore will put a near relation in the place of the promisee because the promisee is bound by the law of nature to provide for such relation and therefore the labour of the relation is a consideration for the promise made to him and the relation hath loss by not receiving the value of his father's labour but the law will not put a stranger in the place of the promisee, because there is no consideration why the payment shall be made to a stranger from whom the consideration did not rise.[64]

This laborious reasoning is not very convincing to the modern reader, and it is of interest in the present context for precisely that reason. Gilbert felt the necessity of formulating a proposition that would explain and justify the decision in *Dutton* v. *Poole*, while maintaining a general rule of privity of contract and excluding the 'stranger'. Several possible propositions are suggested by this passage: the promise is enforceable where promisee and beneficiary are close relatives; the promise is enforceable where the promisee owes a moral duty to confer the benefit on the beneficiary; the promise is enforceable where some asset of the promisee that would otherwise have been transferred to the beneficiary is transferred instead to the promisor in exchange for the promise. All these formulations have difficulties, and it is not the object of the present inquiry to consider which is preferable, or which most accurately represented the law in 1678 or in Gilbert's own time. The significant point is that Gilbert felt the need to articulate a proposition, or principle, that would satisfactorily explain and justify *Dutton* v. *Poole*, while at the same time stating the law as it was perceived to be when he wrote, and laying down a rule that would (in his and his readers' opinion) be satisfactory for the disposition of future cases.

---

could have been entertained in the case of *Dutton* v. *Poole*', Chitty, *A Treatise on the Law of Contracts*, 2nd edn, 48 (though with some reservation).

64 Gilbert, *Of Contracts*, f. 82 (punctuation added, abbreviations expanded – but one abbreviation might be 'provision' or 'portion' – and capitalization removed).

The reason for the conclusion in *Dutton* v. *Poole* plainly had much to do with general considerations of justice, including unjust enrichment. As the report puts it, 'the son hath the benefit by having of the wood, and the daughter hath lost her portion by this means'.[65] The phrase 'unjust enrichment' was not in use in the seventeenth century, but plainer language could scarcely have been found to express the idea that the son had been unjustly enriched at the expense of the daughter. Gilbert also, in the passage just quoted, mentions that 'the son hath benefit by it', and makes the argument that the daughter suffers a loss by the transfer of the value of her father's 'labour' (i.e. a valuable asset, in this case the timber), to the son instead of to her.

In the nineteenth century, *Dutton* v. *Poole* came to seem inconsistent with the principle of consideration, and the case was rejected in *Tweddle* v. *Atkinson*,[66] where an attempt was made by a husband to enforce a post-nuptial agreement made expressly for his benefit between his own father and the father of his wife. The action was brought, after the father-in-law's death, against his estate. Crompton J said in the course of argument that 'we should upset all the principles of the law of contracts if we held that the plaintiff could recover in this action'.[67] But 'all the principles of the law of contracts' had not, until then, been supposed to be inconsistent with cases such as *Dutton* v. *Poole*. Crompton J acknowledged that the law had changed:

> At the time when the cases which have been cited [these included *Dutton* v. *Poole*] were decided the action of assumpsit was treated as an action of trespass upon the case, and therefore in the nature of a tort; and the law was not settled, as it is now, that natural love and affection is not a sufficient consideration for a promise upon which an action may be maintained; nor was it settled that the promisee cannot bring an action unless the consideration moved from him. The modern cases have in effect overruled the old decisions; they show that the consideration must move from the party entitled to sue upon the contract . . . I am prepared to overrule the old decisions, and to hold that, by reason of the principles which now govern the action of assumpsit, the present action is not maintainable.[68]

In the *Law Journal* report the last sentence is given as: 'If it was necessary to do so, I should be ready to overrule these old cases, for they are contrary to all that we have learnt upon the subject, and we may take them not to be law at the present time.'[69] This is a very revealing passage, and shows

65 2 Lev 212. 66 (1861) 1 B & S 393, 30 LJQB 265. 67 30 LJQB 267.
68 (1861) 1 B & S 393, 398. 69 30 LJQB 267.

the self-consciously novel view of principle that came to predominate in the mid-nineteenth century. The 'principles which now govern the action of assumpsit' required the overruling of 'the old decisions' even though no one doubted the justice (as between the parties) of *Dutton* v. *Poole*, the case had stood for nearly 200 years, and the Queen's Bench had no actual power to overrule it.[70] Blackstone's treatment of assumpsit as part of private wrongs, less than a hundred years old, was consigned to an earlier period of ignorance of true contractual principles, an ignorance that prevailed until the nineteenth century when the law was 'settled, as it is now'. These last words reflect both the influence of Pothier and his English followers ('all that we have learnt upon the subject'), and the Victorian confidence in the progressive change of English social institutions, including law. In several ways Crompton J's technique was similar to that of Lord Kenyon in *Goodisson* v. *Nunn*, seventy years earlier.[71] Old cases directly on point were found by both judges to have been impliedly overruled by general propositions in more recent cases. But a significant element is missing from the later case. Lord Kenyon was primarily influenced by the consideration that the determinations in the old cases 'outrage common sense'. Crompton J made no express reference to common sense, or to general considerations of justice or policy. Had he done so, it is unlikely that he would have found himself able to condemn the outcome in *Dutton* v. *Poole*.

It is possible, however, that the court was influenced by an unstated policy concern. The written agreement in *Tweddle* v. *Atkinson* was an undisguised attempt to give retrospective legal enforceability to a pre-nuptial agreement that was unenforceable, not having been evidenced in writing in accordance with the Statute of Frauds. The written agreement was artificial and highly legalistic in its language, and actually anticipated and attempted to foreclose the legal problem by providing that 'it is hereby further agreed by the aforesaid William Guy and the said John Tweddle, that the said William Tweddle has full power to sue the said parties in any court of law or equity for the aforesesaid sums hereby promised and specified'. Since the promisor, Guy, had died, the effect of enforcing the written agreement would have been to allow Guy, by signing the written agreement, to turn an unenforceable promise into an obligation binding on his estate, to the benefit of his daughter and son-in-law but to the potential prejudice of creditors. In the course of argument counsel had suggested that the contract should be enforced so that 'the object of the

---

70 As pointed out by Blackburn J, at 399.   71 Discussed in Chapter 1, above.

parents to make a provision for the children is attained', to which Crompton J replied that 'at the present time all those provisions are made in
a different manner',[72] showing himself markedly unsympathetic to the
artificial legal device attempted to be foisted on the court. There were
other conventional and straightforward ways of transferring property to
children, but these methods (gift, deed, conveyance or settlement) could
not be used to the prejudice of creditors, and the implication of Crompton
J's remark may be that creditors should not be prejudiced (in this or in
possible future cases) by an attempt to disguise a gift as a binding contract. Blackburn J, in the course of argument, remarked that 'a voluntary
settlement of lands, made in consideration of natural love and affection,
is void, under 27 Eliz. c.4', a statute (closely related to the statute protecting creditors) making fraudulent settlements void as against subsequent
purchasers.[73] But, if the purpose of the court was to protect creditors, it
was quite unnecessary to lay down a rule invalidating all contracts for the
benefit of third parties. Denial that policy considerations play a proper
part in judicial decision-making may lead not, in practice, to the exclusion of policy considerations, but to the application of unarticulated and
unanalyzed policies, and hence to the adoption of a legal rule appropriate
from the perspective neither of principle nor of policy, and incapable of
supplying effective guidance in future cases.

Pollock's initial reaction (1876) was to point out that *Tweddle* v. *Atkinson* was a common law decision, and to imply that the result might be
different in equity. Pollock wrote that 'the rule is distinctly established
so far as any common-law right of action is concerned'[74] adding pointedly
that 'the doctrines of equity are not so free from doubt',[75] and discussing
at some length a case (*Gregory* v. *Williams*[76]) indicating that equity would
permit a third party to join with the promisee as co-plaintiff. Pollock
wrote, in a rather complex sentence, that 'it is impossible to say with
confidence that the question how far third persons can acquire equitable
rights under contracts and independent of trust is not to some extent
unsettled',[77] and these words were repeated in the second edition.[78] This
convoluted assembly of qualified and counter-qualified double negatives
reveals Pollock's uneasiness on the question: he was conscious that, after

72 30 LJQB 266–7.
73 30 LJQB 267. He also mentioned this point in his judgment as reported in 4 LT 468 at
    469.
74 Pollock, *Principles of Contract*, 1st edn, 190 (emphasis added).   75 *Ibid.*, at 191.
76 (1817) 3 Mer 582.   77 Pollock, *Principles of Contract*, 1st edn, 193.
78 Pollock, *Principles of Contract*, 2nd edn, 198.

the Judicature Act, equity ought to prevail over a conflicting common law rule,[79] but he was reluctant to grapple with the consequences of this line of thinking. This was the line of thinking that led Professor Corbin fifty years later to conclude that equity, and therefore a modern court, would permit enforcement by a third party wherever justice required it.[80]

Anson in his first edition (1879) followed Pollock on this issue paragraph by paragraph, but where Pollock tended to be cryptic and tentative, Anson was plain and dogmatic. Anson wrote, without limiting his conclusion to the common law, that the old doctrine permitting actions by third parties was 'finally overruled in the case of *Tweddle* v. *Atkinson*'.[81] Having mentioned one of the old cases, he said:

> But there is no modern case in which this proposition has been accepted. On the contrary, it is now established *that no stranger to the consideration can take advantage of a contract, although made for his benefit.*[82]

Anson dealt with the equity cases as follows:

> Until very recently there was no doubt that a third party could not sue alone in equity for benefits intended to be conferred upon him by the contract, although there is authority for saying that he could join as co-plaintiff in a suit brought by the actual promisee.[83]

Gregory v. *Williams* was cited in the sidenote to this paragraph, without discussion.

This treatment was calculated to marginalize, in the reader's mind, the effect of the equity cases. The proposition 'that no stranger to the consideration can take advantage of a contract, although made for his benefit' was printed in italics, signifying its high importance. Reference to *Gregory* v. *Williams* was consigned to a concessive subordinate clause, and for Anson to say that a third party could not sue 'alone' and to mention in passing that he could sue as co-plaintiff in a suit brought by the promisee, without pointing out that the court would, if necessary, compel the promisee to lend his name to the action, conceals the real extent of the beneficiary's right and suggests that the matter was of merely technical or procedural significance. In Anson's second edition (1882) *Gregory* v. *Williams* disappeared altogether.

---

79 Judicature Act 1873, s. 25 (11), Supreme Court Act 1981, s. 49(1) (now the Senior Courts Act 1981).
80 A.L. Corbin, 'Contracts for the Benefit of Third Persons' (1930) 46 LQR 12.
81 Anson, *Principles*, 1st edn, 200.   82 *Ibid.*, at 201 (emphasis in original).   83 *Ibid.*

Pollock's third edition (1881), probably influenced in its turn by Anson, also marginalized *Gregory* v. *Williams* by explaining it as amounting to a declaration of trust of property,[84] and by adding a generalized conclusion, following discussion of another case, that 'the result is that there is no real and allowed authority for holding that rights can in general be acquired by third parties under a contract, unless by the creation of a trust'. The equity cases were further marginalized in the fourth edition (1885) by the insertion of the words 'at first sight', so that the introduction to the discussion of equity was amended to read, 'the doctrines of equity are *at first sight* not so free from doubt'.[85]

One aspect of the separation of law from equity in the English legal system was that the common law judges were able to lay down legal rules in rather absolute terms, knowing that another court had power to mitigate the application of the rules in cases of severe injustice. After the Judicature Act, equity was, in case of conflict, supposed to prevail, but, in respect of several issues in contract law, the opposite occurred, and, oddly enough, equity was marginalized because it came to seem inconsistent with common law rules. This was a curious irony, not only because the Judicature Act provided that, in case of conflict, equity was to prevail, but because the common law rule might never have been asserted in absolute terms had it not been for the existence of the mitigating power of equity, and because it was the very inconsistency with the common law that had justified the Court of Chancery in taking the position it did in the first place.[86] A similar process of marginalization can be discerned in the rules relating to the parol evidence rule, unconscionability and mistake.[87]

The approach of *Tweddle* v. *Atkinson* was confirmed by the House of Lords in 1915. The concept of principle was again very prominent. Viscount Haldane said:

> in the law of England certain principles are fundamental. One is that only a person who is a party to a contract can sue on it. Our law knows nothing of a jus quaesitum tertio arising by way of contract . . . A second principle is that if a person with whom a contract not under seal has been made is to be able to enforce it consideration must have been given by him to the promisor or to some other person at the promisor's request. These two

---

84 Pollock, *Principles of Contract*, 3rd edn, 220. The report of the case, 3 Mer at 590, makes it clear that it was the *benefit of the promise* that was held on trust for Gregory, not any tangible property. Corbin discusses this aspect of the cases, see note 80, above.
85 Pollock, *Principles of Contract*, 4th edn, 220 (emphasis added).
86 See *Tomlinson* v. *Gill* (1756) Amb 330, and Corbin's discussion, note 80, above, at 18.
87 See discussion in Chapter 5, below, at pp. 127–30.

principles are not recognized in the same fashion by the jurisprudence of certain continental countries or of Scotland, but here they are well established.[88]

The link between this conclusion and the doctrine of consideration was emphasized by Lord Dunedin, who, comparing Scots law, to its advantage, with English law, said pointedly:

> I confess that this case is to my mind apt to nip any budding affection which one might have had for the doctrine of consideration. For the effect of that doctrine in the present case is to make it possible for a person to snap his fingers at a bargain deliberately made, a bargain not in itself unfair, and which the person seeking to enforce it has a legitimate interest to enforce. Notwithstanding these considerations I cannot say that I ever had any doubt that the judgment of the Court of Appeal was right [as to English law].[89]

So was the law 'now settled'? Scarcely. In 1919 the House of Lords enforced a contract for the benefit of a non-party, relying on the old equity line of thinking,[90] and in 1924 an exclusion clause in a bill of lading was enforced by a non-party without serious question.[91] In 1930 Corbin published his argument, along the lines suggested in Pollock's first edition about the effect of the older equity cases, in the *Law Quarterly Review* and addressed primarily to an English audience, but it was neither welcomed by English judges[92] nor taken up by English academic writers.

Lord Haldane's assertion that privity of contract was a 'fundamental principle' was, however, challenged by Denning LJ, who said, in 1949:

> Counsel . . . says that the plaintiffs cannot sue. He says that there is no privity of contract between them and the [defendant] board, and that it is a fundamental principle that no one can sue on a contract to which he is not a party. That argument can be met either by admitting the principle and saying that it does not apply to this case, or by disputing the principle itself. I make so bold as to dispute it. The principle is not nearly so fundamental

---

88 *Dunlop Pneumatic Tyre Co Ltd* v. *Selfridge & Co Ltd* [1915] 1 AC 847, 853 (HL).
89 *Ibid.*, at 855.
90 *Les Affreteurs Reunis Societe Anonyme* v. *Leopold Walford (London) Ltd* [1919] AC 801 (HL).
91 *Elder, Dempster Co Ltd* v. *Paterson Zochonis & Co.* [1924] AC 522 (HL). Even the dissenting judge (Viscount Finlay) expressly declined to rely on the ground that the defendant was not a party to the contract, approving, in this respect, the appeal of Scrutton LJ (dissenting in the Court of Appeal), to considerations of commercial convenience: [1923] 1 KB 441–2.
92 *Re Schebsman* [1944] Ch 83 (CA).

as it is sometimes supposed to be. It did not become rooted in our law until the year 1861 . . . and reached its full growth in 1915.[93]

But in 1961 the principle was reasserted by the House of Lords (Lord Denning, then himself a member of the House of Lords, dissenting). Viscount Simonds said:

> Learned counsel . . . met [the argument for enforcement] . . . by asserting a principle which is, I suppose, as well established as any in our law, a 'fundamental' principle, as Lord Haldane called it . . . an 'elementary' principle, as it has been called times without number, that only a person who is a party to a contract can sue upon it. 'Our law', said Viscount Haldane, 'knows nothing of a jus quaesitum tertio arising by way of contract'. Learned counsel . . . claimed that this was the orthodox view and asked your lordships to reject any proposition that impinged upon it. To that invitation I readily respond. For to me heterodoxy, or, as some might say, heresy, is not the more attractive because it is dignified by the name of reform. Nor will I easily be led by an undiscerning zeal for some abstract kind of justice to ignore our first duty, which is to administer justice according to law . . . The law is developed by the application of old principles to new circumstances. Therein lies its genius. Its reform by the abrogation of those principles is the task not of courts of law but of Parliament [two decisions of Lord Denning were cited here and rejected].[94]

This exceeds the forceful, and presses the limits of judicial courtesy. One could scarcely imagine a more powerful assertion of the absolute immutability of legal principle. So, it might appear, the law really was 'now settled'. But, surprising as this may seem, the *Midland Silicone* case was in effect abandoned within a few years, when the opposite result was reached by the Privy Council on very similar facts in the New Zealand case of *The Eurymedon*. Lord Wilberforce, giving the judgment of the majority of the Judicial Committee, said that the conclusion (enforcement by the third party) could 'be given within existing principles', but he had (to say the least) considerable difficulty in explaining the result in conventional terms. The Board was heavily influenced by considerations of commercial convenience and general considerations of fairness. Referring to an American case, Lord Wilberforce said that 'commercial considerations should have the same force on both sides of the Pacific', and said that he desired 'to give effect to the clear intention of a commercial document' adding:

93 *Smith* v. *River Douglas Catchment Board* [1949] 2 KB 500, 514 (CA).
94 *Scruttons Ltd* v. *Midland Silicones Ltd* [1962] 1 AC 446, 467–8 (HL).

It should not be overlooked that the effect of denying validity to the clause would be to encourage actions against servants, agents, and independent contractors in order to get round exemptions (which are almost invariable and often compulsory) accepted by shippers against carriers, the existence, and presumed efficacy, of which is reflected in rates of freight. They see no attraction in this consequence.[95]

This was a clear victory for considerations of commercial convenience and general considerations of justice, and an effective abandonment of what had so very recently been asserted by the House of Lords as 'fundamental principle'.

In a modern case having some parallels with the old case of *Dutton* v. *Poole*, namely, *Beswick* v. *Beswick*,[96] an uncle transferred a coal business (his only substantial asset) to his nephew in exchange for the nephew's promise to pay an annuity to the uncle's widow. The case resembles *Dutton* v. *Poole* in that the promisor had actually gained by receiving a valuable asset that would otherwise have benefitted the plaintiff (because the uncle would otherwise have made other provision for her), differing in this respect from *Tweddle* v. *Atkinson*, where no payments had been made. As Gilbert might aptly have said, the nephew had benefitted by receiving the value of his uncle's labour, and the widow had lost correspondingly. But this feature of the cases, of such obvious importance to every consideration of justice between the parties, was made to appear irrelevant by the principle established in *Tweddle* v. *Atkinson* combined with an over-rigid scheme of categorization that excluded considerations of unjust enrichment.[97] It is little to the credit of the law to establish, in the name of 'principle', rules that require the court to close its eyes to factors crucial to the attainment of justice.

The promise in *Beswick* v. *Beswick* was held to be enforceable, but only because the widow happened to be the administratrix of the uncle's estate, and so entitled, in the opinion of the House of Lords, to a decree of specific performance. It is plain that the court was influenced by the general considerations of justice just mentioned. The law lords described the nephew's conduct as 'an unconscionable breach of faith',[98] and the possibility of there being no remedy as 'grossly unjust',[99] and 'repugnant

---

95 *New Zealand Shipping Co Ltd* v. *A M Satterthwaite & Co Ltd* ('*The Eurymedon*') [1975] 1 AC 154, 169 (PC). This was substantially the same point that had been made by Scrutton LJ (dissenting in the CA) in *Paterson Zochonis & Co* v. *Elder, Dempster Co Ltd*, note 91 above, and by Lord Denning (dissenting) in *Scruttons* v. *Midland Silicones*, note 94, above.
96 [1968] AC 58 (HL).   97 See Waddams, *Dimensions of Private Law*, 49–50.
98 Lord Hodson, note 96, above, at 83.   99 *Ibid.*, Lord Reid, at 73.

to justice and [such as to] fulfil no other object than that of aiding the wrongdoer'.[100] The use of specific performance for this purpose was highly unusual. The remedy was given not because there was anything in the nature of money that could not compensate, but in order to circumvent the rule of privity, which Lord Pearce called 'a mechanical defect of our law'.[101] Lord Reid indicated, contrary to Viscount Simonds' view, that reform of the law would, if necessary, be within the proper power of the court.[102] Statutory reform of English law had been recommended by the Law Revision Committee in 1937, but nothing was done by Parliament until the enactment of the Contracts (Rights of Third Parties) Act 1999. Even after the statute it cannot be said that the law on the point is 'now settled', since it does not abolish the rule that a non-party cannot sue on a contract, but creates new exceptions to it, and, as Professor Stevens has cogently pointed out, the statute poses as many questions as it answers.[103]

In Canada the English law of the late-nineteenth and twentieth centuries was at first strictly followed, leading to a result in *Greenwood Shopping Plaza Ltd* v. *Beattie*,[104] which can, without much exaggeration, be called absurd.[105] The lessor of business premises had covenanted with its tenant to insure against fire. A loss by fire occurred, allegedly caused by the negligence of two of the tenant's employees, and the Supreme Court of Canada held that the lessor (and its insurer) was entitled to sue the two employees individually for the whole of the loss, even if the proper interpretation of the contract was that it had promised not to do so. The Supreme Court of Canada said that 'the rule of privity . . . since *Tweddle* v. *Atkinson* . . . has had decisive effect in this branch of the law. There are many cases which have applied this principle'.[106] But as the Chief Justice of the Nova Scotia Court of Appeal had pointedly commented, this result flew in the face of common sense, modern commercial practice and labour relations.[107]

When the issue arose again in *London Drugs Ltd* v. *Kuehne & Nagel International Ltd*[108] the Supreme Court of Canada took an entirely different

100 *Ibid.*, Lord Pearce, at 89.   101 *Ibid.*
102 *Ibid.*, at 72. To similar effect Lord Scarman in *Woodar Investment Development Ltd* v. *Wimpey Construction UK Ltd* [1980] 1 WLR 277 (HL), 300.
103 R. Stevens, 'The Contracts (Rights of Third Parties) Act, 1999' (2004) 120 LQR 292.
104 [1980] 2 SCR 228, 111 DLR (3d) 257.   105 See note 121, below.
106 Note 104, above, 263 (DLR).
107 *Greenwood Shopping Plaza Ltd* v. *Neil J Buchanan Ltd* (1979) 99 DLR (3d) 289, 295, (NSAD) per MacKeigan CJNS.
108 [1992] 3 SCR 299, (1992) 97 DLR (4th) 261.

view. The facts were similar to those in the *Greenwood* case. The plaintiff
stored a valuable transformer with the defendant warehouser, agreeing to
limit liability to $40. The transformer was damaged by the negligence of
two employees, and, as in *Greenwood*, the owner sued the employees per-
sonally. The plaintiff's counsel relied on 'longstanding, established and
fundamental principles of law', no doubt with some confidence of success
in view of the quite recent decision of the court in *Greenwood*. However,
Iacobucci J, giving the judgment of the majority of the court, decided
in favour of the employees. Iacobucci J could easily have found that the
case fell into one of the established exceptions to the doctrine of privity,
but he chose instead to deal with the issue directly, saying that 'I prefer
to deal head-on with the doctrine of privity and to relax its ambit in the
circumstances of this case'.[109] He considered that the strict rule should be
relaxed for reasons of 'commercial reality and common sense'.[110] Similar expressions were repeated: 'sound commercial practice and justice',[111]
'the reasonable expectations of all the parties to the transaction',[112] 'the
underlying concerns of commercial reality and justice',[113] 'commercial
reality',[114] a result that made 'sense in the modern world',[115] 'sound policy reasons',[116] 'commercial reality and justice'[117] and 'modern notions
of commercial reality and justice',[118] ideas that were contrasted, to their
advantage, with 'a strict application of the doctrine of privity',[119] and 'the
rigid retention of a doctrine that has undergone systematic and substantial attack'.[120] He said that it would be 'absurd in the circumstances of
this case to let the appellant go around the limitation of liability clause
by suing the respondent employees in tort'.[121] These phrases show that
policy considerations were highly influential.

The court did not, however, simply abolish the doctrine of privity, but created a limited exception, which Iacobucci J described as an
'incremental change'.[122] Many commentators and courts had said, as we
have seen, that it was a 'principle' – often indeed called a 'fundamental
principle' – of English and Canadian law that only a party to a contract
could sue on it. Iacobucci J himself described privity of contract as 'an
established principle in the law of contracts [which] should not be discarded lightly'.[123] This phrase demonstrates the elusive meaning of the
idea of principle. Evidently a 'principle', even though 'established', is not

---

109 *Ibid.*, at 341 (DLR).   110 *Ibid.*, at 342.   111 *Ibid.*, at 348.   112 *Ibid.*
113 *Ibid.*   114 *Ibid.*, at 360.   115 *Ibid.*, at 364.   116 *Ibid.*   117 *Ibid.*, at 365.
118 *Ibid.*, at 370.   119 *Ibid.*, at 361.   120 *Ibid.*, at 358.   121 *Ibid.*, at 363.
122 *Ibid.*, at 366.   123 *Ibid.*, at 358 (DLR).

necessarily determinative of legal issues, but can be 'discarded' for sufficient reason (though not 'lightly'). Although in that sentence Justice
Iacobucci called privity of contract a 'principle', more often he described
privity as a 'doctrine' and the *exception* to it as 'principled'.[124] Some might
wish that the court had made a more radical change. On this it may be
remarked first that an exception on such general grounds as 'commercial
reality and justice' *is* in reality a very far-reaching change, and second
that there are good reasons for caution. A simple declaration by the court
that the rule of privity was abolished would have *compelled* future courts
to enforce contracts for the benefit of third parties; the recognition of a
limited exception, on the other hand, has the effect of *empowering* future
courts in appropriate cases to enforce such contracts, but not compelling
them to do so. There are good reasons not to lay down a rule that all
contracts for the benefit of third parties must always be enforced. There
are two particularly difficult cases. One is the case of the incidental beneficiary – one who would have benefitted by performance of the contract but
not a person on whom the contracting parties intended to confer rights.
The other difficult case is where the original contracting parties seek to
rescind or modify the contract. Sometimes it is appropriate for them to
do so, and sometimes it is more appropriate to require the consent of the
third party, but it is not easy to formulate a universal rule on the point.
The effect of the decision in *London Drugs* was to reintroduce flexibility
to the common law, and to enable the lower courts to reach fair and just
results. This approach has advantages over statutory reform, which, as
the English experience shows, is apt to lead to unexpected anomalies and
complexities.[125] In the Canadian context there is the added point that
uniform provincial legislation on the matter could not realistically have
been anticipated.

In the subsequent case of *Fraser River Pile & Dredge Ltd* v. *Can-Dive Services Ltd*[126] Iacobucci J, giving the judgment of the whole court, extended
the *London Drugs* case to a case involving waiver by an insurer of sub-
rogation rights. The decision shows that the recognition of third party
rights in contracts is not limited to any particular class of contract, and
there seems no reason why third party rights should not be recognized in
any case where considerations of justice require it. Iacobucci J described

124 See note 127, below.
125 The complexities of the English statute are forcefully demonstrated by R. Stevens,
note 103, above.
126 [1999] 3 SCR 108, 176 DLR (4ᵗʰ) 257.

the *London Drugs* case as having introduced a 'principled exception to the common law doctrine of privity of contract'.[127] Principle and policy were closely associated in his mind. In *Fraser River* he spoke of 'policy reasons in favour of an exception',[128] and, as in *London Drugs* of 'common sense and commercial reality'.[129] Sometimes a distinction has been made between principle and policy, but it is evident that in Iacobucci J's mind they were not opposed: on the contrary, good policy was an essential aspect of sound principle. The same could be said of many influential judges and commentators in the nineteenth and twentieth centuries.

127 *Ibid.*, para 24.   128 *Ibid.*, para 40.
129 *Ibid.*, at para 25. Parts of an earlier version of this chapter were published in S. Waddams, 'Principle in Contract Law: the Doctrine of Consideration', in Neyers, Bronaugh and Pitel (eds.), *Exploring Contract Law*, and in 'Modern Notions of Commercial Reality and Justice: Justice Iacobucci and Contract Law' (2007) 57 *University of Toronto Law Journal* 331.

4

Unequal transactions

It might be true to say, as a social observation, that most *contracts* involve an exchange of approximately equal value, but this observation is decidedly misleading in respect of contract *law*. Very many contracts that have legally significant consequences involve the exchange of unequal values, and the effect of contract law, where such contracts are enforced, is, therefore, to bring about unequal exchanges. A contract may make a poor person rich; it may make a rich person poor; and it may make a poor person even poorer than formerly. These may be the consequences not only of contracts known to be speculative, but of ordinary contracts, such as sales of goods or land.

This feature of contract law has been limited and constrained to a considerable extent by the reluctance of courts, manifested in a wide variety of circumstances, to enforce transactions that are very unequal, or very disadvantageous to one of the parties, unless the other party appears to have a sufficient interest in enforcement. The fact that the transaction has occurred in accordance with an agreement has not always in itself been conclusive in favour of enforcement. This topic is often considered from the point of view of unfairness, or of inequality of bargaining power, and these are important aspects, but they do not offer a complete explanation: the courts have sometimes refused to enforce extravagant transfers of wealth even when they have occurred (or would occur if the transaction in question were enforced) in accordance with agreements between parties of equal bargaining power. No single principle has evolved to explain or to organize the cases, but, looking at the matter from a broad perspective, they may be considered as instances in which the court has manifested a reluctance to compel the transfer of something for nothing, and, by extension, of much in exchange for little. From this point of view, it is scarcely surprising that courts of justice should have been reluctant to use their powers to enforce drastic and potentially devastating transfers of wealth unless convinced that there is sufficient reason to do so.

The matter must be looked at from the perspective not only of contract law, but also from that of unjust enrichment. The phrase 'unjust enrichment', as mentioned in Chapter 2, like many other legal expressions, has both a general sense (signifying undue advantage) and a specific sense (signifying that branch of private law, sometimes called restitution, concerned with reversing enrichments). From the latter perspective, the existence of a valid contract presents, at first sight, a juridical reason for allowing the enrichment to stand, but the relation of contract law to unjust enrichment (in both its senses) is complex, and the question of the enforceability of contracts is not entirely separable from considerations of unjust enrichment, as appears from the material discussed in this chapter, and also from Chapter 5, on mistake.

It will be recalled from Chapter 3 that Gilbert, writing in the early eighteenth century, gave as the first reason in support of the doctrine of consideration that it tended to protect persons from very disadvantageous transactions. Having said that some opinions favoured 'the punctuall performance of every verbal promise', Gilbert continued:

> Others held that no obligation arises from a naked promise and that the force of the engagement doth totally depend on the consideration and they take it to be a thing of great rigour that a man should dispose of the fruits and effects of a long and painfull industry and all the certain advantages and conveniences of life by the meer breath of a word and the turn of an unwary expression; they also think that the very laws of self-preservation will not permitt it for what reason of conscience can oblige a man to those words that tend to his own destruction, but if a valuable consideration had been received the bargain is compleat for another man's industry comes in the place of his own.

Gilbert continued by saying that English law 'hath held the middle between these two extreames', in that formal contracts were enforceable, but informal contracts required consideration.[1]

The protection of promisors from disadvantageous transactions could not, however, supply a wholly satisfactory explanation, either historically or functionally, of the doctrine of consideration. Consideration has not usually been thought of as a method of protecting persons from disadvantageous bargains, because the consideration need not be of equal value with the promise that is to be enforced: a very small value – conventionally, as was said, a peppercorn – is sufficient. It is true also

---

1 Gilbert, *Of Contracts*, ff. 39–40 (some punctuation added, abbreviations expanded, and capitalization removed).

that courts, where they have been inclined to enforce a transaction, have shown considerable ingenuity in discovering consideration in circumstances where it might at first appear to be absent. But it is also true that one effect of the doctrine of consideration has been to prevent the legal enforcement of a purely gratuitous transaction – the transfer of something for nothing – even though it meets all usual tests of voluntariness, or autonomy, and even though the fact of the promise is convincingly proved, for example by a signed writing.[2] The doctrine of consideration was also employed in the nineteenth century to prevent enforcement of one-sided modifications of obligations.[3] This branch of the law attracted many anomalies and complexities and was, as we have seen, heavily criticized by courts and commentators; recently other approaches to the question have been advanced.[4] Nevertheless, it remains true to say that one effect of the doctrine of consideration has been, in some circumstances, to withhold enforcement of a disadvantageous contractual modification.

A reluctance to enforce one-sided transfers of wealth may be discerned in other aspects of contract law not usually thought of in this context. The discussion will be recalled from Chapter 1 of the rule, established in the late-eighteenth century, that in the case of a simultaneous exchange the defendant's obligation could not usually be enforced unless the claimant had performed or offered to perform the reciprocal obligation. Lord Kenyon's striking phrase will be recalled, that the older cases (those requiring full performance by the defendant even in the absence of performance by the claimant) 'outrage common sense'.[5] The underlying reason for Kenyon's comment was evidently that the effect of the older cases might be, and had sometimes been, to require the defendant to pay something for nothing, that is to render full performance in exchange for a counter-claim that might prove to be worthless.

This topic is closely related to unjust enrichment, an aspect of private law also developing in the latter part of the eighteenth century, though not under that name. Lord Mansfield had said in 1760, in what has become the leading case on the English law of unjust enrichment (*Moses* v. *Macferlan*) that money paid could be recovered back if paid 'upon a consideration which happens to fail'.[6] Looking at contract law and

2 *Rann* v. *Hughes* (1778) 7 TR 350 note.
3 *Stilk* v. *Myrick* (1809) 2 Camp 317, 6 Esp 129, *Foakes* v. *Beer*, (1884) 9 App Cas 605 (HL). See the discussion of this question in Chapter 3, above, and Chapter 6, below.
4 *Williams* v. *Roffey Bros & Nicholls (Contractors) Ltd* [1991] 1 QB 1 (CA) (duress), *Collier* v. *P & MJ Wright (Holdings) Ltd* [2008] 1 WLR 643 (CA) (estoppel).
5 Chapter 1, above, p. 1.   6 (1760) 2 Burr 1005.

unjust enrichment law together, it can be seen that, once this rule is
accepted, the rule established by Lord Kenyon must follow as a necessary
corollary, though Kenyon did not expressly say this. Lord Mansfield's
principle of failure of consideration establishes that if, in the simple case
of a sale of property, the buyer pays the price but does not receive the
property, the price can be recovered back by the buyer: the reason is
that the buyer has paid the price and has received nothing in exchange
for it. If this is accepted as a legal rule it must follow that, if on the
day agreed for completion of the transaction the seller had refused to
convey the property, the buyer would have been justified in withholding
the price, that is to say, in the language of the eighteenth century, that
the covenants were mutually dependent. The law could not coherently
make an order against the buyer to pay the price, which, if complied with,
would create an instant right in the buyer (enforceable in the same court)
to recover the money back again. The link between restitution for failure of
consideration and the question of dependent covenants was not expressly
made by Lord Kenyon, but in *Kingston* v. *Preston*, the decision of Lord
Mansfield chiefly relied on by Lord Kenyon as indicating the change in the
law relating to dependent covenants, successful counsel had argued that
the plaintiff's covenant (i.e. his covenant to give future security *after* the
defendant should have performed his side of the agreement) was 'worth
nothing'.[7] Lord Mansfield, in accepting the argument, used (according to
Lofft's report) very vigorous language:

> It would be the most monstrous case in the world if the [contrary] argu-
> ment . . . was to prevail. It's of the very essence of the agreement that the
> defendant will not trust to the personal security of the plaintiff. A Court
> of Justice is to say, that by operation of law he shall, against his teeth.[?!][8]

The underlying reason for the rule, from the perspective both of contract
and of unjust enrichment, was the same: the reluctance of the court, in
the absence of sufficient reason, to compel one party to render a valuable
performance, or to retain money that had been already paid, in exchange
for what was 'worth nothing'.

   Contract lawyers have commonly used the word 'consideration', as a
criterion of enforceablity, to mean value given or promised in exchange

---

7 James Oldham, 'Detecting Non-Fiction: Sleuthing among the Manuscript Case Reports
  for What was *Really* Said', in Stebbings (ed.), *Law Reporting in Britain*, 133, at 157 (from
  Lincoln's Inn Library). See the discussion of *Kingston* v. *Preston* and *Goodisson* v. *Nunn* in
  Chapter 1, above.
8 Lofft, 194, at 198 (suggested closing punctuation supplied).

for the promise sought to be enforced. It is evident that Lord Mansfield, in *Moses v. Macferlan*, was using the word in another sense, and it has often been said, by way of glossing his phrase, that consideration there meant contractual performance. It is true that, in many contexts, the concepts are equivalent, but it is very probable that Lord Mansfield was using the word in a still wider sense, to mean the reason or basis for the making of the payment. The passage was so understood by Sir William Evans, who equated it with the declaration *causa data causa non secuta* of Roman law,[9] and was understood in this sense also in the mid-nineteenth century, and applied outside the contractual context.[10] Professor Peter Birks, writing in 1985, also understood the word in this wide sense, again noting the influence of Roman law:

> The link between 'consideration' and contracts makes it easy to suppose that 'total failure of consideration' must always refer to a failure in contractual reciprocation, whereas in fact that is only the most common species of the genus so described. In the law of restitution the word 'consideration' should be given the meaning with which it first came into the common law. A 'consideration' was once no more than a 'matter considered', and the consideration for doing something was the matter considered in forming the decision to do it. In short, the reason for the act, the state of affairs contemplated as its basis. Failure of consideration for a payment should be understood in that sense. It means that the state of affairs contemplated as the basis or reason for the payment has failed to materialise or, if it did exist, has failed to sustain itself. The language of the Digest for the same phenomenon is *causa data causa non secuta* (things given upon a consideration, that consideration having failed).[11]

In its widest sense, the principle suggested by Lord Mansfield might be extended to the cases on mistake and frustration, and to embrace the contractual and the restitutionary perspectives on these questions: money transferred on a fundamental basis that happens to fail may be recovered back, and, if in such circumstances the money has been promised but not yet paid, it ceases to be payable.[12]

The need for alignment of contractual and restitutionary principles is shown by the Australian case of *Roxborough v. Rothmans of Pall Mall*

9 Evans, *An Essay on the Action for Money Had and Received* (1802), 25, reprinted in (1998) 25 *Restitution Law Review*, 1, 9 (Digest XII.3.4).
10 *Martin v. Andrews* (1856) 7 El & Bl 1 (money paid for anticipated expenses of subpoenaed witness; expenses not incurred).
11 Birks, *An Introduction to the Law of Restitution*, 223, and note.
12 Birks in *Unjust Enrichment*, 1st edn, suggested failure of basis as the foundation of unjust enrichment.

Australia Ltd.[13] There a retail seller of cigarettes paid to the wholesaler, as part of the price but separately identified and quantified, an amount of money in respect of a tax thought to be payable by the wholesaler to the government. The tax turned out to be invalid, and the retailer claimed repayment of the money paid for that purpose. Sometimes in such cases a persuasive argument can be advanced that there is an implied term that, in the circumstances that have occurred, the money should be repaid. This argument was indeed accepted by one of the majority judges,[14] but rejected by the others. Nevertheless the claim succeeded on the ground of failure of consideration. The argument for restitution is that the money in question was paid for a particular purpose that had failed to materialize, and so was paid 'upon a consideration which happen[ed] to fail'; the contract could not be construed expressly or impliedly to exclude a claim for restitution, and consequently the claim succeeded.

There is room, no doubt, for disagreement on how the contract should be interpreted, but this is no more difficult than other everyday problems of interpretation. A relevant test would be to ask whether, if money corresponding to the tax had not yet been paid when the tax was declared invalid, the retailer would have been obliged to pay it. In this context the question would appear as one of contractual interpretation (not unjust enrichment): did the parties in substance agree on an overall gross price, with the separation of the tax element shown just for information, or was the agreement in substance for two distinct payments for two distinct purposes? The matter is perhaps not entirely free from doubt, but most courts and commentators would probably conclude that, if the payment had not been made before trial, the wholesaler's claim for the tax element would have failed, that is to say that in the circumstances the payment of the tax element was not, as a matter of contractual interpretation, due.[15] To compel the retailer to pay a large sum of money specifically for the purpose of discharging its supposed liability to pay a tax now known to be invalid would be to compel the retailer to pay something for nothing, and would confer a corresponding enrichment on the wholesaler. The grounds on which restitution was sought on the facts of the *Roxborough* case (disappearance of the reason for the payment) are in substance identical to the grounds on which, if the money had not been paid, it would have been argued that payment was not, as a matter of contractual

---

13 (2001) 208 CLR 516.   14 Callinan, J.
15 R. Stevens, 'Is there a law of Unjust Enrichment?' in Degeling and Edelman (eds.), *Unjust Enrichment in Commercial Law*, 11, at 29.

interpretation, due. A consistent result in the two cases is, to say the least, highly desirable. It would be anomalous for the result to vary according to whether the payment was made just before or just after the declaration of the invalidity of the tax, for this would make the substantive rights of the parties depend on accidents of timing.[16] If it is accepted that a payment not yet made would not, under the terms of the contract, have been due, this tends to support the court's conclusion that the payment in respect of the tax was, on the actual facts of the *Roxborough* case, made upon a consideration that had failed.

The question raised here is not whether the payment was due under the original contract, but whether payment would have been due if it had not been made and the matter were now (at time of trial) in dispute, in the light of the events now known to have occurred. In the not uncommon case where a buyer of goods or services agrees to pay the price in advance of delivery and then defaults, the seller is entitled to damages, but not to the price unless property has passed to the buyer, or the contract is specifically enforceable, or it was validly agreed that the price should be paid as a deposit to be forfeited on default.[17] These exceptions show that the crucial question is not whether the payment was due under the original contract (plainly it was), but whether the parties agreed, on a fair interpretation of the contract, that the seller should, in the circumstances now known to have occurred, be entitled to *retain* the payment if made, or to demand it if not. This is a question of contractual interpretation that might in some cases be resolved by implication of a term, but considerations of unjust enrichment cannot be excluded. In seeking the answer to the question of interpretation the court is bound to consider whether the buyer would have been entitled to restitution if the payment had actually been made because, if the answer to that question

---

16 This was the objection to the result in *Chandler* v. *Webster* [1904] 1 KB 493 (CA), and the substantial reason why the case was overruled in *Fibrosa Spolka Akcjyna* v. *Fairbairn, Lawson, Combe, Barbour Ltd* [1943] AC 32 (HL).

17 If the full price is paid in advance and the buyer then repudiates the contract the price is recoverable, subject to the seller's claim for damages (*Dies* v. *British & International Mining Finance Corp Ltd* [1939] 1 KB 724, and American Law Institute, *Third Restatement of Restitution and Unjust Enrichment (Tentative Draft No. 3)* s. 36). It must follow that if the buyer promises to pay the price in advance and fails to do so, the seller is not entitled to the price. It has sometimes been suggested that the seller could refuse to accept the repudiation and retain the price (if paid) or recover it (if not). *White & Carter (Councils) Ltd* v. *McGregor* [1962] AC 413 (HL, Sc) might possibly be read to support this view, but the case has been much criticized and is not likely to be extended, or followed in other jurisdictions.

is yes it must follow that the disputed payment is not, as a matter of contract law, now due. As suggested earlier, the law cannot recognize a contractual right to a payment which, when made, creates an instant right to restitution. The corollary is that where the payment *has* actually been made, the court must consider whether, if the money had not been paid, the seller would have had a contractual right to demand it, because again, if the answer is yes, it must follow that restitution is excluded.[18] If the answer is no, it is desirable that restitution should be available, because otherwise the result will depend on an accident of timing, and the buyer who pays in advance as promised will be less favourably treated than the buyer who defaults.

Where money is paid in advance by a buyer, as in *Dies* v. *British & International Mining and Finance Co,*[19] the buyer, even though in default, is entitled to restitution, subject to any counter-claim for breach of contract, unless the contract can be construed to amount to an actual agreement for forfeiture of the pre-payment. Since the law usually leans against forfeiture, and the pre-payment in the *Dies* case was not described as a 'deposit' or by any equivalent word, the conclusion was that the over-payment (that is, the excess of the payment over the damages for breach) should be restored. Again where, as in *Sumpter* v. *Hedges,*[20] valuable benefits other than money are conferred (a partially completed building in that case), there is a strong argument for restitution, even where the claimant is in default, unless the contract can be construed as actually entitling the recipient to retain the benefit without payment. Some such contracts can be fairly construed to have this effect, for example a contingency contract,[21] where in exchange for a very high reward for success the claimant agrees to receive nothing in case performance is incomplete, but not all contracts can fairly be construed to have this effect, and it seems doubtful that the contract in *Sumpter* v. *Hedges* could be so construed.[22]

In a case, like *Dies,* where a buyer prepays a large proportion of the price and then defaults, if there is an express forfeiture clause (or if the prepayment is called a 'deposit') it is generally accepted that the court will, at least where the amount greatly exceeds a reasonable deposit, grant relief against the forfeiture clause and order restitution of the prepayment,

---

18 *Chandler* v. *Webster,* above, had at least the merit of consistency on this point.
19 [1939] 1 KB 724, *Third Restatement of Restitution (Tentative Draft No. 3),* s. 36.
20 [1898] 1 QB 673 (CA).   21 As, possibly, in *Cutter* v. *Powell* (1795) 6 TR 320.
22 But a contrary view is taken by B. McFarlane and R.H. Stevens, 'In Defence of *Sumpter* v. *Hedges*' (2002) 118 *Law Quarterly Review* 569.

subject to the seller's cross-claim for damages for breach of contract.[23] One speaks of 'setting aside' or 'granting relief against' a forfeiture clause. These are negative concepts from the contractual point of view, which do not, by their own terms, present reasons for restitution. But it has always been taken for granted that the two go together. The setting aside of the forfeiture clause has necessarily implied a right to restitution of the money paid. It would be incoherent to say: the court relieves against forfeiture but will not give restitution.

Let us suppose a case in which relief would be given against an express forfeiture clause[24] and imagine the same case, with the same prepayment but without the forfeiture clause, as in the *Dies* case. The same result must follow (that is, restitution of the prepayment). It would be quite incoherent for the law to set aside an express forfeiture clause but to refuse restitution of a similar prepayment where there was no forfeiture clause: this would be to relieve against a forfeiture where the parties had agreed to it, and to enforce a forfeiture where they had not. This example shows that payments made under a valid contract are sometimes recoverable for reasons related to unjust enrichment.

We are surely on the wrong track if we seek to resolve this issue exclusively by contractual or exclusively by unjust enrichment principles: the ideas are interdependent. Opinions have differed on whether unjust enrichment (as a distinct branch of private law) is subordinate, secondary, supplementary or subsidiary to contract law.[25] Where the forfeiture clause is adjudged valid it could be said, certainly, that contractual principles prevail, but unjust enrichment is not irrelevant because the assessment of the validity of the clause itself involves considerations of unjust enrichment. The validity of the clause is judged by weighing the considerations that favour enforcement of contracts against the desirability of avoiding the unjust enrichment that would be effected by an extravagant forfeiture.

---

23 *Stockloser* v. *Johnson* [1954] 1 QB 476, *Workers Trust & Merchants Bank Ltd* v. *Dojap Investments Ltd* [1993] AC 573 (PC).

24 See below at notes 53–9.

25 See R. Grantham and C. Rickett, 'On the Subsidiarity of Unjust Enrichment' (2001) 117 *Law Quarterly Review* 273: 'While the law of unjust enrichment is a core doctrine of the private law, it is a subsidiary doctrine'; L. Smith 'Property, subsidiarity, and unjust enrichment' in Johnston and Zimmermann (eds.), *Unjustified Enrichment*, 588 at 615: 'It begins to appear that unjustified enrichment is not actually subsidiary to contract law. Rather, it is excluded by an operative distribution of risks and benefits'; and H. MacQueen, 'Unjustified Enrichment in Mixed Legal Systems' (2005) *Restitution Law Review* 21, 33: 'A general test of subsidiarity seems to pose more questions than answers.'

Where the claimant is entitled to restitution, whether to avoid a forfeiture or a result that is otherwise unconscionable, or for undue influence, or for duress, it could be said that unjust enrichment principles prevail over contractual principles, because entitlement to restitution necessarily implies that the contract is unenforceable. No contract can be valid if performance of it would give rise to an immediate right to restitution.[26] Thus contract law and the law of unjust enrichment, though dependent on separate concepts, and though rightly treated for many purposes as separate branches of private law, have not been and cannot be entirely dissociated in their actual operation.

Specific performance, to be discussed further in Chapter 7, is regarded in English law as, conceptually, an exceptional remedy, available only if damages are inadequate. One effect of this approach has been to enable a person who has entered into a very burdensome contract to refrain from performing it, while offering to pay appropriate money compensation to the other party. This aspect of the law has been defended by economists as a recognition of 'efficient breach', and this concept, though criticized by some commentators, has been accepted by several courts.[27] The phrase 'efficient breach' appears on its face to be paradoxical, and Daniel Friedmann has usefully suggested that 'tolerated breach' may be a preferable concept.[28]

In the case of contracts for personal services there is a more fundamental objection to specific enforcement, namely, that it would be unduly restrictive of liberty. *De Francesco v. Barnum*[29] involved an apprenticeship agreement with a dancing teacher whereby the apprentice agreed to serve for seven years and not, during that time, to enter into any professional engagements without the teacher's permission. The contract was set aside primarily because the apprentice was a minor, but in discussing the availability of an injunction, Fry LJ commented generally on specific enforcement of contracts for personal services:

26 See J. Beatson, 'Duress as a Vitiating Factor in Contract' [1974] *Cambridge Law Journal* 97, 106–8, and Waddams, 'Contract and Unjust Enrichment: Competing Categories or Complementary Concepts?' in Rickett and Grantham (eds.) *Structure and Justification in Private Law*, 167.
27 *Bank of America Canada v. Mutual Trust Co.* [2002] 2 SCR 601; *Hillspring Farms Ltd v. Walton (Leland) & Sons Ltd* (2007) 312 NBR (2d) 109 (CA); *Delphinium Ltee v. 512842 NB Inc.* (2008) 296 DLR (4th) 770 at [51].
28 D. Friedmann, 'Economic Aspects of Damages and Specific Performance Compared', in Saidov and Cunnington (eds.), *Contract Damages: Domestic and International Perspectives*, 65, at 82–3.
29 (1890) 45 Ch D 430.

> I have a strong impression and a strong feeling that it is not in the interest
> of mankind that the rule of specific performance should be extended to
> such cases. I think the courts are bound to be jealous, lest they should
> turn contracts of service into contracts of slavery; and, therefore, speaking
> for myself, I should lean against the extension of the doctrine of specific
> performance and injunction in such a manner.[30]

Specific enforcement was refused, not only because it would have been
oppressive to the individual, but because it was 'not in the interest of
mankind'. Fry, who was a treatise-writer as well as a judge, commented
in the edition of his treatise published shortly after this decision that
'it is not for the interests of society that persons who are not desirous
of maintaining continuous personal relations with each other should be
compelled to do so'.[31] These comments, in and out of court, show that
there was thought to be a public interest, as well as a purely private interest
in retention by individuals of some degree of freedom, even where the
exercise of the freedom involved a breach of contract.

It is true that in the well-known case of *Lumley* v. *Wagner*[32] an injunction was issued restraining an opera singer from performing for a competitor of the plaintiff, but the court recognized that a decree of specific
performance actually compelling the defendant to sing for the plaintiff
would have been out of the question, and, in the particular case, the
restraint on the defendant's freedom of action imposed by the injunction
was comparatively slight: the injunction was for a period of three months
only, and it operated only in England, which was not the defendant's
normal sphere of activity. Moreover, there were reasons for the order not
present in most cases: the singer was a star performer for whom there
was no substitute; the plaintiff had invested heavily in her appearance at
his opera house; a money remedy would have been ineffective; and the
defendant was likely (unless restrained by injunction) to confer an unjust
benefit on the plaintiff's competitor. It is these considerations that have
lain behind the rules, adopted in many common law jurisdictions, to the
effect that an injunction will not be issued unless the defendant's services
are unique, and that the plaintiff must have an interest in restraining
the defendant's conduct that is independent of the interest in inducing
performance of the positive side of the contract.[33]

---

30 *Ibid.*, at 438.   31 Fry, *A Treatise on the Specific Performance of Contracts*, 49.
32 (1852) 1 De G M & G 604.
33 See *Whitwood Chemical Co.* v. *Hardman* [1891] 2 Ch 416, CA; *Macdonald* v. *Casein Ltd*
   [1917] 35 DLR 443; *Detroit Football Co.* v. *Dublinski* (1956) 4 DLR (2d) 688, reversed on

A powerful reason for reluctance in granting a decree of specific performance has been that, if the promisee were entitled to specific performance in a case where the burden to the promisor greatly exceeded the benefit to the promisee of actual performance, the promisee would be in a position to extract from the promisor a sum of money approaching the value to the promisor of release, and possibly greatly exceeding the value to the promisee of actual performance, in other words to obtain what might be a very large transfer of wealth.[34] Whatever the terminology, it is a fair summary of the practical effect of the law to say that where a contract imposes a burden on the promisor that is disproportionate to the legitimate interest of the promisee in actual performance, specific performance will not be granted, and the promisee will be restricted to a money remedy. Other legal systems that accept specific performance as a conceptually prior remedy, may achieve a similar result in practice in many cases by use of concepts such as good faith or abuse of rights. The *Draft Common Frame of Reference*, seeking to harmonize English law with civilian systems, provides that 'specific performance cannot . . . be enforced where . . . performance would be unreasonably burdensome or expensive'.[35] This language, if not identical with English law, is readily compatible with English ways of thinking. In their comment, the drafters observe that, despite the opposite conceptual approaches of English and civilian law, 'there is reason to believe . . . that results in practice are rather similar under both theories'.[36] Another comment refers in this context to good faith and 'abuse of remedy'.[37] These examples and references show that one of the principal reasons for placing restraints on the remedy of specific performance has been to avoid the undue enrichment of the promisee.

Mistakes as to the contents of contractual documents, discussed in Chapter 2, have been dealt with by various means, including a very extensive power of the court to reform or rectify the document, techniques of interpretation, and admission of extrinsic evidence to prove the understanding of the parties, or to show misrepresentations or

---

other grounds 7 DLR (2d) 9; *Corbin on Contracts*, s. 1206; Spry, *The Principles of Equitable Remedies*, 537; Sharpe, *Injunctions and Specific Performance*, para. 9.300; Farnsworth, *Contracts*, 825; Trebilcock, *The Common Law of Restraint of Trade*, 156–8; Waddams, 'Johanna Wagner and the Rival Opera Houses' (2001) 117 *Law Quarterly Review* 431.

34 Lord Hoffmann in *Co-operative Insurance Society Ltd* v. *Argyll Stores (Holdings) Ltd* [1998] AC 1 (HL) 15.

35 *Draft Common Frame of Reference*, III – 3:302(3)(b).

36 *Ibid.*, Comment B, vol. 1, 829.   37 *Ibid.*, Comment J, vol. 1, 833–4.

collateral contracts. From the present perspective, these may be regarded as methods of preventing the enforcement of a transaction that would be disadvantageous to one party, in circumstances where the other party has no reasonable expectation that the document truly represents the mistaken party's intention, and therefore no legitimate interest in enforcing the terms of the document.

Where money is paid or value given in the expectation that certain facts exist, or that certain events will occur, and where those facts or events fail to materialize, an unexpected enrichment may occur. This kind of mistake is discussed in the next chapter. As we shall see there, English law has given relief from contracts where unanticipated future events cause a radical change in circumstances.[38] In some cases of mistake as to existing facts relief has been given,[39] though there is considerable doubt about its scope.[40] Relief has been given from a completed gift on proof that the gift was made under the influence of a radical mistake.[41] These cases have often had the effect of granting relief from what would, if it had been enforceable, have been a transaction that had, because of the unexpected facts or events, turned out to be highly disadvantageous to one of the parties.[42] Unexpected disadvantage, standing alone, is not sufficient. But unexpected disadvantage combined with the absence of a legitimate interest in enforcement on the part of the other party has led to the setting aside of contracts.

Since the nineteenth century, writers on English contract law have emphasized the enforceability of contracts, and have tended to marginalize the instances in which contracts have been set aside for unfairness. In dealing with consideration it has been common to point out that inadequacy of consideration is not, in itself, a defence to contractual obligation, and from this 'elementary principle', as Frederick Pollock called it, it has been inferred that, if there is sufficient consideration to meet the test of contract formation, the contract must be enforceable. Pollock in his first edition (1876) wrote that it was:

> a distinguishing mark of English jurisprudence that the amount of the consideration is not material. 'The value of all things contracted for is measured by the appetite of the contractors, and therefore the just value

---

38 E.g. *Krell* v. *Henry* [1903] 2 KB 740 (CA).
39 *Scott* v. *Coulson* [1903] 2 Ch 249 (CA); *Solle* v. *Butcher* [1950] 1 KB 671; *Magee* v. *Pennine Ins. Co.* [1969] 2 QB 507 (CA).
40 *Great Peace Shipping Ltd* v. *Tsavliris Salvage (International) Ltd* [2003] QB 679 (CA).
41 *Lady Hood of Avalon* v. *Mackinnon* [1909] 1 Ch 476.
42 E.g. *Krell* v. *Henry* [1903] 2 KB 740 (CA).

is that which they be contented to give'. It is accordingly treated as an elementary principle that the law will not enter into an inquiry as to the adequacy of the consideration.[43]

Anson (1879) followed the same line, and made the point more forcefully:

> So long as a man gets what he bargained for Courts of law will not ask what the value may be to him, or whether its value is in any way proportionate to his act or promise given in return. This would be 'the law making the bargain, instead of leaving the parties to make it'.[44]

As both writers were aware, however, this was not the whole picture, because courts of equity had often set aside contracts on a variety of grounds related, in general terms, to unfairness. Pollock mentioned this aspect of English law with a somewhat awkward sidenote in his chapter on consideration (chapter IV):

> Inadequacy *plus other things* in Equity: see chap. XI[45]

In the body of the text, he wrote:

> Inadequacy of consideration coupled with other things may however be of great importance as evidence of fraud, &c., when the validity of a contract is in dispute: and it has been considered (though, it is believed, the better opinion is otherwise) to be of itself sufficient ground for refusing specific performance. This subject, which is by no means free from difficulty, will be examined under the head of Undue Influence, Ch XI., *post.*[46]

Anson, closely following both the form and the substance of Pollock's work, but with less nuance, dealt with the matter as follows:

> Equity so far takes adequacy of consideration into account in dealing with contracts, that if a contract is sought to be avoided on the ground of Fraud or Undue Influence, inadequacy of consideration will be regarded as strong corroborative evidence in support of the suit. [Reference followed to what Anson, like Pollock, considered the doubtful power of the court to deny specific performance on this ground.][47]

English courts, after 1875, administered law and equity together, and one of the principal stated purposes of Pollock's book was to consider

---

43 Pollock, *Principles of Contract*, 1st edn, 154, quoting T. Hobbes, *Leviathan*, (1651) pt 1, c. 15.
44 Anson, *Principles*, 1st edn, 63, quoting Alderson B in *Pilkington* v. *Scott* 14 M & W 657, 660.
45 Pollock, *Principles of Contract*, 1st edn, 156 (emphasis in original).   46 *Ibid.*
47 Anson, *Principles*, 65.

English law and equity as a whole. However, his approach to this question, followed in starker form by Anson, tended to marginalize the power of the court to set aside disadvantageous contracts. The statement of the general principle of law, followed by mention two pages later of a power to set aside contracts in 'equity' suggests that the power is exceptional. The categories of 'fraud, &c'. and 'fraud or undue influence' suggest rare and closely defined instances, scarcely affecting the general principles of contract law. The reference to inadequacy of consideration as a matter only of *evidence* tends to suggest that it has little effect on substantive law, and the emphasis of both writers on the power of the court of equity to refuse specific performance (leaving the promisee with a right to full damages) tends to distract the reader from the far more significant power of the court to *rescind* the contract (leaving the promisee with no remedy at all). The postponement of the subject to a later chapter also tends to suggest that it is not directly relevant to the most basic principles of contract law, and that relief on ground of unfairness is conceptually exceptional. The tendency to marginalize the issue reached a peak in Halsbury's *Laws of England* (1907–15) where unconscionable contracts were excluded altogether from the article on 'Contract', and dealt with, anomalously, in a different volume in the article on 'Fraudulent and voidable conveyances' (a quite separate topic).

The power of English courts to set aside contracts on grounds broadly relating to unfairness and inequality of exchange was, however, considerably wider than the extracts from Pollock's and Anson's books suggest. The first published treatise on English contract law (by John Joseph Powell, 1790) included a long chapter entitled 'Of the equitable jurisdiction in relieving against unreasonable contracts or agreements'.[48] Powell stated that the mere fact of a bargain being *unreasonable* was not a ground to set it aside in equity:

> for contracts are not to be set aside, because not such as the wisest people would make; but there must be fraud to make void acts of this solemn and deliberate nature, if entered into for a consideration.[49]

But Powell went on to point out that 'fraud' in equity had an unusual and very wide meaning:

> And agreements that are not properly fraudulent, in that sense of the term which imports deceit, will, nevertheless, be relieved against on the ground of inequality, and imposed burden or hardship on one of the parties to

---

48 Powell, *Essay upon the Law of Contracts and Agreements*, vol. 2, 143.   49 *Ibid.*, at 144.

> a contract; which is considered as a distinct head of equity, being looked
> upon as an offence against morality, and as unconscientious. Upon this
> principle, such courts will, in cases where contracts are unequal, as bearing
> hard upon one party . . . set them aside.[50]

Powell gave as an example the very common provision in a mortgage
that unpaid interest should be treated as principal and should itself bear
interest until paid. Powell wrote that 'this covenant will be relieved against
as fraudulent, because unjust and oppressive in an extreme degree'.[51] The
description of a standard clause of this sort as 'fraudulent', without any
suggestion of actual dishonesty, illustrates how different the concept was
from the modern meaning of fraud.

The very wide meaning thus given to the concepts of 'fraud' and 'fraudulent' indicates that the power to set aside contracts was much wider than
at first appears. Pollock, in his chapter on duress and undue influence,
also explained to his readers that 'fraud' could not be taken at face value:

> The term fraud is indeed of common occurrence both in the earlier and
> in the later authorities: but 'fraud does not here mean deceit or circum-
> vention; it means an unconscientious use of the power arising out of these
> circumstances and conditions' and this does not come within the proper
> meaning of fraud, which is a misrepresentation . . . made with the intent
> of creating a particular wrong belief in the mind of the party defrauded.
> Perhaps the best word to use would be imposition, as a sort of middle
> term between fraud, to which it comes near in popular language, and
> compulsion, which it suggests by its etymology.[52]

It is significant that Pollock, in elucidating the meaning of the word fraud,
should consciously look for an equally ambiguous word (imposition),
suggesting, on the one hand, the taking of unfair advantage, and, on the
other hand, actual compulsion.

The court of equity commonly gave relief against forfeitures of all
kinds. The most clearly established case was that of a mortgage. Mortgage documents usually provided that, on default in repayment, the land
should be forfeited to the mortgagee. The courts consistently refused to
enforce this simple provision, despite the fact that it was well known and
perfectly clear. Whatever form of words was used – even if the document
evidenced an outright conveyance of the land – the court, if convinced
that the substance of the transaction was a mortgage, refused to enforce
the document and permitted the borrower to redeem the land:

---

50 *Ibid.*, at 145–6.   51 *Ibid.*, at 146.   52 Pollock, *Principles of Contract*, 1st edn, 527.

So that in every mortgage the agreement of the parties upon the face of the deed, seems to be, that a mortgage shall not be redeemable after forfeiture . . . and a mortgage can no more be irredeemable than a distress for rent-charge can be irrepleviable. The law itself will control that express agreement of the party; and by the same reason equity will let a man loose from his agreement, and will against his agreement admit him to redeem a mortgage.[53]

No restriction, even by express agreement, was permitted on the right to redeem. In *Spurgeon* v. *Collier* (1758) Lord Northington said: 'The policy of this Court is not more complete in any part of it than in its protection of mortgages . . . ; and a man will not be suffered in conscience to fetter himself with a limitation or restriction of his time of redemption. It would ruin the distressed and unwary, and give unconscionable advantage to greedy and designing persons.'[54] This last sentence compendiously illustrates the impact of the separate but interlocking concepts that have run through the unconscionability cases: lack of consent, avoidance of unjust enrichment, and deterrence of wrongdoing, all linked with 'the policy of this Court'. A few years later the same judge again linked the concepts of reason, justice, freedom of consent and deterrence of trickery:

The court, as a court of conscience, is very jealous of persons taking securities for a loan, and converting such securities into purchases. And therefore I take it to be an established rule, that a mortgagee can never provide at the time of making the loan for any event or condition on which the equity of redemption shall be discharged, and the conveyance absolute. And there is great reason and justice in this rule, for necessitous men are not, truly speaking, free men, but, to answer a present exigency, will submit to any terms that the crafty may impose upon them.[55]

The rule was that the mortgagee could stipulate for no collateral advantage, and so strict was this rule that it came to be applied so as to cause the setting aside of agreements that were perfectly fair and reasonable. It was easier for the nineteenth-century English legal mind to accept a rigid rule that in no circumstances may a mortgagee stipulate for a collateral advantage (a rule that, for better or worse, happened to be the law) than a general power to relieve against unfair transactions (which seemed to admit a dangerous and unprincipled instability). So, ironically, in the name of upholding the sanctity of contracts, transactions were set aside

53 *Howard* v. *Harris* (1683) 1 Vern 190, 192. This passage from the argument of successful counsel was cited, with page reference and near quotation, as having assisted in establishing the law on the point, by Coote, *A Treatise on the Law of Mortgage*, 22.

54 (1758) 1 Eden 55, at 59 (Sir R Henley).   55 *Vernon* v. *Bethell* (1762) 2 Eden 110, 113.

that were *not* unfair. In a decision of the House of Lords in 1904 Lord Halsbury remarked, with evident irritation, that 'a perfectly fair bargain made between two parties to it, each of whom was quite sensible as to what they were doing, is not to be performed because at the same time a mortgage arrangement was made between them'.[56] Ten years later the House of Lords restored flexibility by appealing to the underlying original reason for the intervention of the courts:

> It was, in ordinary cases, only where there was conduct which the Court of Chancery regarded as unconscientious that it interfered with freedom of contract. The lending of money, on mortgage or otherwise, was looked on with suspicion and the courts were on the alert to discover want of conscience in the terms imposed by lenders . . . [I]t is inconsistent with the objects for which [the rules of equity] were established that these rules should crystallise into technical language so rigid the letter can defeat the underlying spirit and purpose.[57]

Forfeiture in its various forms has obvious advantages to the secured party, and it is not surprising that attempts were made by lenders to secure equivalent advantages without the immediate transfer of the property to be forfeited. The growth of the penal bond represented such an attempt. A common form of the bond was a covenant to pay a fixed sum of money unless some other act was performed by a certain date. The effect was to secure the performance of the other act, which might itself be the payment of a sum of money that had been lent by the obligee to the obligor.

The court of equity gave relief from such bonds on much the same principle as in cases of mortgages. The bond was, in substance, a device to secure repayment of a loan, and the legitimate interest of the lender was in repayment (of the principal, together with interest and costs) and no more. In 1880 the law on the point, out of keeping though it was with the spirit of the nineteenth century, was explained by Bramwell LJ (who, though not himself sympathetic, accepted that this was the law) as follows:

> [T]he Court of Chancery said that a penalty to secure the payment of a sum of money or the performance of an act should not be enforced; the parties were not held to their agreement; equity in truth refused to allow to be enforced what was considered to be an unconscientious bargain.[58]

---

56 *Samuel* v. *Jarrah Timber and Wood Paving Co.* [1904] AC 323, 325.
57 *Kreglinger* v. *New Patagonia Meat and Cold Storage Co Ltd* [1914] AC 25, 36–8 per Lord Haldane.
58 *Protector Loan Co.* v. *Grice* (1880) 5 QBD 592, 596.

Another judge said, in 1900:

> The Court of Chancery gave relief against the strictness of the common law in cases of penalty or forfeiture for nonpayment of a fixed sum on a day certain, on the principle that failure to pay principal on a certain day could be compensated sufficiently by payment of principal and interest with costs at a subsequent day.[59]

Important also was the obvious factor that a borrower in urgent need was apt to sign too readily an extravagant penal bond: the need for the funds was always immediate, and the possibility of enforcement of the bond remote.

The English courts of equity relieved against transactions entered into by persons expecting to own property in the future. The typical case was of the 'expectant heir', and this phrase, together with the otherwise obsolete phrase 'catching bargain', is generally used to denote this branch of English law, but the jurisdiction was not restricted to heirs: it extended to every kind of case in which the borrower expected to become the owner of property in the future. Commonly the substance of the transaction was a loan, but the transaction took the form of a sale of the expectancy, or of the reversion. The court would set aside the transaction unless the purchaser proved that he had given full value. As in the case of mortgages and penalties, the situation is one in which experience shows that a person, pressed with the immediate need for money, is apt to sell a future interest at an undervalue – sometimes at a gross undervalue: again, the need for money is immediate, and the interest given up seems remote. So ready was the court to set aside such transactions that the rule came to seem too rigid: a statute of 1867 provided that such transactions should not 'be opened or set aside merely upon the ground of undervalue'.[60] The statute, however, did not affect the general jurisdiction of the court to set aside unconscionable transactions,[61] and this line of cases supplies an important illustration of that wider jurisdiction, before and after 1867.[62] Pollock said, in his first edition, that 'practically the question is whether in the opinion of the court the transaction was a hard bargain'.[63]

Disadvantageous contractual transactions have frequently been set aside for 'undue influence'. This phrase covers a number of different circumstances. It may apply to an openly hostile relationship where one

---

59 *Re Dixon* [1900] 2 Ch 561, 576, per Rigby LJ.   60 31 & 32 Vic c. 4.
61 *Earl of Aylesford* v. *Morris* (1873) LR 8 Ch App 484, 490.
62 See the passage quoted at note 69, below.
63 Pollock, *Principles of Contract*, 1st edn, 534–5.

party threatens the other with adverse consequences if the agreement is not made. Such a case was *Williams* v. *Bayley*[64] where a son had forged his father's signature to promissory notes, and the creditor threatened to prosecute the son unless the father agreed to pay the debt. More commonly the phrase has been applied to situations related to fiduciary duties where one party reposes trust in the other. Certain categories of case have been said to give rise to a presumption of undue influence, but it is not necessary for the weaker party to bring his case into a recognized category: any case in which there is a relationship of trust or confidence may qualify for relief. A twentieth-century instance of a case that does not readily fall into any pre-existing category is one where an employee guaranteed her employer's debts. The guarantee was set aside by the English Court of Appeal. Millett LJ used strong language, very reminiscent of the older equity cases:

> This transaction cannot possibly stand . . . It is an extreme case. The transaction was not merely to the manifest disadvantage of Miss Burch; it was one which, in the traditional phrase, 'shocks the conscience of the court'. Miss Burch committed herself to a personal liability far beyond her slender means, risking the loss of her home and personal bankruptcy, and obtained nothing in return beyond a relatively small and possibly temporary increase in the overdraft facility available to her employer, a company in which she had no financial interest. The transaction gives rise to grave suspicion. It cries aloud for an explanation.[65]

Closely related, and perhaps conceptually indistinguishable,[66] are cases where the relationship between the parties is categorized as fiduciary.

The courts of equity exercised a more general jurisdiction to set aside transactions that they regarded as very unfair. In *Evans* v. *Llewellin*, where a disadvantageous transaction was set aside despite the absence of any kind of misrepresentation, concealment or non-disclosure, Kenyon MR, relying on a cumulation of considerations, had evidently been challenged to explain and formulate an appropriate principle:

> I am called upon for principles upon which I decide this case; but where there are many members of a case, it is not always easy to lay down a principle upon which to rely. However, here, I say, the party was taken by *surprise*; he had not sufficient time to act with caution; and therefore though there was no actual fraud, it is something like fraud, for an undue

---

64 (1866) LR 1 HL 200.
65 *Credit Lyonnais Bank Nederland NV* v. *Burch* [1997] 1 All ER 144 (CA), 152.
66 See *Lloyds Bank* v. *Bundy* [1975] QB 326 (CA).

advantage was taken of his situation. The case of infants dealing with guardians, of sons with fathers, all proceed on the same general principle, and establish this, that if the party is in a situation, in which he is not a *free agent*, and is not *equal to protecting himself* this court will protect him.[67]

In 1818 it was said that:

a court of equity will inquire whether the parties really did meet on equal terms; and if it be found that the vendor was in distressed circumstances, and that advantage was taken of that distress, it will avoid the contract.[68]

In 1888, summarizing the cases, Kay J said:

The result of the decisions is that where a purchase is made from a poor and ignorant man at a considerable undervalue, the vendor having no independent advice, a court of equity will set aside the transaction. This will be done even in the case of property in possession, and *a fortiori* if the interest be reversionary. The circumstances of poverty and ignorance of the vendor and absence of independent advice throw upon the purchaser, where the transaction is impeached, the onus of proving, in Lord Selborne's words, that the purchase was 'fair, just and reasonable'.[69]

Was undervalue alone a sufficient ground for relief at the beginning of the nineteenth century? This question is not easy to answer because of the elusive meaning of 'fraud'. There are, indeed, many statements by courts and commentators to the effect that undervalue alone was insufficient, but these cannot be taken at face value because of frequent indications that a gross undervalue created a 'presumption of fraud': where there was a large inequality of exchange the court could presume, without any separate proof, that the disadvantaged party must have been labouring under some sort of mistake or disability, or else must have been influenced by necessity, or by some sort of pressure, or by a relationship with the stronger party.[70] Some cases and contemporary comments suggest that the presumption was practically irrebuttable. Lord Chancellor Erskine said in *Morse* v. *Royal*, linking protection of the disadvantaged party both with 'principles' and with 'the policy of the law':

The authorities, connected with this Case, are not many; and the Principles are perfectly clear. One class of cases is that of contracts, that may be

---

67 (1787) 1 Cox 334, 340.   68 *Wood* v. *Abrey* (1818) 3 Madd 417, 423, per Leach VC.

69 *Fry* v. *Lane* (1888) 40 Ch D 312, 322. Lord Selborne's words were from *Aylesford* v. *Morris*, note 61 above, 491.

70 *Earl of Chesterfield* v. *Janssen* (1751) 2 Ves Sen 125; *Heathcote* v. *Paignon* (1787) 2 Bro CC 167.

> avoided, as being contrary to the Policy of the law; which are interdicted
> for the wisest reasons. Of that kind are a Deed of Gift, obtained by an
> Attorney while engaged in the business of the author of that Gift; a Deed
> by an Heir, when of Age, to his Guardian; Purchase of Reversions from
> young Heirs, when of age . . . To that Class of Cases I shall add the Case of a
> Trustee selling to himself. Without any consideration of Fraud, or looking
> beyond the Relation of the parties, that Contract is void . . . The Contract
> is interdicted by the Policy of the Law.[71]

In *Lowther* v. *Lowther* the same judge said that 'though inadequacy of
Consideration is not of itself a sufficient ground for setting aside a Contract, it is, when gross, strong evidence of Fraud'.[72] In a note on a case of
1790 it was said that 'under ordinary circumstances even a considerable
inadequacy of price will not invalidate a sale . . . still, the inadequacy may
be so gross as, *of itself*, plainly to demonstrate fraud'.[73] In *A Treatise of
Equity*, published in 1737 and attributed to Henry Ballow, the author
said that 'it is a certain rule, that where the Bargain is plainly iniquitous, and it is against Conscience to insist upon it, as fifty Years purchase
for lands; or an extravagant Price for Stock as was given in the *South-
Sea* Year, Equity can't support it, for that would be to decree iniquity'.[74]
The examples strongly suggest that, in Ballow's mind, 'an extravagant
price' might sometimes itself be a sufficient indicator of iniquity. Joseph
Story (1836) spoke in this context of 'the most vehement presumption of
fraud'.[75]

Summarizing the eighteenth-century cases, it may be said that inequality of exchange, though not, in itself, conclusive, was far from irrelevant:
a large inequality of exchange may be said to have called for some sort
of explanation (which might be that a part-gift was intended, or that the
inequality was caused by risks fairly allocated by the transaction).[76] An
attempt in the twentieth century by Lord Denning[77] to restate a general
principle in terms of unfairness and inequality of bargaining power was
rejected by the House of Lords,[78] but the older cases were not overruled.
Since the beginning of the twentieth century, legislation has empowered

---

71 (1805) 12 Ves 355, 371–2.   72 (1806) 13 Ves 95.
73 *Crowe* v. *Ballard* (1790) 1 Ves Jr Supp 91 (note by John Hovenden; emphasis added).
74 Ballow, *A Treatise of Equity*, 11.   75 Story, *Commentaries on Equity Jurisprudence*, 250.
76 *Rotheram* v. *Browne* (1747), 8 Bro PC 297 (part gift); *Mortimer* v. *Capper* (1782), 1 Bro
   CC 156 (inherent risk).
77 *Lloyd's Bank* v. *Bundy* note 66, above.
78 *National Westminster Bank Plc* v. *Morgan* [1985] AC 686 (HL).

the court to set aside loan and credit transactions that are found to be (broadly speaking) very unfair.[79]

A common situation arising in cases of loan guarantees is that the guarantor is induced to enter the transaction because of some kind of influence exercised by the principal debtor. The problem is whether, and in what circumstances, the lender, not having precise knowledge of the relationship between the guarantor and the principal debtor, should be precluded from enforcing the contract of guarantee. The typical case has been a guarantee given by a wife to secure her husband's debts, or those of his business. But many kinds of relationship raise the same problem. In *Credit Lyonnais* v. *Burch*, mentioned earlier, where an employee gave a guarantee to secure the debts of her employer, the English Court of Appeal held that the bank was precluded from enforcing the guarantee, and that it was not sufficient for the bank to recommend independent advice:

> The bank had actual notice of the facts from which the existence of a relationship of trust and confidence between Mr. Pelosi and Miss Burch could be inferred. It knew that they were respectively employer and junior employee working in a small business and should have 'appreciated that the possibility of influence exist[ed]'.[80]

In a later case the House of Lords laid down detailed rules for the guidance of lenders in such circumstances. Dealing with the case of husband and wife, Lord Nicholls said:

> For the future a bank satisfies these requirements if it insists that the wife attend a private meeting with a representative of the bank at which she is told the extent of her liability as surety, warned of the risks she is running and urged to take independent advice. In exceptional cases the bank, to be safe, has to insist that the wife is separately advised.[81]

The House of Lords was conscious of conflicting policies, desiring, on the one hand, to protect the vulnerable guarantor, and, on the other hand not to make it practically impossible for spouses to raise money on jointly owned property.[82] Despite the genuine endeavours of the court to

---

79 Money-lenders Act 1900 (excessive...harsh and unconscionable), Consumer Credit Act 1974, ss. 137–40 (extortionate, grossly exorbitant, grossly contravenes ordinary principles of fair dealing), Consumer Credit Act 2006, s. 140A (unfair).

80 See note 65, above, at 155.

81 *Royal Bank of Scotland Plc* v. *Etridge (No. 2)* [2002] 2 AC 773 (HL).

82 See the comments of Lord Browne-Wilkinson in *Barclays Bank plc* v. *O'Brien* [1994] 1 AC 180 (HL), 188–9.

satisfy these conflicting objectives, it is difficult to avoid doubts as to the
feasibility of the court's enterprise, because a guarantor who is truly under
the influence of a stronger spouse will not be effectively protected by the
measures proposed. A short private meeting in an office at a bank cannot
realistically be expected to displace the continuing influence of a stronger
spouse in whose company the weaker spouse will be immediately before
and after the meeting. Then there is the consideration that the transaction
can easily be restructured in the form of a direct advance of cash to the
weaker spouse; if he or she is truly under the influence of the other spouse
documents can readily be prepared and executed whereby money is paid
into the account of the weaker spouse and paid over, after a shorter or
longer interval of time, to the other; the precautions imposed by the
House of Lords would not apply in those circumstances. Moreover there
is the awkward consideration that, in the case of a guarantee secured
by a mortgage on the matrimonial home, it will, if the spouses are still
living together, be the stronger spouse – the very party who allegedly has
been responsible for the impugned transaction – who will benefit from
having it set aside, thus creating an incentive for self-serving evidence and
self-serving admissions. From the public policy point of view difficult
questions arise: is it an essential aspect of freedom that persons should
have unrestricted power to borrow money on security of their assets, or
are some restraints acceptable or desirable, and if so what restraints, and
on whom, and in respect of what assets? These are questions on which
social and judicial consensus was lacking and which, therefore, could not
readily be resolved by propositions recognizable as legal principles.

There are several other techniques that have been used by English law
to control potentially unfair contracts, which cannot be discussed here in
detail. One of these is the invalidation of disclaimer, or exemption clauses,
a topic with a long and convoluted judicial and legislative history in the
twentieth century. Another is the use of implied terms, which often have
the effect of importing obligations of good faith, and of converting an
apparently one-sided transaction into a more equal exchange. Another
method is to find that insufficient consent has been given, in particular
circumstances, to a burdensome contractual term. One twentieth-century
judge said that 'we do not allow printed forms to be made a trap for the
unwary'.[83]

The *Draft Common Frame of Reference* incorporates several of these
concepts in its provision on unfair terms. An unfair term, which is 'not

---

83 *Neuchatel Asphalte Co Ltd* v. *Barnett* [1957] 1 WLR 356, 360 (CA) (Denning LJ).

binding on the party who did not supply it', is defined differently according to whether the contracting parties are consumers or businesses. The definitions refer to 'transparency', 'significant disadvantage', 'good faith', 'fair dealing' and to whether terms are individually negotiated. A list is supplied of terms presumed to be unfair in consumer-business contracts.[84] The comments and notes to these articles show that this was a difficult and controversial question for the drafters.[85] Although no general duty of good faith has been adopted by English law, many of the concepts mentioned in the Articles and comments are reflected also in English cases.

Very often it has been asserted that the underlying reason for refusal to enforce unfair contracts is absence of consent on the part of the promisor, and this is implied by such concepts as cognitive incapacity, undue influence and coercion. Consensual capacity is, no doubt, a relevant, necessary and useful perspective on the problem, but it does not supply a complete explanation, and in certain respects it is misleading.

The principal attraction of the 'consent' approach is that it apparently enables relief for unfairness to be reconciled with a theory that requires enforcement of all voluntary agreements. Thus sanctity of contracts can be maintained in theory, those contracts that are not enforced being not, truly speaking, contracts at all. The objections to this, as a complete explanation, are that it is fictitious, artificial and circular, and that it distorts the concept of consent in cases where that concept is really needed, such as mistake.

In many cases where relief is given consent, in every ordinary sense of the word, is present. The vendor of land who sells for a tenth of its value, or the accident victim who settles a claim for a small sum in cash, or the employee who guarantees her employer's debts usually knows what the terms of the agreement are, and intends to agree to those terms. Relief has been regularly given against forfeitures and penalties, even to sophisticated and knowledgeable parties. It is not plausible to say here that the party seeking to set aside the contract has not assented to its terms. The ordinary tests of assent, subjective and objective, are fully met in most such cases. If it were argued that, where the contract is unfair, there is no 'true' assent,[86] the answer would be that a test would then be needed of what amounts to 'true' assent, and this necessarily reintroduces some test of fairness.

---

84 *Draft Common Frame of Reference*, II – 9:401–10.   85 *Ibid.*, vol. 1, 628–67.
86 J. Murray, 'Unconscionability, Unconscionability' (1969) 31 *University of Pittsburgh Law Review* 1.

A second general approach to unconscionability has been to focus on the wrongful conduct of the party seeking enforcement. This is suggested by concepts such as equitable fraud, and duress. There is confusion in the usage of the word 'unconscionable'. The older usage was to refer to the *transaction* as unconscionable; the attitude of the party seeking enforcement might be described as 'unconscientious' or 'unconscionable' or 'fraudulent', but these usages referred to the impropriety of seeking enforcement (now that the transaction has been adjudged unfair) not to any wrongful conduct at the time of the transaction itself.[87] On the other hand a number of modern courts have suggested that it is the *conduct* of the party seeking enforcement that must be shown to be unconscionable, thereby implying the need to establish some kind of wrongdoing.[88]

Many older cases cannot be explained as depending on the defendant's wrongful conduct. In 1864, in setting aside a sale of land at a large under-value, Turner LJ said:

> I say nothing about improper conduct on the part of the appellant; I do not wish to enter into the question of conduct...I am content to believe that in this case there has been no actual moral fraud on the part of the appellant in the transaction; but, for all that, in my judgment an improvident contract has been entered into.[89]

In 1873, in granting relief to a plaintiff from an improvident bargain, Lord Selborne said that the defendant:

> is not alleged or proved to have been guilty of deceit or circumvention, and the plaintiff has no merits of his own to plead. He comes into court to be relieved from the consequences of a course of very wilful and culpable folly and extravagance. I think him entitled to the relief which he asks; but I think it is not unjust that he should obtain it at his own expense.[90]

Costs were refused, and in some analogous cases a successful claimant has actually been ordered to pay the defendant's costs.[91] These cases show

---

87 See Sheridan, *Fraud in Equity*.
88 E.g., *Hart v. O'Connor* [1985] AC 1000 (PC); *National Westminster Bank v. Morgan*, note 78, above.
89 *Baker v. Monk* (1864) 4 De G J & S 388, 393–4. See James Devenney, 'Book Review of *Re-examining Contract and Unjust Enrichment: Anglo-Canadian Perspectives* by Paula Giliker (ed.)' (2008) 28 *Legal Studies*, 477, 480.
90 *Earl of Aylesford v. Morris*, note 61, above, at 499.
91 Field and others, Daniell, *The Practice of the Chancery Division*, 1180: 'Where securities are ordered to be delivered up because the bargain has been unconscientious judgment is generally given for the plaintiff upon the terms that he shall repay the defendant the amount actually advanced or paid by him, with interest; and the defendant being looked

plainly that proof of wrongdoing on the part of the stronger party was not required. Even though the party seeking enforcement has acted perfectly properly and entirely in good faith, there are cases where the transaction has been set aside. If, as in the 1873 case mentioned, the plaintiff has 'no merits of his own' and has caused the difficulties entirely by his own 'wilful and culpable folly and extravagance' he may still be entitled to relief. He should pay the expenses attributable to his folly, but this does not mean that he should suffer the consequences of full enforcement of what might be a disastrous contract or that the other party should receive an extravagant gain; justice is sufficiently done if the party seeking relief pays the costs (to both parties) of the legal proceedings that his folly has made necessary. So formulated, this is recognizable as a coherent and defensible principle.

There are many other cases in which relief has been given despite the absence of wrongful conduct on the part of the party seeking enforcement. Maritime salvage cases supply two kinds of examples. Salvage agreements were not infrequently set aside both on the ground that too small a sum had been agreed (undue advantage being taken of the salvors) and on the opposite ground that too large a sum had been agreed (undue advantage thereby being taken of the ship in distress). Wrongdoing, in any ordinary sense, was not required in either kind of case. In one of the cases setting aside a receipt 'in full payment' of salvage services on the ground that the payment was too small, the judge (Dr Lushington) said: 'I do not mean to say that this receipt was not honestly obtained, but the inclination of the court is to look at the circumstances of the case, and not to allow a paper to operate as a bar.'[92] 'So jealous was the law that no man should be deprived of his fair share of this reward, that even before the passing of [the Merchant Shipping Act, 1854, making assignments of salvage money void] it was a general doctrine of this court, that no seaman could enter into a stipulation of an inequitable nature.'[93] In the opposite case, where a salvor took advantage of a ship's difficulties in order to obtain what the court considered to be an extravagant payment, the agreement was again set aside.[94] The agreement was described by the court as 'inequitable',

---

upon as a mortgagee for that amount, he was treated as such, and the plaintiff ordered to pay him his costs.'
92 *The Silver Bullion* (1854) 2 Sp 70, 75. Also *Akerblom* v. *Price Potter Walker & Co.* (1881) 7 QBD 129 (CA).
93 *The Pride of Canada* (1864) 9 LT 564 (Dr Lushington).
94 *The Port Caledonia and The Anna* [1903] P 184.

'unjust', 'unreasonable' and 'extortionate',[95] but it does not appear that the salvor had committed or threatened any legal wrong. Again, undue influence may be established without proof of wrongdoing.[96]

The concept of unjust enrichment (in its general sense), though not before the twentieth century under that name, has been very influential. In the treatise of 1737 attributed to Henry Ballow, the author asserted the power of the court of equity to set aside very burdensome contracts, giving as the reason that 'no man should be a Gainer by another's Loss'.[97] This phrase, like phrases in many of the cases, old and modern, such as 'advantage taken of weakness',[98] and 'deriving immoderate gain',[99] strongly suggests that the principal underlying value to be weighed against the value of enforcing the contract is the avoidance of unjust enrichment. In *Moses* v. *Macferlan*,[100] Lord Mansfield gave, among the instances where restitution of money paid was available, 'money got through imposition (express or implied); or extortion; or oppression; or an undue advantage taken of the plaintiff's situation'. Unjust enrichment has been, since the middle of the twentieth century, recognized as a source of obligations independent of contract, but there is, in this context, a close interrelation between the two concepts: if the contract is enforceable the enrichment is not unjust, but if the enrichment is unjust the contract must be unenforceable. It is not satisfactory to say that, before unjust enrichment can be considered, the contract must *first* be set aside, because the concept of unjust enrichment (in its general sense) has itself been highly relevant in determining the enforceability of the contract. Nevertheless, unjust enrichment, standing alone, does not explain every case. A person who agrees to sell or to purchase property or services, even at fair market value, may be entitled to set aside the contract if it was induced by undue influence,[101] or by wrongful threats.[102] Thus the concepts of consent and of wrongdoing cannot be entirely dispensed with.

Inequality of bargaining power seems to offer an attractive principle, but this feature does not supply a complete explanation of past decisions.

95 *Ibid.*, at 189–90 (Bucknill J).
96 *Allcard* v. *Skinner* (1887) 36 Ch D 145; *Williams* v. *Bayley* (1866) LR 1 HL 200. See P. Birks, 'The Burden on the Bank' in Rose (ed.), *Restitution and Banking Law*, 199–200.
97 Ballow, *A Treatise of Equity*, 11.
98 *Earl of Chesterfield* v. *Janssen*, note 70, above, at 157.
99 See B. Crawford, 'Comment' (1966) 44 *Canadian Bar Review* 142.
100 See note 6, above.
101 See *Griesshammer* v. *Ungerer* (1958) 14 DLR (2d) 599 (agreement to purchase dancing lessons).
102 See Trebilcock, *The Limits of Freedom of Contract*, 81.

The cases on forfeitures and penalty clauses have frequently given relief to parties of equal or superior bargaining power, and, in more general terms, many instances have shown that a party of equal or even of inferior bargaining power may be found to have been unjustly enriched by transfers of wealth in accordance with or in association with agreements.

Public policy, discussed in Chapter 6, has sometimes been directly invoked to set aside disadvantageous contracts. Contracts in restraint of trade,[103] in restraint of marriage,[104] or otherwise unduly restrictive of personal liberty[105] have been held to be unenforceable. These cases involve a mixture of public and private considerations. Contracts in restraint of trade were said to be void unless reasonable, not only in the public interest, but 'in reference to the interests of the parties concerned'.[106] As Lord Diplock said, in relation to contracts struck down for restraint of trade:

> If one looks at the reasoning of 19th-century judges . . . one finds lip service paid to current economic theories, but if one looks at what they said in the light of what they did, one finds that they struck down a bargain if they thought it was unconscionable as between the parties to it, and upheld it if they thought it was not.[107]

In a more general sense, policy has often been invoked in support of the avoidance of unfair transactions. As mentioned, Lord Northington referred to 'the policy of this court' in reference to protection of mortgagors. In *Chesterfield* v. *Janssen* counsel for the successful plaintiff combined principle with policy and public with private considerations in his argument:

> The principle, on which the court has gone in these cases, is an unconscionable bargain, and it being clearly contrary to public convenience to encourage it. Such contracts are generally founded in oppression by taking undue advantage of the borrower's necessity; which is the general ground of the malignancy of usury; they are of public mischief by encouraging the extravagance of young men.[108]

---

103 *Mason* v. *Provident Clothing & Supply Co.* [1913] AC 724. See Trebilcock, *The Common Law of Restraint of Trade.*

104 *Lowe* v. *Peers* (1768) 4 Burr 2225.

105 *Horwood* v. *Millar's Timber & Trading Co. Ltd* [1917] 1 KB 305 (CA). See P. Saprai, 'The Principle against Self-Enslavement in Contract Law' (2009) 26 *Journal of Contract Law* 25.

106 *Nordenfelt* v. *Maxim Nordenfelt Guns & Ammunition Co.* [1894] AC 535, 565.

107 *A. Schroeder Music Publishing Co.* v. *Macaulay* [1974] 1 WLR 1308, 1315 (HL).

108 See note 70, above, at 129.

In *Gwynne* v. *Heaton* Thurlow LC said that an unconscionable bargain made with an heir dealing with an expectancy 'shall not only be looked upon as oppressive in the particular instance, and therefore avoided, but as pernicious in principle'.[109] The sentence demonstrates the close alliance in Thurlow's mind between principle and policy, and between individual justice and the public interest. Lord Hardwicke said in 1840, speaking of the same subject, that 'the court will give relief merely to discourage attempts of this nature'.[110] Colebrooke, perhaps the most purely principled of the nineteenth-century writers, was uncharacteristically vigorous in stressing the policy implications of this branch of the law, calling it a 'principle of national policy':

> Upon the principle of national policy, bargains with heirs, reversioners, or expectants, dealing with their expectancies, are treated as intrinsically corrupt, and repressed as radically pernicious; and therefore set aside, because they tend to encourage disobedience and imprudence on one side, and avarice and imposition on the other, and are attended with deceit on third persons not privy to the agreement, who, having the disposing power over the estate, were induced to leave it, as they supposed, to their heirs or families, and are misled into leaving it to persons succeeding to it under unconscionable and oppressive bargains made with necessitous expectants.[111]

In *Allcard* v. *Skinner* where a transfer of wealth to a religious order by a member of the order was held liable to be set aside, Cotton LJ said:

> the court interferes, not on the ground that any wrongful act has in fact been committed by the donee, but on the ground of public policy, and to prevent the relations which existed between the parties and the influence arising therefrom being abused.[112]

In a twentieth-century case where a mortgage to a bank was set aside on the ground that the bank had taken undue advantage of the trust reposed in it by the mortgagor, Sir E. Sachs said that:

> the word ['abused'] in the context means no more than that once the existence of a special relationship has been established, then any possible use of the relevant influence is, irrespective of the intentions of the persons possessing it, regarded in relation to the transaction under consideration as an abuse unless and until the duty of fiduciary care has been shown to be fulfilled and the transaction is shown to be truly for the benefit of the

---

109 (1778) Bro Ch 1, 10.   110 *Brooke* v. *Gally* (1740) 2 Atk 34, 36.
111 Colebrooke, *Treatise on Obligations and Contracts*, 62.
112 (1887) 36 Ch D 145, 171. Relief was refused for another reason.

person influenced. This approach is a matter of public policy . . . Once the
relevant duty is established it is contrary to public policy that the benefit
of the transaction be retained by the person under that duty.[113]

The law relating to fiduciary relationships, which commonly, though not
always, arise out of contracts, has often been said to be influenced by
considerations of public policy. The 'safety of mankind requires' strict
enforcement of fiduciary duties.[114]

There is much debate, and little consensus, about the theoretical basis
of contract law.[115] To every theory that seeks to explain why contracts
are enforced, unfairness, as a ground of relief, appears as an exception,
anomaly, or limitation: the criteria of enforceability have been apparently
satisfied, yet the contract is not enforced. This is true whether the fundamental purpose of contract law is taken to be giving effect to the will of
the promisor, or protecting the reliance or expectation of the promisee,
whether dealing with promises or bargains, whether resting on principles
of morality or of social utility, and whether primarily concerned with
justice between individuals or with social welfare.

Some attempts have been made to discern in the willingness of courts
to relieve against unfairness the positive implementation of social policy.
It has been suggested that the willingness of courts to set aside contracts
reflects the egalitarian values of the welfare state.[116] There is undoubtedly some substance in this suggestion: a society that acknowledges a
duty to give positive assistance to its poorest members can hardly fail to
sympathize with a poor and weak person who seeks relief from a very
disadvantageous contract.

Nevertheless, standing alone, the redistribution of wealth could not
qualify as a principle of contract law, partly because contract law could
not effectively achieve that object, and partly because no generalizable

---

113 *Lloyd's Bank* v. *Bundy* [1975] 1 QB 333, 343–6 (CA).
114 *Parker* v. *McKenna* (1874) LR 10 Ch App 96, 125. 'The desire to protect and reinforce the
  integrity of social institutions and enterprises is prevalent throughout fiduciary law' per
  La Forest J in *Hodgkinson* v. *Simms* (1994) 117 DLR (4th) 161, 186 (SCC). Wedderburn,
  'The Social Responsibility of Companies', (1985) 15 *Melbourne University Law Review* 4,
  24 wrote that 'fiduciary duty is imposed in private law but with a public function'. See
  also *Keech* v. *Sandford* (1726) Cas t King 61.
115 The principal theories are discussed by Stephen Smith, *Contract Theory*.
116 See Brownsword, Howells and Wilhelmsson (eds.), *Welfarism in Contract Law*; E. Posner,
  'Contract Law in the Welfare State: a Defense of the Unconscionability Doctrine, Usury
  Laws, and Related Limitations on the Freedom to Contract' (1995) 24 *Journal of Legal
  Studies* 283, S. Waddams, 'Unconscionable Contracts: Competing Perspectives' (1999)
  62 *Saskatchewan Law Review* 1.

proposition could be articulated in a form suitable for fair and consistent application by judges in private litigation. With some exceptions (mainly in monopoly situations) the law does not compel the making of contracts. Even where power is given to reopen or to rewrite a contract, there is usually no power to compel parties who have not dealt with each other at all to enter into a contract. Because of this, the ability of contract law to redistribute wealth in society has always been very strictly limited. Its scope of operation has been restricted, on the whole, to granting relief to those who happen to have entered into disadvantageous transactions. Moreover, the extent of relief for mistake or unconscionability is usually the restoration of the status quo before the contract was made. If there was an inequality of wealth between the parties before the contract was made, the most that the court has done, where it has granted relief, is to restore that situation. It may have prevented some persons from throwing away the little wealth that they had, but it has not made them wealthier.

Contract law gives attention to individual transactions, not, generally, to the overall wealth of the parties. Thus, wealthy parties benefit at the expense of the poor by doctrines of mistake, as where a bank erroneously credits a customer's account, or where a wealthy party signs a contract that contains a clerical error. Even in the case of relief for unconscionability, a wealthy party may benefit at the expense of a poorer party, as in the case of a wealthy farmer who sells the farm to an impecunious speculator for one-tenth of its value. The court, if inclined to give relief, has not been deterred by the consideration that the farmer was wealthier than the buyer, and would remain wealthier even if the transaction were enforced.

It should be noted too that the court, in a contract case, lacks the mechanism to assess the wealth of the parties. If redistribution of wealth were to become a central feature of contract law, the court would have to contemplate a full examination of both parties' wealth, with assessment of income and valuation of capital assets, with opportunity for the other party to dispute the evidence. Such a process would, to say the least, be inconvenient in the course of a civil action. Relief from contractual obligation is specific to the parties. Even if the court had the means to judge the wealth of the parties, it could not compare the plaintiff with other potential recipients of welfare, who might be more deserving, nor could it compare the defendant with other potential contributors, who might have a greater ability to pay. Apart from the fact that the court lacks the machinery to operate a means test and a system of taxation, there are grave political and institutional objections to ad hoc taxation and distribution of the proceeds by individual judges.

The beneficiaries of the relief that contract law can give are rarely the very poor. They are people with something to lose, and with the means and energy to seek to retain or to regain it. As we have seen, the courts gave relief to expectant heirs who squandered their inheritance, and to landowners who sold their land at an undervalue. These were deserving cases, but they were by no means representative of the poorest members of their society. The greater the wealth lost, the more useful has been the law to the party seeking relief. Thus, the benefit of a judicial power to set aside contracts increases with the wealth of the weaker party. Litigation is often inaccessible to the poor. The law of insolvency must also be considered. If a debtor has many creditors, but only one is before the court, as is usual in a contract case, it cannot be right for the court to give relief against one creditor only. The effect will probably be to benefit, not the debtor, but the other creditors. There may well be a case for consumer bankruptcy, or a stay of proceedings against a needy debtor, but such a stay should bind all the creditors, and the court, in contract litigation, lacks the mechanism to achieve that result.

The considerations mentioned in the preceding paragraphs tend to suggest reasons why policy, standing alone, has not been adopted by courts as the primary criterion for setting aside unfair contracts: redistribution of wealth, however desirable it might be, from some points of view, in the interests of society, could not rank as a principle of contract law. But it does not follow that policy has been irrelevant. The word 'policy' has often been used in the sense of general residual considerations of justice between the parties, and in this sense it weighs in favour of giving relief from very harsh transactions. 'Policy' has also been used in the sense of giving due attention to the effect that a proposed rule or principle is likely to have on future cases. In this latter sense policy considerations have been adduced sometimes as a reason for granting relief, but also as a reason for restraint lest, in the words of an eighteenth-century judge, the court should 'throw every thing into confusion and set afloat all the contracts of mankind'.[117]

---

117 *Griffith* v. *Spratley* (1787) 1 Cox Ch 383, 388 (Eyre LCB).

The provisions of the *Draft Common Frame of Reference* on unfair terms have already been mentioned. The *Draft Common Frame of Reference* also includes a general provision entitled 'unfair exploitation', which includes several concepts very familiar to English lawyers,[118] including dependence, trust, economic distress, urgent needs, improvidence, ignorance, inexperience, and lack of bargaining skill.[119] These factors largely echo expressions used in English courts and tend to suggest lack of consent. The *Draft Common Frame of Reference* speaks of whether the advantaged party 'knew or could reasonably be expected to have known' of the factors, echoing the equitable concept of constructive notice. The phrases 'excessive benefit' and 'grossly unfair advantage' appear in the *Draft Common Frame of Reference*, and echo phrases like 'immoderate gain' and 'undue advantage' suggestive of unjust enrichment. But lack of consent, wrongdoing and unjust enrichment are not expressly required to be proved. The inclusion of these various elements in a carefully considered international document suggests that it has not been possible to reduce the issue to a single governing concept: several concepts, not wholly commensurable, appear to be simultaneously in play. The fact that these provisions have been included in a draft to which European civil and common lawyers have both contributed strongly suggests that it is no less important now than it was 250 years ago to avoid transactions that would 'ruin the distressed and unwary, and give unconscionable advantage to greedy and designing persons'.[120]

The *Draft Common Frame of Reference* includes the phrase 'given the circumstances and purpose of the contract',[121] which invites the court to look at the real substance of the transaction and to ask whether the enrichment can be justified by the allocation of risks properly inherent in the particular kind of transaction. The sale of a reversionary interest in land was, on the face of it, a sale of an interest in land. If that were the real substance of the transaction, that is, if the seller were dealing in a fair market for the purchase and sale of future property interests, a very large enrichment to *either* party would be wholly defensible if it arose from risks inherent in the purchase and sale of property, for example an unexpected rise in land values after the date of the contract. The allocation of that risk is the very nature of the contract, and the buyer takes a corresponding

---

118 The English law on undue influence and unconscionability is referred to, as is the Consumer Credit Act, *DFCR*, Note 4, vol. 1, 511–12.
119 *Draft Common Frame of Reference*, II – 7: 207. 120 See note 54, above.
121 *Draft Common Frame of Reference*, II – 7:208(1)(b).

risk of a fall in values: general contractual principles give strong support for enforcement *even if there is a substantial enrichment to the buyer*. The buyer, in that case, would simply have made a profitable, legitimate bargain. But, if the real substance of the transaction is a loan, the court will compare the net effect of the transaction with the terms on which money could be borrowed in a fair market for the lending of money, and will not allow the lender to extract what is, in effect, an extravagant rate of interest. The point was made in an eighteenth-century case:

> An annuity may be purchased at as low a rate as you can, provided it was the original negotiation to purchase and sell an annuity: but if the treaty began about borrowing and lending, and ends in the purchase of an annuity, it is evident, that it was only a method or contrivance to split the payment of the principal and usurious interest into several instalments, and consequently that it was a shift . . . So, in the case of goods or merchandise it is lawful to sell as dear as you can, on a clear bargain by the way of sale: but if it is first proposed to borrow, and afterwards to sell goods beyond the market price, this is usurious.[122]

No single or simple principle can explain these cases, nor can any single or simple view of policy. Policy, in this context, has had several meanings. Sometimes it has referred to a residual sense of justice between the parties, as in some of the cases on undue influence and unconscionability discussed above. The courts have been reluctant to use their powers to enforce large transfers of wealth unless the party who benefits has a sufficient and legitimate interest in enforcement: the transaction must be looked at from both sides.[123] The cases on forfeitures and penalty clauses reflect the courts' view that the legitimate interest of the party seeking to enforce such clauses lies in receiving performance of the primary obligation, not in gathering an unexpected and disproportionate windfall from a clause that was secondary to the main purpose of the transaction. As many of the cases indicate, a primary objective has been the avoidance of unjust enrichment, though not referred to by that name until the middle

---

122 *Earl of Chesterfield* v. *Janssen*, note 70, above (Lord Hardwicke). For further discussion, see Waddams, 'Protection of Weaker Parties in English Law', in Kenny, Devenney and Fox O'Mahoney (eds.), *Unconscionability in European Private Financial Transactions*, 26; Waddams, 'Autonomy and Paternalism from a Common Law Perspective; Setting Aside Disadvantageous Transactions' (2010) 3 *Erasmus Law Review* 121; Waddams, 'Abusive or Unconscionable Clauses from a Common Law Perspective' (2011) 49 *Canadian Business LJ* 378.
123 This concept was developed in respect of tort law in Ernest Weinrib's influential *The Idea of Private Law* (1995).

of the twentieth century. This has been perceived both as a requirement of justice between the parties, and as desirable in the sense of establishing rules likely to be beneficial for the future. In this last sense the concept of policy has been deployed both as a reason for setting aside contracts, and as a reason for restraint in setting them aside. All of these considerations have, at times, also been called principles.

5

Mistake

If contractual obligation depended on consent, it would seem to follow that a material mistake on any matter that induced the consent would prevent the formation of a contract. It was by application of this principle that Pothier asserted that 'error is the greatest defect that can occur in a contract, for agreements can only be formed by the consent of the parties, and there can be no consent when the parties are in an error respecting the object of their agreement'. He did not hesitate to spell out the far-reaching consequences of this line of thinking: 'error annuls the agreement, not only when it affects the identity of the subject, but also when it affects that quality of the subject which the parties have principally in contemplation, and which makes the substance of it', adding, as an illustration, 'therefore if, with the intention of buying from you a pair of silver candlesticks, I buy a pair which are only plated, though you have no intention of deceiving me, being in equal error yourself, the agreement will be void, because my error destroys my consent; for my intention was to buy a pair of silver candlesticks'.[1] Even where there was reasonable reliance by one party on the apparent consent of the other, as in the case of an artist commissioned to paint a picture by a person privately mistaken as to the artist's identity, Pothier thought that the mistaken party could not be liable on contractual principles, though he might be liable on a non-contractual principle: 'in this case I am obliged not by the agreement, which was void, and therefore could not produce any obligation; the reason of my obligation is the principle of equity which obliges me to indemnify the person whom I have imprudently led into an error'.[2]

Despite Pothier's very high reputation, this line of thinking could not be assimilated by nineteenth-century English law. The idea that any material mistake destroyed consent and made the contract void would have seemed too wide, because almost every case of a disadvantageous contract might

---

1 Pothier, *A Treatise on the Law of Obligations: or Contracts*, 12.
2 *Ibid.*, at 1, 1, III, 19 (Evans, 13).

be analysed as having been caused by a mistake. Notably in cases of mistake of quality of goods sold, as in Pothier's candlestick example, the English law was that the contract was enforceable, a result that might be explained (or perhaps merely restated) by saying that, in the absence of warranty or misrepresentation, the buyer takes the risk of the error. Moreover, the idea that reliance might be protected, as in Pothier's painter example, by a non-contractual principle having the same result as though there were a contract but depending on principles of equity could not be assimilated to English legal thinking. It would have seemed convoluted and artificial to deny that there was a contract and then to create an equivalent obligation derived from a non-contractual source. And no such source was available in nineteenth-century English law: no tort liability existed in such a case, and English equity could not have imposed such an obligation (to pay money as compensation for loss caused by imprudence) as Pothier contemplated.[3]

Nevertheless, English equity did have a very important role in respect of contractual mistake: the court had a wide power to rescind an agreement for mistake. The existence of such a power was not doubted before the Judicature Acts. Thus Story wrote that 'the general rule is that an act done or a contract made under a mistake or ignorance of a material fact is voidable and relievable in equity'.[4] This power was recognized by Leake[5] and Benjamin,[6] and was affirmed in wide terms by the House of Lords in *Cooper v. Phibbs* (1867).[7] Lord Westbury said:

> at the time of the agreement . . . the parties dealt with one another under a mutual mistake as to their respective rights . . . In such a state of things there can be no doubt of the role of a Court of equity with regard to the dealing with that agreement . . . If the parties contract under a mutual mistake and misapprehension as to their relation and respective rights, the result is, that the agreement is liable to be set aside as having proceeded upon a common mistake.[8]

The headnote writer also read the decision as affirming a wide general power: 'the agreement having been made in mutual mistake, the plaintiff, though there was no fraud, was entitled to have it set aside'.[9] Relief was

---

3 Compare Pothier's suggestion, discussed in Chapter 2, above, that an uncommunicated withdrawal of an offer would give rise to non-contractual liability.
4 Story, *Commentaries on Equity Jurisprudence*, 155, maintained in subsequent editions, 13th edn, vol. 1, 149–50.
5 Leake, *The Elements of the Law of Contracts*, 178.
6 Benjamin, *A Treatise on the Law of Sale*, 1st edn, 303.   7 (1867) LR 2 HL 149.
8 *Ibid.*, at 170.   9 *Ibid.*, at 149.

given, as Catharine MacMillan has said, 'for reasons related to conscience and not consent':[10] in some circumstances it was unconscientious to insist on enforcement of an agreement made by the other party under a mistake. Although the phrase 'mutual mistake' was used in *Cooper v. Phibbs*, the equitable perspective implies that it cannot be a requirement of relief that the mistake should be shared. As George Palmer wrote, 'it takes a peculiar sense of justice'[11] to regard the case of a party damaged by mistake as weaker where the party who profits knows the truth. The equitable principle of preventing an unjust result indicates that the crucial question is not whether the mistake was shared, but whether the party damaged by the mistake could fairly be said to have agreed to take that risk.

Though the existence of the power was not doubted, its limits were ill-defined. The power of the court to rescind a contract was, like all equitable remedies, 'discretionary', and the discretion would not be exercised in the absence of what seemed to the court to be sufficient reason. Where the agreement fairly allocated the risk to the mistaken party, the court would not intervene. But a large and accidental enrichment did present a strong case for rescission. In *Bingham* v. *Bingham*,[12] an eighteenth-century case expressly approved by the House of Lords in *Cooper* v. *Phibbs*, where there was a mistake as to the title to land, the court said, 'though no fraud appeared and the defendant apprehended he had a right, yet there was a plain mistake such as the court was warranted to relieve against, and not to suffer the defendant to run away with the money in consideration of the sale of an estate, to which he had no right'.[13] Though the phrase 'unjust enrichment' was not in use at the time, the concept could hardly have been more vividly expressed than by the phrase 'run away with the money'. Professor George Palmer has said that 'overhanging all problems of mistake . . . is the element of enrichment'.[14]

A case decided by the Court of Queen's Bench a few weeks after *Cooper v. Phibbs* suggests that even at common law a very radical mistake, going to the substance of what was contracted for, might nullify a contract, though the decision itself might be read to imply that such circumstances rarely arise. In *Kennedy* v. *Panama New Zealand and Australian Royal Mail Co.*[15] the buyer of shares in a company sought to avoid the contract on

---

10 MacMillan, *Mistakes in Contract Law*, 38. See also 53, 68 and 136.
11 Palmer, *Mistake and Unjust Enrichment*, 94.   12 (1748) 1 Ves Sen 126.
13 *Ibid.*, 126–7 (Fortescue, MR).   14 Palmer, *Mistake and Unjust Enrichment*, 96.
15 (1867) LR 2 QB 580.

account of a mistake as to whether the company had a binding contract
with the New Zealand government for delivery of mail. The buyer's claim
was dismissed on the ground that the shares were in substance the same
as those intended to be purchased,[16] but the court went on to formulate
a principle on which contracts might be set aside for radical mistake.
Blackburn J, giving the judgment of the whole court, referred extensively
to Roman law, saying that the relevant principle there was the same as in
English law:

> The principle is well illustrated in the civil law, as stated in the Digest, lib.
> 18, tit. 1. De Contrahendâ Emptione, leges, 9, 10, 11. There, after laying
> down the general rule, that where the parties are not at one as to the
> subject of the contract there is no agreement, and that this applies where
> the parties have misapprehended each other as to the corpus, as where an
> absent slave was sold and the buyer thought he was buying Pamphilus and
> the vendor thought he was selling Stichus, and pronouncing the judgment
> that in such a case there was no bargain because there was 'error in corpore
> [error as to the body]', the framers of the digest moot the point thus . . . and
> the answers given by the great jurists quoted are to the effect, that if there
> be misapprehension as to the substance of the thing there is no contract;
> but if it be only a difference in some quality or accident, even though the
> misapprehension may have been the actuating motive to the purchaser,
> yet the contract remains binding. Paulus says: 'Si æs pro auro veneat, non
> valet, aliter atque si aurum quidem fuerit, deterius autem quam emptor
> existimarit: tunc enim emptio valet [a sale of bronze for gold is not valid,
> but it is otherwise in the case of real gold but of quality inferior to what
> the buyer thought: for in that case the purchase is valid]'. Ulpianus, in the
> eleventh law, puts an example as to the sale of a slave very similar to that of
> the unsound horse in *Street* v. *Blay* . . . And, as we apprehend, the principle
> of our law is the same as that of the civil law; and the difficulty in every
> case is to determine whether the mistake or misapprehension is as to the
> substance of the whole consideration, going, as it were, to the root of the
> matter, or only to some point, even though a material point, an error as to
> which does not affect the substance of the whole consideration.[17]

The extracts from the Digest, the lengthier parts of which have been
omitted from this quotation, are significant: the court evidently thought

---

16 Catharine MacMillan, *Mistakes in Contract Law*, 201, writes that 'Kennedy's action was
   refused on policy grounds', the court being anxious, in the commercial and financial
   context of the time, to prevent disappointed shareholders from too easily avoiding their
   obligations. From this perspective, it is striking that the court went out of its way to
   elaborate the circumstances in which radical mistake *would* have been recognized as a
   contractual defence.
17 (1867) LR 2 QB 580, 587–8.

that 'the principle of our law is the same as that of the civil law', and
that English law could be derived from, or at least be usefully illustrated
by Roman law. *Cooper* v. *Phibbs* was not cited by counsel, but *Taylor* v.
Caldwell was; this was the leading case on what came later to be called
frustration, in which Blackburn J had also given a judgment relying heavily
on Roman law.[18] The fact that counsel cited the case shows that a link
between mistake and frustration was recognized at the time.

After the Judicature Acts it might have been expected that the new court,
uniting as it did the powers of the courts of law and equity, with equity to
prevail in case of conflict, would exercise the power of the former court of
equity to rescind contracts for mistake. However, despite the Judicature
Acts, there was a reluctance by English writers and judges to recognize the
full breadth of the equitable power to rescind for mistake. The main reason
for this reluctance was probably that the limits of the equitable power had
not been clearly defined,[19] and so recognition of the power, without
the ability to state clear limits, appeared to jeopardize the stability and
certainty of contracts. Another reason was that it appeared unnecessary,
and therefore undesirable, to separate the concept of relief for mistake
from that of contract formation: it seemed an attractive simplification
to apply a single principle (consent) to both, and thereby to eliminate
altogether the need for discussion of the old equitable jurisdiction. But
looking at the question in terms of contract formation was wholly alien
to the methods of thought of the old equity cases. Equity intervened in
order to prevent an unconscionable result, but not because the contract
was void. On the contrary, the contract was assumed to be valid at law,
and this was precisely why the intervention of equity was both justified
and required. Here, as elsewhere, the effect of merging the equitable and
legal jurisdictions was, ironically, to suppress the former equitable powers
to grant relief.[20]

The apparent attraction of a single simple principle to resolve this
problem ran into two fundamental and related difficulties. The first was
that the adoption of consent as the sole determining test had the effect
of excluding other relevant dimensions of the question. These might be
summarized as whether the risk of the mistake could fairly be said to
have been allocated by the contract to the mistaken party. The same
point might be stated in terms of whether the promisee had a reasonable

18 See discussion below, pp. 135–6.   19 See MacMillan, *Mistakes in Contract Law*, 49.
20 See the discussion in Chapter 3, above, of third party beneficiaries, and in Chapter 4,
  above, of unconscionability.

expectation of receiving the benefit of the transaction, and whether any enrichment caused by enforcement of the transaction should be considered unjust.

The second and related difficulty was that a test based solely on consent was, as Pothier's examples show, potentially far too wide. Almost every disadvantageous contract involves a mistake of some sort, and in almost every such case it is possible for the disadvantaged party to show that in the absence of the mistake the contract would not have been made. To set aside contracts for this reason alone would undermine the security of transactions. Before the Judicature Acts this danger was avoided by the self-restraint of equity in exercising the power to rescind. It seems, at first sight, to be an advance in legal thinking to formulate a single simple principle that will determine all cases without the need to resort to 'discretion'. But to say that the only test is whether the purported contract is 'void' for lack of consent conceals the need for the exercise, by the court, of judgment in determining the question of whether the risk can fairly be said to have been allocated by the contract to the mistaken party. This process undoubtedly involves an element of uncertainty, but uncertainty cannot satisfactorily be eliminated because addressing the question of risk allocation is crucial to the attainment of results that are fair to the individual parties, and that maintain the stability of transactions, while avoiding very large fortuitous enrichments. The attempt to make consent the sole relevant principle runs the risk of concealing or eliminating other equally important principles.

The collapse of the distinction between law and equity had other consequences. The concept of a contract that is not necessarily void, but that may be set aside by the judgment of the court for sufficient reason (i.e. one that is voidable), admits the possibility of enforcement by the mistaken party if that party so chooses. It admits also the possibility of partial relief, or relief on terms, which the court can fashion in order to meet the justice of the particular case. And it admits the possibility of denying or restricting relief in order to protect third parties who may have relied on the validity of the contract. These important objects were familiar features of equity, but they tend to be lost if the only and decisive question is formulated in terms of whether the contract is 'void' for lack of consent. It is not necessary, and may well be undesirable in seeking to summarize the law applicable in the twenty-first century, to link these marks of flexibility with the history of equity. But for present purposes it should be noted that one of the hidden effects of the adoption of consent as the sole test of mistake in English law has had the effect of depriving the courts of important elements of flexibility that had existed in English law as it was (taking the two systems together) on the eve of the Judicature Acts. This loss of flexibility was not intended or authorized by the Judicature Acts, and, partly because the former flexibility has not generally been recognized by modern courts or writers on English law, no serious justification of its removal has ever been advanced.

Pollock, as the influential author of the first book to examine the effects on contract law of the unification of the courts, must take some of the responsibility for the weakening of the old equitable jurisdiction. Catharine MacMillan's severe but carefully considered and justified conclusion is that 'the equitable treatment of mistake was sometimes overlooked, sometimes misunderstood and sometimes marginalised in Pollock's treatment of it'.[21] Pollock's first edition (1876) included a chapter on mistake, which, though lengthy,[22] was rather discursive, inconclusive and, at times, self-contradictory. He wrote that 'mistake does not *of itself* affect the validity of contracts at all' adding in a footnote that 'as fear is to coercion so is mistake to fraud',[23] words that imply that mistake is irrelevant without fraud. He then added: 'But mistake may be such as to prevent any real agreement from being formed; in which case the agreement is void both at law and in equity.'[24] These words indicate an attempt to assimilate law and equity under a single principle of contract formation, and this theme was reflected in the principal sub-heading of the chapter, 'Mistake as excluding true consent'.

The danger, mentioned above, of adopting a test that is too wide, which, when rejected, causes a swing to the opposite extreme of a very narrow test is illustrated by Pollock's treatment of consent. In his first edition Pollock cited, with full approval,[25] the following proposition, from the Indian Contract Act: 'Where both parties to an agreement are under a mistake as to a matter of fact essential to the agreement, the agreement is void.'[26] This proposition was too wide to be an accurate description of English law in 1876, or to be acceptable as a test for the future, and Pollock must soon have realized this for, by degrees, he distanced himself from the proposition. In the third edition it was introduced with the words, 'The Indian Contract Act gives the rule in *rather wide* language',[27]

21 MacMillan, *Mistakes in Contract Law*, 153.   22 88 pages, in a book of 577.
23 Pollock, *Principles of Contract*, 1st edn, 357 (emphasis in original).   24 *Ibid.*
25 'We cannot do better than begin with the rule and illustrations as given in the Indian Contract Act.'
26 Pollock, *Principles of Contract*, 1st edn, 397.
27 Pollock, *Principles of Contract*, 3rd edn, 455 (emphasis added).

and in the fifth edition (1885) it was reduced to a footnote.[28] In English law the adoption of consent as the only relevant criterion led, for the reasons just mentioned, to the assertion, in *Bell v. Lever Bros* (1932) of a very narrow view of mistake.[29] The old equitable jurisdiction was reasserted by the Court of Appeal in 1950,[30] but denied by the same court in 2002 in the name of coherence with the principles of *Bell v. Lever Bros*.[31] It is a curious irony that the equitable jurisdiction (which was supposed to prevail after 1875) should have been suppressed by reliance on the very feature (validity of the contract at common law) that had given jurisdiction to the courts of equity in the first place.[32] Wherever equity intervened to set aside a contract, whether for mistake, or for unconscionability, undue influence, or misrepresentation, the contract was valid at common law (otherwise equity could not have intervened). Coherence was attained before the Judicature Acts by the predominance of equity (enforced, if necessary, by the common injunction), and was supposed to be attained afterwards by express statutory provision.[33] As George Palmer has justly commented, 'in modern times English judges have sometimes remembered earlier English equity, but often it seems to be either forgotten or consciously discarded'.[34] In other jurisdictions a more flexible view has been preserved. The American Second Restatement of Contracts provides that 'a party bears the risk of mistake when . . . the risk is allocated to him by agreement of the parties . . . or . . . by the court on the ground that it is reasonable to do so'.[35] Canadian courts have accepted the survival of the equitable jurisdiction, with the consequence

---

28 Pollock, *Principles of Contract*, 5th edn, 469 note.
29 *Bell* v. *Lever Bros* [1932] AC 161 (HL), where large sums of money were paid to terminate employment contracts that could have been terminated without any compensation had the employer known of the employees' earlier misconduct. Catharine MacMillan, 'How Temptation led to Mistake: an Explanation of *Bell* v. *Lever Brothers, Ltd*' (2003) 119 *Law Quarterly Review* 625 examines the decision in its historical context, and concludes (659) that the particular circumstances of the litigation led to 'an overly rigid doctrine of contractual mistake'. The result though not the reasoning might, perhaps, be defended on the ground that the payments were made largely in recognition of past services that had been of real value to the employer (as to which there was no mistake) and only in part to compromise a potential claim for dismissal.
30 *Solle* v. *Butcher* [1950] 1 KB 671 (CA).
31 *Great Peace Shipping Ltd* v. *Tsavliris Salvage (International) Ltd (The Great Peace)* [2003] QB 679, para 157 (CA).
32 See at notes 19–20, above.
33 Judicature Act 1873, s. 25(11), Supreme Court Act 1981, s. 49(1).
34 Palmer, *Mistake and Unjust Enrichment*, 14.
35 American Law Institute, *Second Restatement of Contracts*, s. 154.

that the court may take account of such factors as the allocation of risk and the degree of enrichment.[36]

The *Draft Common Frame of Reference* provides for relief for fundamental mistake in certain circumstances unless the mistaken party had assumed the risk of the mistake.[37] The comment indicates that there is no uniformity among civil law systems, observing that 'there are substantial differences between the laws of the Member States in the way in which such cases are conceptualised and also in substantive outcomes'. The drafters add that the article 'does not purport to lay down rules which are "common principles" to be found in different laws, though it reflects what is found in many of them'.[38]

Pollock may have come to regret his treatment of the subject, for he was extremely critical of *Bell* v. *Lever Bros.* Shortly after the decision he wrote in a private letter that he thought it was 'wrong in law . . . and mischievous in fact as encouraging shifty people to say they forgot the things it was their business to remember'.[39] In the next edition of his treatise (the last published in his lifetime) he included an extended criticism of the case, concluding that '*Bell* v. *Lever Bros., Ltd* cannot be regarded as a satisfactory case; and I will even venture to hope that in the next generation our successors will put it on the shelf as one of those decisions on peculiar facts in which it is unsafe to put one's trust as settling any general principle'.[40] It cannot be said that this hope has been fulfilled in respect of English law, where *Bell* v. *Lever Bros* was regularly cited throughout the twentieth century in support of an extremely narrow view of the scope of relief for mistake,[41] but the case was 'put on the shelf' in respect of American law, and no discussion of it appeared in Corbin's comprehensive treatise (1950).[42]

Whenever a contract is induced by a false statement by one of the parties a mistake occurs – on the part of both parties if the misrepresentation is innocent. An innocent misrepresentation does not necessarily justify the

---

36 See *Miller Paving Ltd* v. *B Gottardo Construction Ltd* (2007) 285 DLR (4th) 568 (Ont CA) rejecting *The Great Peace.*

37 *Draft Common Frame of Reference*, II – 7:201(2)(b).

38 *Ibid.*, comment A, vol. 1, p. 457.

39 Pollock to O. W. Holmes Jr., 23 March, 1932, *Holmes-Pollock Letters*, vol. 2, 306.

40 Pollock, *Principles of Contract*, 10th edn, 498.

41 Its continuing influence was reaffirmed in the twenty-first century in *The Great Peace*, note 31, above.

42 The case was discussed and severely criticized by Palmer in *Mistake and Unjust Enrichment*, a book that influenced the *Second Restatement of Contracts*. See Reporter's Notes, *Second Restatement of Contracts*, American Law Institute, 383, 392, 400.

imposition of any obligation on the representor. If the statement in question does not meet the test of contractual formation there is no ground for imposing contractual liability,[43] and if the statement does not meet the test of tortious liability there is no ground for imposing liability in tort.[44] These propositions are clear, coherent and logical – indeed, practically self-evident, and may well be called principles. But it does not follow from them that an innocent misrepresentation is legally irrelevant. There is another relevant principle, namely that a misrepresentation inducing a contract, even though it does not justify the *imposition* of any obligation on the misrepresentor, affords an *excuse* from contractual obligation to the party misled.

The existence of this last principle was recognized by equity, which exercised a power to rescind a contract that had been induced by misrepresentation, even where the representation was entirely innocent. The reasons in support of this power were articulated in *Redgrave* v. *Hurd*:

> According to the decisions of the Courts of Equity it was not necessary, in order to set aside a contract obtained by material false representation, to prove that the party who obtained it knew at the time when the representation was made that it was false. It was put in two ways, either of which was sufficient. One way of putting the case was, 'a man is not to be allowed to get a benefit from a statement which he now admits to be false ...' The other was of putting it was this: 'Even assuming that moral fraud must be shewn in order to set aside a contract, you have it where a man, having obtained a beneficial contract by a statement which he now admits to be false, insists upon keeping that contract. To do so is a moral delinquency; no man ought to take advantage of his own false statements.'[45]

The phrases 'get a benefit', 'obtained a beneficial contract' and 'take advantage of' show that the avoidance of unjust enrichment, though not at that time by that name, was very prominent – overhanging, as Palmer said, all problems of mistake.

The equitable jurisdiction to rescind a contract was expressly recognized in the later case of *Derry* v. *Peek*,[46] and distinguished from the question of imposition of liability on the representor for deceit. Lord Herschell said that the action in deceit:

---

43 *Heilbut, Symons & Co.* v. *Buckleton* [1913] AC 30 (HL).
44 *Derry* v. *Peek* (1889) 14 App Cas 337 (HL). Negligence, recognized as a ground of liability for misrepresentation in *Hedley Byrne & Co.* v. *Heller & Partners Ltd* [1964] AC 465 (HL), required proof of fault.
45 (1881) 20 Ch D 1, 12–13.   46 Note 44, above.

differs essentially from one brought to obtain rescission of a contract. . . . The principles which govern the two actions differ widely. Where
rescission is claimed it is only necessary to prove that there was misrepresentation, then, however honestly it may have been made, however free
from blame the person who made it, the contract, having been obtained
by misrepresentation, cannot stand.[47]

He went on to contrast the tortious action for deceit, where proof of
dishonesty was required.

In *Heilbut, Symons & Co.* v. *Buckleton*[48] the House of Lords held that
a statement inducing a contract did not amount to a warranty in the
absence of contractual intention. Insofar as the case decided that before
contractual liability can be imposed the tests for imposing contractual
liability (whatever they may be) must be met the decision may, as suggested above, be accepted as principled, and indeed self-evident. But Lord
Moulton formulated a very different principle when he said that 'it is
of the greatest importance . . . that this House should maintain in its full
integrity the principle that a person is not liable in damages for an innocent misrepresentation, no matter in what way or under what form the
attack is made'.[49]

It may be accepted, as mentioned above, that an innocent misrepresentation does not in itself justify the imposition on the misrepresentor
of any contractual or tortious obligation, and this is what Lord Moulton
probably intended to convey by use of the phrase 'not liable in damages'.
But it does not follow from the absence of contractual or tortious liability
that a monetary obligation ought never to be imposed. Where there is
sufficient reason to rescind or set aside the contract in order to prevent
unjust enrichment, but where it is impractical to forestall or reverse the
transaction, it may be appropriate to require the party who has profited by the transaction to make a money payment in lieu of rescission
in order to bring about an equivalent effect. Such a payment, probably
not best described as 'damages', would not be measured by principles of
compensation for breach of contract or for tort, but by the need to avoid
or reverse an unjust enrichment. The whole question of innocent misrepresentation, and its relation to money remedies, which has given so
much trouble to the common law, is neatly resolved by the *Draft Common
Frame of Reference*, which provides that 'a party may avoid a contract for
mistake of fact or law existing when the contract was concluded if . . . the
other party caused the mistake', and adds that 'the question whether either

47 *Ibid.*, at 359.   48 [1913] AC 30 (HL).   49 *Ibid.*, at 51.

party has a right to the return of whatever has been transferred or supplied under a contract which has been avoided under this section, or a monetary equivalent, is regulated by the rules on unjustified enrichment'.[50] Lord Moulton said, in very forceful language, that it was a principle that a person is not liable in damages for an innocent misrepresentation and, so important was this principle that it was 'of the greatest importance' to maintain it 'in its full integrity' and 'no matter in what way or under what form the attack is made'.[51] But by looking at the matter from a different perspective the principle is displaced. The relevant principle in the *Draft Common Frame of Reference* is neither that a misrepresentation gives rise to an obligation, nor, on the other hand, that an innocent misrepresentor can never be required to pay money, but that a person who causes a mistake should not profit from it. The comment emphasizes that the provision is not based on the concept of wrongdoing: 'even if the party giving the information reasonably believed it to be true, that party chose to give the information; and cannot complain if the recipient is allowed to avoid the contract provided that the resulting misapprehension was serious enough'.[52]

Where unexpected events occur after the making of the contract, problems arise that seem closely analogous to those arising from mistake, but whether or not the analogy is recognized depends on what are supposed to be the governing principles. In the *Draft Common Frame of Reference*, mistake is dealt with as a ground of invalidity, under the heading 'Vitiated consent or intention', whereas the power of the court to vary or terminate an obligation on a change of circumstances is dealt with, not as part of contract law at all, but in a different book under general provisions affecting obligations.[53] The effect is to separate questions that are fundamentally similar. Nevertheless, the drafters, in a passing reference, recognized the link, writing in a note to the mistake provisions:

> in some systems, as an alternative to relief on the ground of mistake, relief may be given on the basis of *clausula rebus sic stantibus* [an implied condition that circumstances remain unchanged] e.g., GERMAN law, where the doctrine may apply to changes which have already occurred when the contract was made if the parties were not aware of the change.[54]

In English law the problem of mistake came, as we have seen, to be regarded as an aspect of contract formation, whereas the problem of

50 *Draft Common Frame of Reference*, II – 7:201 and II – 7: 212.   51 [1913] AC 30, 51.
52 *Draft Common Frame of Reference*, comment D, vol. 1, 459. *Redgrave* v. *Hurd* is mentioned in Note I, 1, at 464.
53 *Ibid.*, at III – 1:110.   54 *Ibid.*, Note 1, 2 to II – 7:201, vol. 1, 164.

subsequent changes of circumstances came to be seen as an aspect of the discharge of contracts. Yet, from the point of view of justice, and particularly of unjust enrichment, the problems are indistinguishable. A number of legal disputes arose from the cancellation of the coronation procession of King Edward VII in 1902. Large sums had been promised and in some cases pre-paid for the hire of rooms or seats with a view of the procession, which was unexpectedly cancelled because the king fell ill. Cases where the cancellation was announced before the contract was made (but unknown to the parties) were cases of mistake, whereas cases where the cancellation was announced after the contract were treated as cases of frustration. From the point of view of justice between the parties, the two kinds of case are scarcely distinguishable, and even those cases in which the cancellation was announced after the contract might be analysed as mistake cases if medical evidence showed that the king's illness, though undiagnosed, existed at the time of the contract, or that the decision to cancel had been made, though not yet announced. Relief was given to the hirers in both kinds of case.[55] If the relevant principle is perceived to be the avoidance of unjust enrichment, the cases are substantially alike, but if the relevant principle is thought to be one of contract formation, or construction of implied terms, the cases fall into entirely separate categories.

The idea of approaching the question through the concept of implied terms can be traced to what turned out to be the very influential decision of the Court of Queen's Bench in 1863 in *Taylor* v. *Caldwell*.[56] The contract was for the letting of a concert hall for a series of four concerts. The hall was destroyed by fire, and the plaintiffs brought an action to recover wasted expenses. At the trial, a verdict was given for the plaintiffs, but with leave to the defendants to move to set it aside. After argument before the whole court the verdict was set aside. Blackburn J, giving the judgment of the court, expressed the relevant principle, not very compendiously, as follows:

> [T]here are authorities which, as we think, establish the principle that where, from the nature of the contract, it appears that the parties must from the beginning have known that it could not be fulfilled unless when the time for the fulfilment of the contract arrived, some particular specified thing continued to exist, so that, when entering into the contract, they must

---

55 *Krell* v. *Henry* [1903] 2 KB 740; *Griffiths* v. *Brymer* (1903) 19 TLR 434. In *Clark* v. *Lindsay* (1903) 88 LT 198 the contract was made at 12.00 and the cancellation announced at 12.30. Relief was refused for another reason.

56 (1863) 3 B & S 826, Catharine MacMillan, '*Taylor* v. *Caldwell* (1863)' in C. Mitchell and P. Mitchell (eds.), *Landmark Cases in the Law of Contract*, 167.

have contemplated such continuing existence as the foundation of what was to be done; there, in the absence of any express or implied warranty that the thing shall exist, the contract is not to be construed as a positive contract, but is subject to an implied condition that the parties shall be excused in case, before breach, performance becomes impossible from the perishing of the thing without default of the contractor.[57]

Later in the judgment, the principle was condensed to the following proposition:

The principle seems to us to be that, in contracts in which the performance depends on the continued existence of a given person or thing, a condition is implied that the impossibility of performance arising from the perishing of the person or thing shall excuse the performance.[58]

The underlying justification for the result was that it seemed to accord with the intention of the parties, 'for in the course of affairs, men, in making such contracts, in general would, if it were brought to their minds, say that there should be such a condition'.[59]

However, there is an element of fiction in the highly abstracted notion of what 'men, in making such contracts, in general would, if it were brought to their minds, say' and it is by no means obvious that, if the matter had been raised in respect of the particular contract in question, the plaintiffs would readily have agreed that they should bear the whole loss of wasted expenses. As Catharine MacMillan has commented, 'from a judicial perspective, this fictitious device allowed courts to impose a rule of law while appearing to do so on the grounds of the parties' intentions'.[60]

Blackburn J said that 'there are authorities which, as we think, establish the principle', favoured by the court, but English law offered little in the way of authorities,[61] and Blackburn J looked for support from civil law sources, including Pothier and the Digest. He evidently felt a need to explain his resort to the civil law, and was slightly apologetic about his invocation of cases from Roman law involving the sale of slaves. But his use of these examples suggests that he perceived the existence of fundamental principles common to the civil law and English law:

Although the civil law is not of itself authority in an English court, it affords great assistance in investigating the principles on which the law is grounded. And it seems to us that the common law authorities establish

---

57 3 B & S 833–4.   58 Ibid., at 839.   59 Ibid., at 834.
60 Macmillan, note 56, above, at 202.
61 MacMillan writes (note 56, above, at 191) that, as a matter of prior English law, 'the plaintiffs should have succeeded', and describes the decision as 'extraordinary' (199).

that in such a contract the same conditions of the continued existence of
the thing is implied by English law.[62]

Early in the twentieth century the concept of 'continued existence of the
thing' was extended to cover cases where the parties had expected a certain event to occur in the future, as in the coronation cases, mentioned
earlier, where high prices had been agreed for seats or rooms overlooking
the route of the anticipated coronation procession. In his eighth edition
(1911), Pollock included these cases in the chapter entitled 'Impossible
agreements', but he recognized in the preface that this was scarcely satisfactory, since there was nothing in any way impossible about the actual
performance of the agreements in the coronation seat cases; the problem was not that performance was impossible, but that enforcement was
unjust. Pollock wrote in the short preface:

> Few recent decisions have affected any point of principle. Perhaps the most
> remarkable are those known as the coronation cases. They strengthen my
> belief that 'Impossible Agreements' is really not a legal category at all. If
> I could now rewrite the whole book, I should break up the contents of
> the chapter so named, and assign them partly to the head of Duties under
> Contract, and partly to a new chapter on Conditional Agreements.[63]

In a review published in 1906, Pollock said of the coronation cases that
'these decisions, except so far as they are purely on the construction
of special contracts, extend the rule laid down in *Taylor* v. *Caldwell* far
beyond its original scope; for the failure of the event contemplated by the
parties did not, in the coronation cases, make it impossible to perform
the agreement according to its terms'.[64]

A considerable number of cases arose in which contracts were found
to have been frustrated by circumstances connected with the First World
War. These cases had the effect of consolidating 'frustration' as an important and independent category in English contract law. Pollock, realizing
this, wrote to Holmes in 1920:

> I am revising the old book on contract, rather dramatically in parts –
> some of it seems to me but callow stuff now. I have in my mind some
> large rearrangement, such as a new head of Conditional Contracts with

---

62 See note 56, above, at 835.
63 Pollock, *Principles of Contract*, advertisement to 8th edn (1911).
64 Pollock, 'Book Review of *Principles of the Law of Contracts* by S.M. Leake [5th edn]' (1906)
   22 *Law Quarterly Review* 322, 323.

'frustration of adventure' prominent, but have not made up my mind whether it is worth the pains.[65]

When the coronation cases were taken into account, it had become increasingly difficult to explain the cases in terms of implied conditions, or on the basis of the implied intention of the parties, as suggested in *Taylor* v. *Caldwell*, and Pollock was very conscious of this difficulty. He added, in his letter to Holmes, that:

> After all, is not the implied condition in these cases something of a fiction to screen rules of policy imposed on the parties ... ?

This is a striking comment from several perspectives. 'Fiction' suggests that the reasons given by courts were false, and 'screen' suggests deception, though not necessarily a conscious or deliberate deception. The use of the word 'policy' in this context is also significant. By it Pollock appears to have meant that the results of the cases depended on a general judgment made by the court the reasons for which were not articulated. The word 'policy' here embraces general considerations of justice between the parties, as well as considerations of public interest, which, as we have seen, and will see in the next chapter, may operate directly or indirectly.

In the ninth edition, published in the following year, Pollock put his ideas into execution. The chapter on 'impossible agreements' was replaced by a new chapter entitled, somewhat awkwardly, 'Conditions, and herein of frustration'. In the preface he wrote, referring back to his preface to the previous edition:

> In the advertisement to the eighth edition I said in effect that I should like to rewrite the chapter headed 'impossible agreements' and abolish its heading. What then seemed a counsel of perfection hardly worth the pains of executing it has been made a necessity by the rapid development of the 'frustration of the adventure' doctrine in cases arising out of the war of 1914.[66]

The express reference to the cases arising out of the war may suggest that Pollock was not excluding direct considerations of the public interest in his use of the word 'policy' in the letter to Holmes of the previous year. In a note published in 1936 Pollock wrote that 'no branch of the law of contract is so difficult to explain or so uncertain in its effect as that dealing with frustration. It is in large part a comparatively recent development,

---

65 Pollock to Holmes 14 March 1920, *Holmes-Pollock Letters*, vol. 2, 38.
66 Pollock, *Principles of Contract*, 9th edn, preface, viii.

having been introduced to mitigate the harshness of the strict law.'[67] The reference to harshness indicates that 'policy' also included considerations of justice between the contracting parties.

Pollock's opinion that the theory of implied terms was 'something of a fiction' was soon taken up by the judges themselves. The traditional view that 'no court has absolving power'[68] gave way quite rapidly to another perspective. Lord Sumner said in *Hirji Mulji* v. *Cheong Yue SS Co.*[69] (1926) that frustration was 'a device by which the rules as to absolute contracts are reconciled with a special exception which justice demands',[70] a phrase expressly adopted by Pollock in the note just mentioned.[71] Writing extra-judicially, Lord Wright said in 1935 that:

> this whole doctrine of frustration has been described as a reading into the contract of implied terms to give effect to the intention of the parties. It would be truer to say that the Court in the absence of express intention of the parties determines what is just.[72]

In the following year in another lecture he described the theory of implied terms as 'a fiction'.[73] In a review of Williston's treatise he described it again in 1939 as a 'fiction' that was 'not very useful'.[74] In court he said, in 1942, that 'the court is exercising powers, when it decides that a contract is frustrated, in order to achieve a result that is just and reasonable'.[75] In a review of the eleventh edition (posthumous) of Pollock's book he said:

> The convenient phrase 'implied condition' generally said to justify the court's interference, is artificial and may be misleading. The 'condition' which is here meant is one implied by law, not agreed to by the parties. It is imposed by the court *ab extra* [from outside], though with due regard to the actual terms of the contract and the surrounding circumstances. But, if I may quote a pithy phrase used by Williston . . . 'the qualification of the literal terms of the promise is imposed by law, on principles of justice'.[76]

Two years later, he said, again rejecting the implied term approach, that frustration was 'a substantive and particular rule which the common law

---

67 Pollock, 'Note' (1936) 52 *Law Quarterly Review* 7.
68 Lord Loreburn in *F.A. Tamplin Steamship Co. Ltd* v. *Anglo-Mexican Petroleum Products Co. Ltd* [1916] 2 AC 379, 404 (HL).
69 [1926] AC 497 (PC).   70 *Ibid.*, at 510.   71 (1936) 52 LQR 7.
72 Wright, *Legal Essays and Addresses*, 258.   73 *Ibid.*, at 379.
74 (1939) 55 LQR 189, reprinted in *Legal Essays and Addresses*, 202, 248.
75 *Joseph Constantine Steamship Line Ltd* v. *Imperial Smelting Corp. Ltd* [1942] AC 154, 186.
76 Lord Wright, 'Book Review of *Pollock on Contracts*' (1943) 59 *Law Quarterly Review* 122, 124.

has evolved'.[77] Judicial statements to this effect reached a culmination in Lord Radcliffe's striking comments in a decision of the House of Lords in 1956. After referring to some of the First World War cases, he said that:

> the legal effect of frustration 'does not depend on their [the parties'] intention or their opinions, or even knowledge, as to the event' ... On the contrary, it seems that when the event occurs 'the meaning of the contract must be taken to be, not what the parties did intend (for they had neither thought nor intention regarding it), but that which the parties, as fair and reasonable men, would presumably have agreed upon if, having such possibility in view, they had made express provision as to their several rights and liabilities in the event of its occurrence' ... By this time it might seem that the parties themselves have become so far disembodied spirits that their actual persons should be allowed to rest in peace. In their place there rises the figure of the fair and reasonable man. And the spokesman of the fair and reasonable man, who represents after all no more than the anthropomorphic conception of justice, is and must be the court itself. So perhaps it would be simpler to say at the outset that frustration occurs whenever the law recognizes that without default of either party a contractual obligation has become incapable of being performed because the circumstances in which performance is called for would render it a thing radically different from that which was undertaken by the contract. Non haec in foedera veni. It was not this that I promised to do.[78]

It is generally supposed that the school of thought known as American legal realism had little or no influence on English legal thinking, but the line of thought here examined that led to the rejection of the implied term theory of frustration was plainly influenced, if not by legal realism itself, then by the same underlying ideas that had also influenced legal realism. Moreover, the links between Pollock and Holmes, and between Wright and Williston, show that Pollock and Wright were well aware of American thinking. Rejection of the implied term theory has been generally accepted by subsequent courts in England and in other common law jurisdictions. The English Court of Appeal, making a connection between frustration and mistake, commented in 2002 that 'the theory of the implied term is as unrealistic when considering common mistake as when considering frustration'.[79]

One of the difficulties with resting the doctrine of frustration on the implied intention of the parties is that it tends to the conclusion that

---

77 *Denny, Mott & Dickson Ltd* v. *James B. Fraser & Co. Ltd* [1944] AC 274 (HL).
78 *Davis Contractors* v. *Fareham UDC* [1956] AC 696, 728–9 (HL).
79 *Great Peace Shipping Ltd* v. *Tsavliris Salvage Int Ltd*, note 31, above, at para. 73, and see para. 61 also making the connection.

the contract remains fully valid until the occurrence of the frustrating
event, and then is suddenly and entirely dissolved at that point: the
principle is taken to be that the parties impliedly agreed that, if the
frustrating event occurred, the contract should be dissolved. To approach
the matter in terms of the implied intention of the parties tends to exclude
any mechanism appropriate for dealing with complexities. The fiction of
implied intention seems tolerable so long as it is a simple intention that
the contract should be dissolved in certain circumstances, but it places too
much strain on the theory to suppose a fictitious intention to deal with
matters such as restitution and reliance, in various ways, or in various
hypothetical circumstances. This seemed to the courts to be making a
contract for the parties, and to go beyond the proper judicial function.
Wills J put it in this way in one of the coronation cases:

> The process of constructing a hypothetical contract by supposing what
> terms the parties would have arrived at if they had contemplated the
> possibility of what was going to happen is, to my mind, very unsatisfactory.
> It is very difficult to construct such a contract for them. Probably, in
> the present case, the defendants would have stipulated for compensation
> for their outlay, and the plaintiffs for a return of their money; but it is
> impossible to say with any certainty what the result of their bargaining
> would have been.[80]

A related problem was that the theory of implied intention distracted
attention from the overall justice of the disposition of the case, tending
particularly to suppress the concept of unjust enrichment. If the result
was seen to depend on the parties' agreement, there was no need for the
court to concern itself with the justice of the result, for the result followed
from the agreement of the parties themselves. But if the result were seen
to be imposed by the court for reasons of justice, then the court would
be bound to address the question of whether the result was, indeed, just
and, particularly, whether it brought about an unjust enrichment.

The problem was starkly illustrated by another of the coronation cases.
In *Chandler* v. *Webster* the plaintiff had agreed to pay a sum of £141,15s for
rooms overlooking the route of the procession. The money was payable
in advance, and, at the time of the cancellation of the procession, £100
had been actually paid. The plaintiff sought recovery of the £100, and the
defendant counterclaimed for the balance of the agreed sum. The plaintiff's claim failed and, to add insult to injury, the counterclaim succeeded
in the Court of Appeal. The plaintiff argued that there had been a total

80 *Blakely* v. *Muller & Co.* [1903] 2 KB 760.

failure of consideration, but this argument was rejected by an appeal to principle:

> The principle on which it [the claim based on total failure of considera-
> tion] has been dealt with is that which was applied in *Taylor* v. *Caldwell* –
> namely, that, where, from causes outside the volition of the parties, some-
> thing which was the basis of, or essential to the fulfilment of, the contract,
> has become impossible, so that, from the time when the fact of that impos-
> sibility has been ascertained, the contract can no further be performed by
> either party, it remains a perfectly good contract up to that point, and
> everything previously done in pursuance of it must be treated as rightly
> done, but the parties are both discharged from further performance of it.
> If the effect were that the contract were wiped out altogether, no doubt the
> result would be that money paid under it would have to be repaid as on a
> failure of consideration. But that is not the effect of the doctrine; it only
> releases the parties from further performance of the contract. Therefore
> the doctrine of failure of consideration does not apply.[81]

The counterclaim succeeded on the principle – in itself perfectly defensible – that, since the money was payable before the dissolution of the contract, the plaintiff should not be in a better position by his default than he would have occupied had he paid what was due. Thus the result on both branches of the case seems to be demanded by principle. But from the point of view of unjust enrichment, the result is indefensible, for the plaintiff, who had paid the large sum of £100 for something that was practically worthless, was compelled by the judicial process to pay a further £41,15s. Collins MR evidently felt some of the force of this point, since he added, a little apologetically, that:

> The rule adopted by the Courts in such cases is I think to some extent an
> arbitrary one, the reason for its adoption being that it is really impossible in
> such cases to work out with any certainty what the rights of the parties in the
> event which has happened should be. Time has elapsed, and the position
> of both parties may have been more or less altered, and it is impossible to
> adjust or ascertain the rights of the parties with exactitude. That being so,
> the law treats everything that has already been done in pursuance of the
> contract as validly done, but relieves the parties of further responsibility
> under it. [Collins MR then referred to the comments of Wills J, above, on
> the difficulties of making up a hypothetical contract.][82]

Pollock initially defended *Chandler* v. *Webster* saying in his eighth edition (1911) that the result was 'in aid of the presumed intention of the parties',[83] a comment that demonstrates the far-reaching and, in this

81 [1904] 1 KB 493, 499.   82 *Ibid.*, at 499–500.
83 Pollock, *Principles of Contract*, 8th edn, 441.

instance, pernicious influence of the implied intention theory, even on so flexible and fertile a legal mind as Pollock's, a point that he effectively conceded in subsequent editions. In the ninth edition (1921) the words just quoted disappeared, and Pollock wrote (though only in a footnote) that 'the rule is admitted to be to some extent arbitrary, and justifiable only because a perfect adjustment of rights is impracticable', adding, prophetically, that 'it is not clear that a less arbitrary one could not be devised'.[84] In 1921 the House of Lords applied the rule in *Chandler* v. *Webster*, describing it as a 'principle', though commenting that 'it may not in all cases provide an equitable settlement'.[85]

In 1923 a Scottish case, arising out of the First World War, reached the House of Lords.[86] It was held that, by Scots law, based on Roman law, an advance payment to a shipbuilder was recoverable. *Chandler* v. *Webster* was expressly held not to be part of Scots law, and there were strong hints that, when an opportunity arose, it was likely to be reconsidered by the House of Lords as a matter of English law.[87] Lord Shaw took the opportunity to make a rather forceful criticism of the English law on the point:

> Thus the rule, admitted to be arbitrary, is adopted because of the difficulty, nay the apparent impossibility, of reaching a solution of perfection. Therefore, leave things alone: potior est conditio possidentis [the position of the possessor is the stronger]. That maxim works well enough among tricksters, gamblers, and thieves; let it be applied to circumstances of supervenient mishap arising from causes outside the volition of parties: under this application innocent loss may and must be endured by the one party, and unearned aggrandisement may and must be secured at his expense to the other party. That is part of the law of England. I am not able to affirm that this is any part, or ever was any part, of the law of Scotland.[88]

Pollock, emboldened, it would seem, by this decision, then fortified his criticism of *Chandler* v. *Webster*. In his tenth edition (1936), the last in his lifetime, he attacked the rule by invoking another principle, that of restitution:

84 Pollock, *Principles of Contract*, 9th edn, 324 note.
85 *French Marine* v. *Cie Napolitaine d'eclairage et de chauffage par le gaz* [1921] 2 AC 494 (HL).
86 *Cantiare San Rocco SA* v. *Clyde Shipbuilding & Engineering Co. Ltd* [1924] AC 226 (HL, Sc).
87 *Ibid.*, Earl of Birkenhead, at 233, Viscount Finlay, at 241, Lord Dunedin, at 247, Lord Shaw, at 257–8.
88 *Ibid.*, at 259.

The rule is, however, admitted to be at best a rough one, and in fact the law of Scotland, following the wider principle of restitution embodied in the Roman law of Condiction, allows the recovery of payments for which there has been no return . . . *Chandler* v. *Webster*, which would have been decided the other way in Scotland, certainly did not produce a reasonable result.[89]

This approach was accepted in 1942 in an English case on somewhat similar facts to the Scottish case, arising out of the Second World War. In *Fibrosa Spolka Akcyjna* v. *Fairbairn Lawson Combe Barbour Ltd*,[90] the House of Lords expressly overruled *Chandler* v. *Webster* and held that a claim lay for recovery of advance payments in cases of frustration, not on the basis of the intention of the parties, but on the extra-contractual principle of 'total failure of consideration'. This was the ground of restitution for avoidance of unjust enrichment (then in the form of indebitatus assumpsit) mentioned by Lord Mansfield nearly 200 years earlier, and in turn based on Roman law, of money paid 'upon a consideration which happens to fail'.[91] Lord Wright's speech in the *Fibrosa* case, expressly recognizing restitution as an independent part of English law, and adopting the approach of the American Restatement of Restitution,[92] has formed the foundation for the revival of the subject in the twentieth century both in England and in other Commonwealth jurisdictions.[93]

The *Fibrosa* case left a number of problems unresolved, as the judges themselves recognized. Lord Simon said:

While this result [overruling *Chandler* v. *Webster*] obviates the harshness with which the previous view in some instances treated the party who had made a prepayment, it cannot be regarded as dealing fairly between the parties in all cases, and must sometimes have the result of leaving the recipient who has to return the money at a grave disadvantage. He may have incurred expenses in connexion with the partial carrying out of the contract which are equivalent, or more than equivalent, to the money which he prudently stipulated should be prepaid, but which he now has to return for reasons which are no fault of his. He may have to repay the money, though he has executed almost the whole of the contractual work, which will be left on his hands. These results follow from the fact that the English common law does not undertake to apportion a prepaid sum in such circumstances . . . It must be for the legislature to decide

89 Pollock, *Principles of Contract*, 10th edn, 297 and footnote (last sentence of quotation).
90 [1943] AC 32 (HL).   91 *Moses* v. *Macferlan* (1760) 2 Burr 1005.
92 See Lord Wright, 'Book Review of *Restatement of the Law of Restitution*' (1937) 51 *Harvard Law Review* 369, reprinted in *Legal Essays and Addresses*, 34.
93 *Deglman* v. *Guarantee Trust Co. of Canada* [1954] SCR 725.

whether provisions should be made for an equitable apportionment of prepaid moneys which have to be returned by the recipient in view of the frustration of the contract in respect of which they were paid.[94]

There is a curious irony in these words. The House of Lords felt sufficiently emboldened to overrule a decision that had stood for forty years, and to do so on a very general principle derived from the broadest considerations of justice, and yet found that it lacked the power to define or articulate the principle in such a way as to avoid foreseeable future cases of admittedly serious injustice.

The questions unresolved by the *Fibrosa* case included the following: is restitution available for money paid where the failure of consideration is not *total*, but partial; is restitution available for benefits conferred other than money; can the reliance of the recipient or of the other party be protected, and to what extent; to what extent can relief be given where the unexpected event causes partial but not total frustration of the contract? In response to the *Fibrosa* case, legislation was enacted in England,[95] and copied in several Commonwealth jurisdictions,[96] but, as often happens when legislation addresses a particular perceived defect of the common law, not all the problems were resolved, and new anomalies were created. The legislation excluded several types of contract from its scope. It codified the reversal of both branches of *Chandler* v. *Webster*, and provided for restitution in case of benefits other than money. The matter of expenses was dealt with to some extent, but the Act gave protection only to a party to whom an advance payment was paid or payable. Thus no provision was made for expenses incurred where there was no advance payment made or promised, or where expenses were incurred by the party who was to make the payment, as in *Taylor* v. *Caldwell*. The statute did not address the question of partial frustration.

The drafters of the statute could scarcely be expected to have escaped the prevailing framework of thought on this branch of the law, and naturally they addressed the questions that had been called to their attention by the remarks of Lord Simon in the *Fibrosa* case. But, from a later perspective, it is apparent that the whole framework of thought on the matter was too narrow. If a broader basis for the court's intervention

94 [1943] AC 32 (HL).
95 Law Reform (Frustrated Contracts) Act 1943. As Paul Mitchell has pointed out, the question had been on the legislative agenda for several years, P. Mitchell, '*Fibrosa Spolka Akcyjna v. Fairbairn Lawson Combe Barbour, Ltd*', in Mitchell and Mitchell (eds.), *Landmark Cases in the Law of Restitution*, 245.
96 E.g. Frustrated Contracts Acts in Ontario and British Columbia.

had been recognized, the statute would have been unnecessary. If the principle is, as it now is generally accepted to be, that, where unexpected circumstances cause injustice, the court may fashion an appropriate solution, several consequences would follow. First, unjust enrichment should be avoided; secondly, in case of partial frustration, partial relief may be appropriate; thirdly, relief may be made conditional on the protection of reliance by either party. The American Second Restatement of Contracts embodies all these ideas. Section 272, entitled 'Relief including restitution' provides:

> (1) In any case governed by the rules stated in this Chapter, either party may have a claim for relief including restitution under the rules stated in ss 240 [apportionment] and 377 [restitution for benefits conferred]
> (2) In any case governed by the rules stated in this Chapter, if those rules together with the rules stated in chapter 16 [remedies] will not avoid injustice, the court may grant relief on such terms as justice requires including protection of the parties' reliance interests.

The European *Draft Common Frame of Reference* has very similar provisions:

> III – 1:110: Variation or termination by court on a change of circumstances
>
> (1) ...
> (2) If ... performance of a contractual obligation ... becomes so onerous because of an exceptional change of circumstances that it would be manifestly unjust to hold the debtor to the obligation a court may:
> (a) vary the obligation in order to make it reasonable and equitable in the new circumstances; or
> (b) terminate the obligation at a date and on terms to be determined by the court.

These provisions recognize that relief from contractual obligations because of unexpected changes in circumstances depends on the judgment of the court, not on the prior intention of the parties, that the underlying reason for the court's intervention is to avoid manifest injustice,[97] and that the extent of the court's intervention must be governed accordingly. If these simple propositions had been accepted as legal principles, many of the difficulties attending the English law of frustration in the twentieth

---

97 The comment uses the phrase 'grossly unjust', *Draft Common Frame of Reference*, Comment A, vol. 1, p. 711.

century would have been avoided. The law of mistake would also have benefited, because formulation of these principles in respect of subsequent unexpected changes in circumstances would probably have prompted the acceptance of similar principles in respect of similarly manifest injustice caused by similarly radical mistakes as to facts existing at the time of the contract.

6

Public policy

One aspect of contract law plainly demands an open and direct engagement with questions of public policy. This is the question of when, for policy reasons, the courts have refused to enforce agreements that otherwise meet all the requirements of valid contracts. Modern accounts of contract law have tended to marginalize this aspect of the subject, visualizing it as impliedly a small island in a wide sea of enforceability. But this is not the only way of looking at the matter. Compliance with public policy might plausibly be presented as a primary, or even a threshold requirement for the creation of enforceable obligations.

On either approach considerations of justice as between the parties would be outweighed by the public interest. Lord Mansfield said, in 1775, that the defence that a contract was immoral or illegal:

> sounds at all times very ill in the mouth of the defendant. It is not for his sake, however, that the objection is ever allowed; but it is founded in general principles of policy, which the defendant has the advantage of, contrary to the real justice as between him and the plaintiff, by accident, if I may so say.[1]

Principles of justice between plaintiff and defendant were outweighed by considerations of public policy, which, however, were also themselves called 'general principles'. The subject is of enormous practical as well as theoretical importance. The kinds of contract that have been held to be unenforceable constitute, practically as well as conceptually, a very large and miscellaneous group that has not been precisely limited or defined.

Many judges, in various past periods, have openly defined and enforced what they have perceived to be sound public policy. *Omychund* v. *Barker*[2] (1744) was a contract case, but one that is known for establishing not any point of contract law, but a very important point of evidence law, namely, the admissibility of the evidence of a witness who could not take the

---

1 *Holman* v. *Johnson* (1775) 1 Cowp 342, 343.   2 (1744) 1 Atk 21.

Christian form of oath. Counsel (William Murray, later Lord Mansfield), arguing in favour of admissibility, said that the question was 'whether upon principles of reason, justice and convenience this witness ought to be admitted'.[3] His fellow counsel (Dudley Rider, also, like Murray, a future Chief Justice of the King's Bench) said that 'trade requires it [admission of the testimony]; policy requires it'. The Lord Chancellor (Hardwicke) relied both on the principle of justice between the parties and on the overt policy consideration that 'if we did not give this credence, courts abroad would not allow our determinations here to be valid'.[4] This was also the case in which Murray said, in urging judicial reform of the law, that the common law 'works itself pure'.[5] The remark has often been quoted to suggest that Murray favoured a purity of formal legal principle, but it is evident from the context that 'purity' did not, in Murray's mind, nor in the Chancellor's, exclude considerations of utility and policy. *Omychund* v. *Barker* itself was plainly decided for policy reasons, but the rule it established (that evidence could be authenticated by the practices of the witness's own religion), never since doubted, has in all subsequent applications been called a principle.

Many other assertions of Lord Mansfield offer evidence of the close association in his mind between the concepts of principle and policy in contract law. In *Jones* v. *Randall*,[6] in discussing the enforceability of a wager on the outcome of litigation in which the parties had an interest, he said, in a passage quoted in an earlier chapter,[7] that 'it is argued, and rightly, that notwithstanding it is not prohibited by any positive law, nor adjudged illegal by any precedents, yet it may be decided to be so upon principles; and the law of England would be a strange science indeed if it were decided on precedents only. Precedents serve to illustrate principles, and to give them a fixed certainty. But the law of England, which is exclusive of positive law, enacted by statute, depends upon principles; and these principles run through all the cases'. He then addressed himself to the question of whether the particular wager was enforceable:

> The question then is, whether this wager is against principles? If it be contrary to any, it must be contrary either to principles of morality: for the law of England prohibits every thing which is contra bonos mores; or it must be against principles of sound policy; for many contracts which are not against morality, are still void as being against the maxims of sound policy.[8]

3 *Ibid.*, at 32.   4 *Ibid.*, at 33.   5 *Ibid.*   6 (1774) 1 Cowp 37.
7 Chapter 1, above, p. 8.   8 *Ibid.*, at 39.

Lord Mansfield added that the wager was 'not prohibited by any positive law nor contrary to any principle of sound policy or morality', and concluded, with the concurrence of the three other judges, that the wager was enforceable.

Though the decision in *Jones* v. *Randall* was in favour of enforceability, the reporter (Cowper) highlighted the corollary that principle and policy might, in appropriate cases, *prevent* the enforceability of contracts, saying in the headnote: 'Contracts not prohibited by positive law, nor adjudged illegal by precedent, may nevertheless be void as against principles.' Many other judicial statements of this period are to similar effect, and include the close association of the concepts of principle and policy. In *Harris* v. *Watson*[9] the issue was the enforceability of a promise, made during a voyage, to increase the previously agreed rate of sailors' wages. Lord Kenyon, refusing enforcement, said that 'if this action was to be supported it would materially affect the navigation of this kingdom. It has been long since determined that when the freight is lost, the wages are also lost. This rule was founded on a principle of policy'. In *Stilk* v. *Myrick* (1809),[10] Lord Ellenborough, dealing with the same question, is reported by 'Espinasse as saying that he 'recognised the principle of the case of *Harris* v. *Watson* as founded on just and proper policy'. In another case the same judge said, speaking in very wide terms, that 'wherever the toleration of any species of contract has a tendency to produce a public mischief or inconvenience, such a contract has been held to be void'.[11]

Stilk v. *Myrick*, the case of the promise to increase the sailors' wages, was reported also by Campbell, who quotes Lord Ellenborough as expressly rejecting the ground of public policy:

> I think that *Harris* v. *Watson* was rightly decided; but I doubt whether the ground of public policy, upon which Lord Kenyon is stated to have proceeded, be the true principle on which the decision is to be supported. Here, I say that the agreement is void for want of consideration.[12]

In evaluating the comparative accuracy of the two reports it may be said that 'Espinasse had a lesser reputation as a reporter,[13] but, against that, it may be pointed out that he was counsel in the case, and so had good opportunity to know what Lord Ellenborough actually said. Moreover,

---

9 (1791) Peake 102.   10 (1809) 1 Esp 129, 2 Camp 317.
11 *Gilbert* v. *Sykes* (1812) 16 East 150, 156–7 (wager on when Napoleon would die).
12 (1809) 2 Camp 318.
13 This was remarked on by Mocatta J in *North Ocean Shipping Co. Ltd* v. *Hyundai Construction Co. Ltd* [1979] QB 705, 712.

Campbell's reporting is known to have been selective. He himself described his reporting method as 'my "garbling process"', adding that:

> Lord Ellenborough ought to have been particularly grateful to me for suppressing his bad decisions . . . Before each number was sent to the press I carefully revised all the cases I had collected for it, and rejected such as were inconsistent with former decisions *or recognised principles.*[14]

In 1866 Lord Cranworth said, of Campbell's reports, that 'they really do, in the fewest possible words, lay down the law, very often more distinctly and more accurately than it is to be found in many lengthened reports and what is so laid down has been subsequently recognised as giving a true view of the law as applied to the facts of the case'.[15] To say that Campbell's reports were *subsequently* recognized as 'giving a true view of the law' more accurate than longer reports contemporary with the cases reported suggests that Campbell might have strayed somewhat beyond the role of reporter. At the end of the century, Darling J referred, with more than a hint of irony, to 'such decisions at nisi prius as had the good fortune to be reported by Lord Campbell'.[16] It seems probable, accepting the accuracy of as much as possible from each report, that both reasons were mentioned by Lord Ellenborough, and that Campbell emphasized the reason that seemed to him the more principled.[17]

The question of enforceability of such contractual modifications has been explained and justified on the basis of three quite different concepts. In the eighteenth century the governing principle was one of public policy, in the nineteenth century absence of consideration, and in the late-twentieth century economic duress.[18] Each of these concepts may be deployed to justify the same result, and each may claim to be a 'principle', but they are quite different and, indeed, incompatible with each other. Though the first and the last approaches have both been called 'policy', they are quite distinct. Ironically, it is the earlier view of public

---

14 Hardcastle (ed.), *Life of John, Lord Campbell, Lord High Chancellor of Great Britain*, 215 (emphasis added). Garbling (sorting) implies purposive selection of what is meritorious, and rejection of inferior material, though not deliberate distortion.

15 *Williams* v. *Bayley* (1866) LR 1 HL 200, 213.

16 *Sharman* v. *Mason* [1899] 2 QB 679, 689, mentioned in Megarry, *A Second Miscellany-at-law*, 133.

17 Garrow's argument for the defendant, according to Campbell's report, was very forceful, and based solely on public policy, which suggests that it probably constituted, at the least, one ground for the decision. See also P. Luther, 'Campbell, Espinasse and the Sailors: Text and Context in the Common Law' (1999) 19 *Legal Studies* 526.

18 See Chapter 3, above, at pp. 64–8.

policy – apparently a dangerously wide concept – that would have had the least extensive effect on enforceability of contracts in general. If the principle was, as Lord Kenyon said, that contracts are not to be enforced if they 'materially affect the navigation of the kingdom' the direct effect of the decision would have been confined to a narrow range of transactions. But if the 'true principle' is supposed to be, as in Campbell's report of *Stilk* v. *Myrick*, that modifications of contracts require consideration, many transactions will be affected, and agreements struck down, where there is no policy justification for doing so. The solution in Campbell's report was apparently more simple, logical, precise and elegant than the vague notion of public policy, but the practical consequences of adopting it have been to invalidate, without sufficient reason, business transactions that most persons would expect to be enforceable, as the convoluted history of this aspect of Anglo-American contract law amply demonstrates. But, curiously enough, the principle in Campbell's report was, from the public policy perspective, too narrow, as was shown by the decision of the Admiralty Court in *The Araminta*[19] where the extra money was actually paid in advance, and so the doctrine of consideration was of no assistance to the shipowner. Dr Lushington, the Admiralty Court judge, upholding a deduction from the seamen's wages corresponding to the extra payment, found it necessary to say that 'the payment itself was illegal',[20] thus reasserting the primacy in this context of public policy. The differing opinions from time to time of what is the 'true principle' of decisions do not show that the concept of principle has been useless or unimportant: on the contrary, they show the opposite, for the result in many cases will differ and has differed according to which principle has been selected as applicable. But they do suggest that there has been no infallible and constant method of determining what is the correct principle to apply to a particular legal issue.

Writers on contract law in the late-eighteenth and early-nineteenth centuries recognized a large and potentially indeterminate scope for judicial invalidation of contracts on policy grounds. Powell (1790) wrote that 'the subject of every contract must not only be a thing *naturally* possible to be accomplished, but it must be *morally* so'.[21] Comyn (1807) wrote that 'all contracts and agreements which have as their object any thing contrary to principles of sound policy are void by the common law'.[22]

---

19 (1854) 1 Sp 224.   20 *Ibid.*, at 230.
21 Powell, *Essay upon the Law of Contracts and Agreements*, 164 (emphasis in original).
22 Comyn, *A Treatise of the Law Relative to Contracts*, 32.

Chitty (1826) wrote, using very wide language, that 'the common law prohibits every thing which is unjust, or *contra bonos mores*', adding that 'the object of all laws is to suppress vice, and promote the general welfare of the state, and society; – and an individual shall not be assisted by the law, in enforcing a demand, originating in a breach or violation on his part, of its principles or enactments'.[23]

But for nineteenth-century courts and commentators seeking to formulate principles that defined the circumstances in which enforceable contracts arose, a large and undefined judicial power to refuse enforcement was a considerable embarrassment. 'Public policy' was said to be 'a very unruly horse, and when once you get astride it you never know where it will carry you'.[24] Judges and commentators sought to limit and make precise those instances in which contracts were not enforceable for policy reasons, so that the principles thought to govern contractual enforceability could be stated confidently and authoritatively (subject to exceptions, which, however, should, so far as possible, be precise and knowable).

Pollock, whose book was entitled *Principles of Contract Law*, wrote, in introducing his chapter on 'unlawful agreements', that 'we have already seen that an agreement is not in any case enforceable by law without satisfying sundry conditions: as being made between capable persons, being sufficiently certain, and the like'. He added that 'if it does satisfy these conditions it is in general a contract which the law commands the parties to perform'.[25] Thus Pollock presented enforceability of agreements as the general rule, and the chapter on unlawful agreements as the exception. The next paragraph, not surprisingly in the context, commences with the word 'But', and the extent of the exception with which Pollock found that he had to grapple is indicated by the length of the chapter (103 pages), occupying almost one-fifth of the entire treatise.

Pollock found considerable difficulties in organizing the topic and classifying the material. His first category was contracts where the subject matter was prohibited by law, and his second was contracts that violated 'established rules of decency, morals or good manners'.[26] In addition to these categories he recognized that 'there are a good many transactions which cannot fairly be brought within either of the foregoing classes and yet cannot *conveniently* be admitted as the subject-matter of valid contracts', adding that 'it is doubtful whether these can be completely

---

23 Chitty, *A Treatise on the Law of Contracts*, 1st edn, 214.
24 *Richardson* v. *Mellish* (1824) 2 Bing 229, 252, per Burrough J.
25 Pollock, *Principles of Contract*, 1st edn, 218.   26 *Ibid.*, at 219.

reduced to any general description, and how far judicial discretion may go in novel cases'.[27] This third category, which he called agreements 'against public policy', included many miscellaneous kinds of agreement, among them the large and very important area of restraint of trade.

Pollock evidently considered that public policy was not something to be contrasted with, or opposed to principle, but was itself a principle, and was, in its application, to be governed by principles. Speaking of the consequences of unlawful agreements Pollock wrote that 'the general principle is, of course, that an unlawful agreement cannot be enforced'.[28] He quoted with approval the United States Supreme Court to the effect that 'no principle is better settled than that no action can be maintained on a contract the consideration of which is wicked in itself or prohibited by law'.[29]

By the middle of the nineteenth century a wide judicial power to invalidate contracts had come to be seen by most of the judges as an unwelcome burden. A striking example is the assertion of Parke B, representing nine of the eleven judges summoned to advise the House of Lords in *Egerton* v. *Brownlow*[30] that:

> It is the province of the judge to expound the law only; the written from the statutes, the unwritten or common law from the decisions of our predecessors and of our existing courts, from text writers of acknowledged authority, and upon the principles to be clearly deduced from them by sound reason and just inference; not to speculate upon what is best, in his opinion, for the advantage of the community. Some of these decisions [past decisions on public policy] may no doubt have been founded upon the prevailing and just opinions of the public good; for instance the illegality of covenants in restraint of marriage or trade. They have become part of the recognized law, and we are therefore bound by them, but we think we are not thereby authorized to establish as law everything which we may think for the public good, and prohibit everything which we think otherwise.[31]

It was easier on this view – and paradoxically made to seem more principled – to accept an anomalous rule simply because it was a binding rule than to examine, accept or apply the reason on which the rule had originally been based.

Egerton v. *Brownlow* concerned a bequest in a will conditional on acquisition by the beneficiary of a peerage. Though not a contract case, it has always been treated as directly applicable to similar provisions in

27 *Ibid.* (emphasis added).   28 *Ibid.*, at 292.
29 *Ibid.*, at 294, referring to *Armstrong* v. *Toler* (1826) 11 Wheat 258, 272.
30 (1853) 4 HLC 1.   31 *Ibid.*, at 123.

contracts. The view of Parke B, just quoted, led him to conclude that the bequest was valid. But this opinion, though held by the large majority of the judges, did not prevail. Pollock LCB summarized the contrary view of the other two judges by saying:

> My Lords, it may be that judges are no better able to discern what is for the public good than other experienced and enlightened members of the community; but that is no reason for their refusing to entertain the question, and declining to decide upon it.[32]

He thought that upholding the bequest was likely, not in this case but in possible future cases, to lead to corruption in the creation of peerages, and the majority of the law lords agreed.[33] This is, in the broadest sense, a judgment on a question of social policy. Pollock LCB, in a forceful passage, invoked the concept of principle in support of his assertion that it was not only permissible but mandatory for judges, on occasion, to determine new question of policy:

> My Lords, after all these authorities, am I not justified in saying that, were I to discard the public welfare from my consideration, I should abdicate the functions of my office – I should shrink from the discharge of my duty? I think I am not permitted merely to follow the particular decisions of those who have had the courage to decide before me, but in a new and unprecedented case to be afraid of imitating their example. I think I am bound to look for the principles of former decisions, and not to shrink from applying them with firmness and caution to any new and extraordinary cases that may arise.[34]

Lord Chief Baron Pollock did not hesitate, indeed, to describe the court's function as 'political'. Adopting the words of Lord Hardwicke from a case a century earlier, he said that:

> Political arguments, in the fullest sense of the word, as they concern the government of a nation, must be, and always have been of great weight in the consideration of this Court.[35]

This reference to 'political arguments' was expressly adopted in the House of Lords by Lord Lyndhurst, who, at the age of 81, gave the leading speech for the majority also invoking the concept of principle in support of flexibility in respect of policy: 'I strongly advise you . . . not to lay down on

32 (1853) 4 HLC 151.
33 Lords Lyndhurst, Brougham, Truro and St Leonards (Cranworth LC dissenting).
34 (1853) 4 HLC 149.   35 *Earl of Chesterfield* v. *Janssen* (1751) 2 Ves Sen 125.

this occasion any abstract rules. Let each case be decided upon principle.'[36] *The Times* praised the result, describing the will as 'most iniquitous' and saying that the decision 'will be received with unqualified satisfaction by the public'. The writer of the leading article had some difficulty in explaining the difference of opinion between the common law judges and the law lords:

> The point has been decided by the House of Lords in a manner contrary to the opinions delivered by the judges of the land. These learned persons had, of course, but one point to consider – what the law was – not what it should be. They are interpreters, not makers of the law, and cannot be charged with its defects or shortcomings.

But this distinction was not helpful to the writer's line of thought because, if true of the common law judges, the same should have been true of the House of Lords in its judicial capacity. The editorial writer was constrained to add, rather lamely: 'We must notice it as a curious fact that this opinion should have been overruled by that of the law Lords in the Upper House.'[37]

Frederick Pollock, writing in 1876 and differing sharply from the opinion expressed by his grandfather the Lord Chief Baron, found the decision in *Egerton* v. *Brownlow* highly embarrassing. He posed to his readers the question 'whether it is at the present day open to courts of justice to hold transactions or dispositions of property void simply because in the judgment of the court it is against the public good that they should be enforced, although the grounds of such judgment may be novel', and answered immediately as follows: 'The general tendency of modern ideas is no doubt against the continuation of such a jurisdiction.' This last sentence – a transparent formula for conveying Pollock's own opinion – was cast in the form of a reference to recent history (the general tendency of modern ideas), but the historical evidence was not very favourable to it. Recognizing this, Pollock immediately added, with more honesty than elegance: 'On the other hand there is a good deal of modern and even recent authority which makes it difficult to deny its continued existence.'[38] Pollock went on to criticize Lord St Leonards' reference to principle ('with all submission to so great an authority') writing that if he meant to say 'that the court may lay down new principles of public policy without any warrant or even analogy, it seems of doubtful and dangerous latitude'.[39] Pollock then wrote that 'the view here put forward, that there is really

---

36 (1853) 4 HLC 239.   37 *The Times*, 20 August 1853, 8d.
38 Pollock, *Principles of Contract*, 1st edn, 251–2.   39 *Ibid.*, at 255.

nothing in the case to warrant the invention of new heads of "public policy"' seems to be borne out by remarks of Sir George Jessel in the then recent case of *Printing & Numerical Registering Co.* v. *Sampson*[40] to the effect that freedom of contract was itself a paramount public policy. Anson (1879) followed Pollock's view, writing that 'the policy of the law, or public policy, is a phrase of frequent occurrence and somewhat attractive sound, but it is very easily capable of introducing an unsatisfactory vagueness into the law'.[41] Following Pollock closely, but with fewer qualifications and less diffidence, he wrote, after regretting the overuse of the doctrine in the eighteenth century, and, like Pollock, claiming the support of more recent history, that 'modern decisions, however, while maintaining the duty of the Courts to consider the public advantage, have tended to limit the sphere within which this duty has been exercised'.[42] In subsequent editions Pollock shortened the discussion of *Egerton* v. *Brownlow*, and endorsed Jessel's view (in favour of freedom of contract) as 'the prevailing modern view'.[43] Whereas, in the early editions *Egerton* v. *Brownlow* was called 'the great case' and 'the leading modern authority', by the eighth edition (1911) it was described, with evident disapproval, as the 'most remarkable modern case on the general doctrine of "public policy"'.[44] In the same edition Pollock, citing a decision of the House of Lords of 1902,[45] wrote that 'we may be pretty sure, therefore, that no further attempts in this direction will be made in our time; nor will the particular doctrine of *Egerton* v. *Brownlow* be extended'.[46] The forceful tone of this assertion is somewhat impaired by the use of the confidential 'we', the colloquialism 'pretty sure', and the curious and ambiguous limitation 'in our time' (it is unclear whether the readers' or the author's time is meant, and the three words could well have been omitted).

As it happened, an important case on public policy reached the House of Lords a few months after Pollock's death, thirty-five years later, in 1937.[47] The issue, on which the judges were almost evenly divided,[48] was the enforceability of a contract to marry, made by a man married to another person, after a conditional but before a final decree of divorce. Lord

---

40 (1875) LR 19 Eq. 462, 465.   41 Anson, *Principles*, 1st edn, 173.   42 *Ibid.*, at 174.

43 Pollock, *Principles of Contract*, 6th edn, 303.

44 Pollock, *Principles of Contract*, 8th edn, 330.

45 *Janson* v. *Driefontein Consolidated Mines* [1902] 2 AC 484.

46 Pollock, *Principles of Contract*, 8th edn, 333.

47 Pollock died in January 1937. *Fender* v. *St John Mildmay* was argued in April and decided in June of the same year.

48 The trial judge, the majority of the Court of Appeal and two of the law lords held the contract to be unenforceable.

Wright, one of the majority in the House of Lords, following Frederick Pollock's opinion that the court could not formulate new heads of public policy, said that 'it is, I think, clear that this dictum of Pollock CB [quoted above] and certain observations in *Egerton* v. *Brownlow* to a similar effect cannot be regarded as fixing the modern law, which is in my opinion as stated by Parke B'.[49]

Lord Wright wrote extra-judicially at some length about this case. He presented the legal issue as follows:

> The question was whether the principle of public policy, which was assumed to apply to [former cases where there had been no conditional decree] applied also to the facts in *Fender* v. *St. John-Mildmay*. The question had to be decided on ordinary common-law principles, subject only to this, that the doctrine of public policy was not to be unduly extended.[50]

He concluded his discussion of the case by saying:

> The broad public policy invoked in all these cases is the public interest in the promotion of the married state. The practical limits which good sense and convenience require are elucidated by the conflicting decisions. If, however, the demands of public policy do not clearly apply, then the contract must be enforced. The presumption should be in favour of the validity of the contract.[51]

These passages reveal multiple associations and cross-associations between principle and policy. Public policy was itself a principle ('the principle of public policy'); so also was freedom of contract: *pacta sunt servanda*, which, Lord Wright had said in his judicial opinion, was also a 'paramount policy';[52] reasoned evaluation of the cases also involved the application of principles ('ordinary common law principles') but these principles in their turn did not exclude considerations of 'good sense and convenience'.

These comments formed part of a lecture delivered by Wright at Harvard University in 1938. The general theme of the lecture sought to minimize the extent to which individual judges resorted, and should resort, to general considerations of policy. Wright introduced the issue, and the perceived difficulty that he had to explain, by saying that:

> It is prima facie anomalous that a judge should attempt in settling private disputes to introduce into law the principles of state policy, or to depart from the rules of the common law in order to invent doctrines of what is

---

49 *Fender* v. *St John Mildmay* [1938] AC 1, 42 (HL).
50 Wright, *Legal Essays and Addresses*, 81.   51 *Ibid.*, at 84–5.   52 [1938] 1 AC 37–8.

good for the common weal. Modern judges, I think, neither desire nor are qualified to fill such a role.[53]

He added that, in novel cases, it was the function of the judges:

> to apply the recognized principles to the new conditions, along the lines of logic and convenience, just as they do when dealing with any other rule of the common law or equity.[54]

It is notable that, even in minimalizing the role of the judges, Wright left room for considerations of 'convenience'. He concluded the lecture by saying that:

> public policy is not a matter depending on the personal views of the individual judge, but a body of rules in some cases fixed, in others flexible, but governed by precedent and authority like other branches of the common law.[55]

Parts of the lecture, however, were difficult to reconcile with this overall thesis. Wright said that 'public policy changes with the times',[56] and that 'what public policy requires in the circumstances of one time may not be required in the circumstances of another age'.[57] He defended a recent decision of the House of Lords, upholding a judgment of his own in the Court of Appeal, refusing to enforce a life insurance contract when the insured had committed suicide, even though the contract itself clearly contemplated liability in these circumstances, having excluded liability only in case of suicide occurring within twelve months of its issue (that period having expired before the suicide). Lord Wright, in defending the result, said that:

> it is the general principle of English public policy that a criminal or his representative will not be allowed by the judgment of the Court to reap the fruits of his crime. That principle rests on a broad rule of public policy.[58]

There being no cases directly in point:

> the Court in deciding this question of public policy had to proceed on recognized principles according to logic and convenience and according to the nearest authorities.[59]

This approach was adduced in support of Wright's general argument that public policy is governed by precedent and authority just like any other question of private law, but the argument was weakened to some degree

---

53 Wright, *Legal Essays and Addresses*, 71.   54 *Ibid.*, at 78.   55 *Ibid.*, at 95.
56 *Ibid.*, at 93.   57 *Ibid.*, at 94.   58 *Ibid.*, at 86.   59 *Ibid.*, at 87.

by recognition that public policy was constantly changing and that novel cases continually arose. Lord Wright, quoting Lord Halsbury's assertion that no court 'can invent a new head of public policy',[60] commented astutely that 'it is really a question of what is meant by a new head'.[61] Since there has been no consensus on how to classify cases on public policy, or on how many categories they might occupy, the comment draws attention to the inherent uncertainty of this area of contract law, and to the inescapable exercise of very general judgment on broad social questions. Somewhat paradoxically, attempts at precision and comprehensiveness, admirable in themselves, have led to a multiplication of numerous narrowly defined categories, or 'heads' of public policy, and this, in turn, has made it more likely that a novel question will not fall into a pre-existing category and will therefore require the creation of a new one, and so a continual proliferation of categories.[62]

In the first half of the twentieth century many writers and judges adopted the approach of Frederick Pollock and Lord Wright, asserting that the heads of public policy in English law were closed, or frozen, much as Parke B had suggested in his opinion, quoted earlier, in *Egerton* v. *Brownlow*. Lord Halsbury said in 1902: 'I deny that any Court can invent a new head of public policy.'[63] But not all the judges, even in the early-twentieth century, agreed with this approach. In 1918 McCardie J doubted 'if this dictum [of Lord Halsbury] be consistent with the history of our law or with many modern decisions'. Giving several instances of novel heads of policy created by the courts, he said: 'The truth of the matter seems to be that public policy is a variable thing. It must fluctuate with the circumstances of the time', adding that 'the principles of public policy remain the same, though the application of them may be applied in novel ways.'[64] Perhaps McCardie J thought it necessary, or advisable, to say that 'the principles . . . remain the same', but it is difficult to give a high degree of precision to this proposition if his view is also accepted that public policy is 'a variable thing', and that the courts have frequently and consistently asserted power to create new and very miscellaneous heads of policy. From a historical perspective, it cannot be seriously doubted that judicial perceptions of public policy have indeed varied from time to

---

60 *Ibid.*, at 76, from *Janson* v. *Driefontein Consolidated Mines Ltd* [1902] AC 484, 491.
61 Wright, *Legal Essays and Addresses*, 77.
62 Pollock, in his first edition, had about thirty categories, but none that included racial discrimination.
63 [1902] AC 484, 491 (HL).
64 *Naylor, Benzon & Co.* v. *Krainisch Industrie Gesellschaft* [1918] 1 KB 331.

time and from place to place: 'public policy is necessarily variable',[65] as subsequent decisions in the twentieth century have demonstrated.[66]

An earlier example of this variability was the changing judicial attitude in the nineteenth century to separation agreements between husband and wife. Of such agreements Sir George Jessel himself had said, in 1879:

> Judicial opinion has varied a great deal . . . For a great number of years, both ecclesiastical Judges and lay Judges thought it was something very horrible, and against public policy, that the husband and wife should agree to live separate, and it was supposed that a civilized country could no longer exist if such agreements were enforced by Courts of law, whether ecclesiastical or not. But a change came over judicial opinion as to public policy; other considerations arose, and people began to think that after all it might be better and more beneficial for married people to avoid in many cases the expense and the scandal of suits of divorce by settling their differences quietly . . . and that was the view carried out by the Courts when it became once decided that separation deeds *per se* were not against public policy.[67]

A few years earlier Jessel had, in the case mentioned earlier on which Pollock had relied, rejected an appeal to *overt* considerations of public policy, but this does not show that public policy had in fact no influence, for the conclusion itself rested on the judge's perception of what public policy required:

> If there is one thing which more than another public policy requires it is that men of full age and competent understanding shall have the utmost liberty of contracting and that their contracts when entered into freely and voluntarily shall be held sacred and shall be enforced by courts of justice.[68]

The context of this last case was restraint of trade, a doctrine that has reflected differing views of the importance of a free market in various commodities and services.[69] All contracts in restraint of trade are said to be

---

65 P. Winfield, 'Public Policy in the English Common Law' (1929) 42 *Harvard Law Review* 76, 93. In *Henningsen* v. *Bloomfield Motors* 32 NJ 358 (1960) the New Jersey Supreme Court said that public policy 'is not static and the field of application is an ever increasing one. A contract or a particular provision therein, valid in one era, may be totally opposed to the public policy of another.'

66 Contracts contemplating cohabitation outside marriage (formerly condemned as immoral) are now enforceable, and racially discriminatory contracts (formerly clearly enforceable) are now unenforceable.

67 *Besant* v. *Wood* (1879) 12 Ch D 605, 620. See also *Davies* v. *Davies* (1886) 36 Ch D 359, 364 (Kekewich J).

68 *Printing & Numerical Registering Co.* v. *Sampson* (1875) LR 9 Eq 462, 465 (Sir George Jessel, MR).

69 Trebilcock, *The Common Law of Restraint of Trade*, 1–59.

void, unless shown to be reasonable. This formulation inevitably requires an element of judgment, for almost all contracts restrain freedom of action to some degree. There are many other instances of changes in perceptions of public policy. The attitude to racially discriminatory contracts, and similar provisions in wills, clearly enforceable until the mid-twentieth century,[70] were, by the end of the century just as clearly unenforceable.[71] Contracts of financial support between unmarried cohabitants, clearly immoral in the nineteenth century[72] were, by the last quarter of the twentieth century clearly enforceable in most jurisdictions.[73]

In some cases courts have refused to enforce agreements, not because there is anything objectionable in the substance of what has been agreed, but because, for a variety of reasons, it has been considered that the dispute is of a kind that should not be resolved in the courts. Agreements that the courts have been unwilling – or at least reluctant – to enforce, although they appear to meet the usual requirements of contract formation, include bets and wagers, domestic agreements, labour agreements, agreements to conform to religious practices and political promises. What is, or may be, contrary to public policy in such cases is neither the making nor the performance of the agreement itself, but the use of the courts to resolve the dispute that arises from it.

In the eighteenth century the law as to bets and wagers was complex. The general rule was that wagers were enforceable, but a variety of statutes modified this rule in respect to particular games, and particular sums of money that might be lost at play.[74] However, even where an action for a gaming debt was barred, money that had been 'fairly lost at play', if actually paid, could not be recovered back in an action of indebitatus assumpsit, the predecessor of the modern law of restitution, because, Lord Mansfield said, 'the defendant may retain it with a safe conscience'.[75] Wagers not affected by the statutes were said to be enforceable, unless contrary to public policy. As we have seen, a wager on the outcome of a lawsuit in which the parties had an interest was enforced in *Jones* v. *Randall*. One

---

70 See, for example, *Essex Real Estate Co.* v. *Holmes* (1930) 37 OWN 392, affd 38 OWN 69, Div Ct; *Re McDougall and Waddell* [1945] 2 DLR 244; *Re Noble and Wolf* [1949] 4 DLR 375, revd on other grounds [1951] SCR 64.

71 See *Canada Trust Co.* v. *Ontario Human Rights Commission* (1990) 69 DLR (4th) 321 (Ont. CA).

72 See *Fender* v. *St John Mildmay*, note 49, above, at 42.

73 See *Chrispen* v. *Topham* (1986) 28 DLR (4th) 754, affd 39 DLR (4th) 637, (Sask. CA).

74 See Burns, *Justice of the Peace*, vol. 2, 408–25, s.t. Gaming.

75 *Moses* v. *Macferlan* (1760) 2 Burr 1005.

eighteenth-century judge, Buller J, thought that it was not too late for English law to adopt what he called the rule and principle of Scottish law, that 'all idle wagers were void'.[76] But Buller J's was a dissenting opinion, and the accepted legal view in the early years of the new century was that wagers were generally enforceable.[77]

In many cases in this period, however, judges showed a marked reluctance in practice to enforce wagers, and the decision not to enforce was often justified on grounds of public policy. Fine distinctions arose as judges hostile to wagers sought reasons to avoid enforcing them, so that Parke B remarked that the judges had become 'astute even to an extent bordering upon the ridiculous to find reasons for refusing to enforce them'.[78] Thomas Starkie, Downing professor of law at Cambridge, in a paper prepared for a parliamentary committee in 1844, thought that the trend of judicial decisions was against enforcement:

> The general rule of the common law is, that a wager is a valid contract, but there are many exceptions to it, founded upon the principle that wagers so excepted are against sound policy and convenience . . . But although the general rule be as above stated, yet in modern times the courts have gone further than formerly in making exceptions on grounds of policy; and it is probable that several cases of wagers which formerly were held to be valid within the general rule, would now be deemed to fall within the principle of the exception.[79]

Chitty said in 1826 that judges were so hostile to wagers that they resorted to informal methods to avoid having to enforce them:

> And many judges at nisi prius have recently exercised a very extended discretion in refusing to try actions on wagers, which, though not strictly illegal, have been of a trifling, ridiculous, or contemptible nature.[80]

Though Chitty cited no authority for this observation, it is supported by other evidence. In a case of 1811 Lord Ellenborough is reported as saying that:

> there is . . . another principle on which, I think, an action on such wagers cannot be maintained. They tend to the degradation of courts of justice. It

---

76 *Good* v. *Elliott* (1790) 3 TR 693, 697.
77 See Edward Christian's note to Blackstone's *Commentaries on the Laws of England*, 15th edn, vol. 2, 173, note 11.
78 *Egerton* v. *Brownlow* 4 HLC 1, 124.
79 *Report from Select Committee on Gaming*, PP 1844 vi 1, 223 (appendix I, 'Substance of the Common and Statute Law relating to Gaming' prepared by T Starkie, Esq QC).
80 Chitty, *A Treatise on the Law of Contracts*, 1st edn, 156.

is impossible to be engaged in ludicrous inquiries of this sort, consistently with that dignity which it is essential to the public welfare that a court of justice should always preserve. I therefore will not try the plaintiff's right to recover the four guineas [wagered].[81]

In a later case the same judge made similar comments, adding a further consideration, namely 'the misapplication . . . of public time, by occupy-ing the attention of the Court in deciding upon foolish wagers of this description, to the prejudice of more important business'.[82] The other members of the court agreed, Abbott J saying that: 'I think that a Judge at nisi prius would best exercise his discretion by refusing to try questions arising out of them [wagers].'[83]

This invitation seems to have been taken up by a number of judges, as is suggested by the passage quoted above from Chitty, and from another quotation relied on by the parliamentary committee of 1844:

> The Judges have . . . refused to try actions with relation to wagers not falling within any of the above exceptions [of policy] where they have considered the matter to be of a frivolous or improper nature.[84]

The use of such informal methods indicates failure to formulate a principle on which the actions could be excluded, and this manner of dealing with the problem did not endure. In a note in the second edition (1834) Chitty said that judges could use discretion to *defer* cases, but doubted whether they could properly refuse absolutely to try a case on these grounds.[85] In a case of 1839 counsel suggested in argument that 'wagers dicountenanced by the law are divided into two classes. There are some which a Judge may refuse to try, as unlawful and improper'. Two judges interrupted at this point. Lord Abinger CB said that 'the first class of cases is exploded', and Parke B commented that 'the Judge is bound to try them at some time, though he may postpone them until after cases of more importance have been tried'.[86] In the third edition of Chitty's treatise (1841, by Tompson

---

81 *Squires* v. *Whisken* (1811) 3 Camp 140.   82 *Eltham* v. *Kingsman* (1818) 1 B & A 683.
83 *Ibid.*, at 688 per Abbott J.
84 *Report from Select Committee on Gaming*, note 79, above, appendix II, Extracts from Seventh Report of Commissioners on Criminal Law, 61. The Seventh Report of the Commissioners on Criminal Law (of whom Starkie was one) is in PP 1843 xix 1, but the extract quoted by the 1844 committee was not found there at the page mentioned.
85 Chitty, *A Treatise on the Law of Contracts*, 2nd edn, 394–5 note, citing *Bate* v. *Cartwright* (1819) 7 Price 540.
86 *Evans* v. *Jones* (1839) 5 M & W 77, 80. The issue in *Evans* v. *Jones* was the enforceability of a wager on whether a person charged with forgery would be convicted. The wager was held to be contrary to public policy as tending to interfere with the course of justice.

Chitty) the opinion of Parke B was elevated to the text, introduced, somewhat grudgingly, by the words 'but it seems that'.[87] However, the fact that counsel thought, in 1839, that his argument was plausible, and the dramatic metaphor chosen by Lord Abinger to contradict this view ('is exploded') indicate that the opinion expressed by Joseph Chitty in his first edition had played a role.

By a statute of 1845,[88] following the report of the parliamentary committee of 1844, all wagers were declared void, and this settled the matter for the next century-and-a-half in jurisdictions that adopted the statute, but the statute has been repealed in England and in several other jurisdictions, and the question of enforceability of bets and wagers might again have to be resolved judicially for the twenty-first century. An overriding principle that agreements are always to be enforced would appear to demand the enforcement of bets and wagers: there is offer, acceptance, consideration and, by the usual tests, intention; the transactions are not illegal, and the actual payment of a wager by the loser after the event is not contrary to any definable public policy. Yet it seems very probable that modern courts, like their predecessors, would, if pressed, seek a way not to use their powers to enforce huge and random transfers of wealth on personal bets.

The proposition that judges may exercise a discretion to refuse to try cases that they consider to be 'frivolous or improper', or, in Chitty's words, 'trifling, ridiculous, or contemptible', was rejected, partly because it could not rank as a principle. It lacked reasoned support, it left individual judges without precise guidance, and it would have been likely to affect all kinds of contracts in wholly unpredictable ways. Moreover a simple discretionary refusal to try an action would have been potentially unjust to the claimant because it would have prevented any opportunity to adduce argument that the case should be heard, or that the transaction was not a wager at all, or to know the reasons why the judge had rejected the claim, or to appeal from such a rejection.

A legal rule that wagers were unenforceable might have been supported on some such grounds as the following: the practice of making bets and wagers where the parties have no independent interest in the result serves no discernible public purpose; it causes random transfers of wealth that may give unmerited enrichment to the winner and may have devastating consequences for the loser; experience has shown that gambling may

---

87 Chitty, *A Treatise on the Law of Contracts*, 3rd edn by T. Chitty, 496.
88 Gaming Act, 8 & 9 Vic. c. 109, s. 18.

become an addictive practice that causes harm to individuals, to their families and to society at large; even though the practice is not so harmful as to have been prohibited with penal sanctions, yet there is good reason why the courts should not use their powers positively to enforce wagers. A rule that wagers were unenforceable for these reasons, essentially those given by Buller J in *Good* v. *Elliott*, and echoed by other contemporary commentators,[89] would probably have been recognized as a principle. The reasons for it could have been persuasively articulated; they reflected a judicial and social consensus; the rule would have been stable and likely to lead to predictable results; the crucial questions (what is a wager, and what is a legitimate independent interest?) were questions well-fitted for judicial determination, as is shown by the resolution of analogous questions in the insurance context; the rule would not have affected the enforceability of contracts generally; it would have corresponded with very many results reached in the past, before and after the statute of 1845; it would not usually be considered unjust to the winner of a particular wager to withhold enforcement; the rule would be likely to be adjudged to lead to satisfactory results in the future for society at large and for litigants; if such a rule were to make it difficult to gamble on credit, this result would be consistent with various statutory provisions over several centuries, and would generally be regarded as a social merit rather than as a demerit. But after the statute of 1845 the judicial development of such a principle was unnecessary.

Enforceability of domestic agreements has been restricted, in English law, by holding that spouses normally have no intention to create legal relations in their dealings with each other. The difficulty with this approach is that proof of subjective intention to create legal relations has not been a general requirement of English contract law: if the requirements of contract formation are satisfied, it is irrelevant to show that one or both parties gave no thought to legal consequences, or that one or both detested litigation. Nor, as indicated by the discussion in Chapter 2, would the subjective intention of the promisor (not to be legally bound) be relevant, unless apparent to a reasonable person in the position of the promisee. The conclusion, therefore, that domestic agreements are not normally enforceable must rest on some other principle than lack of intention in the ordinary legal sense of that word. The leading case

---

89 E.g., Blackstone, *Commentaries on the Laws of England*, 1st edn, vol. 4, 171–4, in support of the gaming statutes.

on the issue demonstrates that this was so. Atkin LJ said, in *Balfour* v. *Balfour:*[90]

> The common law does not regulate the form of agreements between spouses. Their promises are not sealed with seals and sealing wax. The consideration that really obtains for them is that natural love and affection which counts for so little in these cold courts. The terms may be repudiated, varied or renewed as performance proceeds or as disagreements develop, and the principles of the common law as to exoneration and discharge and accord and satisfaction are such as find no place in the domestic code. The parties themselves are advocates, judges, courts, sheriff's officer and reporter. In respect of these promises each house is a domain into which the King's writ does not seek to run, and to which his officers do not seek to be admitted.

The rather high-flown and rhetorical style of this passage shows clearly that other considerations were involved than an inquiry into intention, either on a subjective or on an objective basis. Evidently Atkin LJ thought, in the social and legal context of his time, that it was undesirable for broad reasons of social policy that family agreements should, as a general class of agreements, be enforced by the courts. Changing social and legal views of the family, and of the relations between husband and wife, during the twentieth century have necessarily altered this conclusion.

Religious ceremonies associated with marriage often include mutual promises, and the question has arisen whether such ceremonies create legally enforceable contracts. Some cases have held such ceremonial contracts to be not 'justiciable'.[91] The presence of a religious element will not necessarily prevent the enforcement of an agreement between spouses, as shown by a decision of the Supreme Court of Canada where a promise to give a religious divorce was held to be enforceable under Quebec law,[92] but this case involved an arm's-length separation agreement, not a promise that was an integral part of a religious ceremony.

Collective labour agreements have been held to be unenforceable by English courts. In *Ford Motor Co.* v. *Amalgamated Union of Engineering and Foundry Workers*[93] Geoffrey Lane J said, in refusing an interlocutory injunction to enforce a collective agreement:

90 [1919] 2 KB 571, 579.
91 *Re Morris and Morris* (1973) 42 DLR (3d) 550 (Man., CA); *Kaddoura* v. *Hammoud* (1998) 168 DLR (4th) 503.
92 *Bruker* v. *Marcovitz* [2007] 3 SCR 607, 288 DLR (4th) 257.   93 [1969] 2 QB 303.

> The conclusion which I have reached is this; it is necessarily a preliminary
> view as this of course is not the hearing of the action proper. If one applies
> the subjective test and asks what the intentions of the various parties were,
> the answer is that so far as they had any express intentions they were
> certainly not to make the agreement enforceable at law. If one applies an
> objective test and asks what intention must be imputed from all the cir-
> cumstances of the case, the answer is the same. The fact that the agreements
> prima facie deal with commercial relationships is outweighed by the other
> considerations, by the wording of the agreements, by the nature of the
> agreements, and by the climate of opinion voiced and evidenced by the
> extra-judicial authorities. Agreements such as these, composed largely of
> optimistic aspirations, presenting grave practical problems of enforcement
> and reached against a background of opinion adverse to enforceability, are,
> in my judgment, not contracts in the legal sense and are not enforceable at
> law. Without clear and express provisions making them amenable to legal
> action, they remain in the realm of undertakings binding in honour. None
> of the authorities cited by Mr. Neill, on behalf of the plaintiffs, dissuades
> me from this view. In my judgment, the parties, none of them, had the
> intention to make these agreements binding at law.[94]

It is evident from this passage that this was not solely, or even primarily,
an inquiry into actual intention, either on a subjective or on an objective
test: considerations of policy, as perceived by the judge in the context of
English labour relations at the time, were also influential. Differing social
and legal views of labour relations in other jurisdictions and at other
times may alter the conclusion.

Political promises have also been held to be unenforceable. Often the
form in which a political promise is made will suggest that no legally
enforceable contract is contemplated. The promise may often be construed as amounting merely to an aspiration, or as representing present
intention only, or as subject to modification in changed political circumstances. But in a Canadian case a candidate for political office made
a solemn promise, incorporated in a document that was deliberately
designed to have the appearance of a binding contract, signed in public
with considerable ceremony and publicity. Despite the deliberate adoption of the appearance of contract, the document was held not to be
enforceable.[95] The reason was not that there was anything objectionable
in the substance of what was promised (not to impose new taxes), nor

---

94 *Ibid.*, at 330–1.
95 *Canadian Taxpayers Federation* v. *Ontario* (2004) 73 OR (3d) 621 (Sup Ct).

that intention was lacking – all the indicia of intention were present – but the court's opinion that enforcement of such promises as contracts would interfere improperly with the political process.

As mentioned in an earlier chapter, public policy has sometimes been directly invoked to set aside disadvantageous contracts. Contracts in restraint of trade,[96] in restraint of marriage,[97] or otherwise unduly restrictive of personal liberty[98] have been held to be unenforceable. Comyn wrote, of restraint of trade, that 'all such obligations are contrary to principles of national policy; one great object of which is to enable and promote trade'.[99] These cases involve a mixture of public and private considerations. As Lord Diplock said, in relation to contracts struck down for restraint of trade,

> If one looks at the reasoning of 19th-century judges . . . one finds lip service paid to current economic theories, but if one looks at what they said in the light of what they did, one finds that they struck down a bargain if they thought it was unconscionable as between the parties to it, and upheld it if they thought it was not.[100]

There is a public interest in the freedom of persons not being unduly restrained by law, and this interest has been reflected in the setting aside of transactions that are in unreasonable restraint of trade, or unreasonable restraint of other freedoms. These cases have reflected both considerations personal to the contracting parties, and also a public interest that individuals should be free of undue restraints – not only for their own good, but for the good of the community. The two kinds of consideration are not entirely separable, because it has been perceived to be in the public interest that individuals should retain a certain degree of freedom. More generally, the words 'policy' and 'public policy' have also often been associated with a residual sense of justice between the parties, because avoidance of oppression and of unjust enrichment have themselves been thought of as public policies.[101]

96 *Mason* v. *Provident Clothing & Supply Co.* [1913] AC 724. See Trebilcock, *The Common Law of Restraint of Trade.*
97 *Lowe* v. *Peers* (1768) 4 Burr 2225.
98 *Horwood* v. *Millar's Timber & Trading Co. Ltd* [1917] 1 KB 305 (CA).
99 Comyn, *A Treatise of the Law Relative to Contracts*, 32.
100 A. Schroeder Music Publishing Co. v. Macaulay [1974] 1 WLR 1308, 1315 (HL). See Chapter 8, below, at note 47.
101 See Chapter 4, above, at pp. 108, 115–17, Chapter 5, at p. 138, and Chapter 8, at p. 224, below.

The *Draft Common Frame of Reference*, in dealing with this aspect of contract law, avoids the use of the word 'policy' altogether, and relies entirely on the concept of principle. The relevant section is headed 'Infringement of fundamental principles or mandatory rules', and the first provision, headed 'Contracts infringing fundamental principles', is that:

> A contract is void to the extent that:
>
> (a) it infringes a principle recognised as fundamental in the laws of the Member States of the European Union; and
> (b) nullity is required to give effect to that principle.[102]

The comments to this section state that:

> the subject matter is sometimes described as 'illegality' . . . However, 'illegality' is not necessarily the most appropriate term for some infringements of fundamental principles or mandatory rules . . . The formulation of the first Article is similarly intended to avoid the varying national concepts of immorality, illegality at common law, public policy, *ordre public*, and *bonos mores*, by invoking a necessarily broad idea of fundamental principles found across the European Union . . . [103]

It is instructive to observe that the topic generally thought of as 'public policy' by Anglo-American lawyers and sometimes contrasted with principle, may equally be envisaged as an *application* of fundamental principles.

The interactions between private and public considerations, and between principle and policy are complex, and they run in both directions. Freedom of contract has usually been called a principle of private law, and has been justified mainly by considerations of justice between the parties. But freedom of contract is also perceived to be in the public interest, and the operation of contract law has been perceived to be for the public benefit, and has been said to be required by public policy. On the other hand, public policy does not require enforcement of all contracts, in some cases because the contracts themselves are contrary to the public interest, and in other cases because they offend residual considerations of justice between the parties, or would cause the undue enrichment of one at the expense of the other. Public policy itself has often been

---

102 *Draft Common Frame of Reference*, 2009, II – 7:301.
103 *Ibid.*, Full Edition (2009, 6 vols) comments A and B, vol. 1, 536.

called a principle,[104] and the implementation of it has been governed, where possible, by generalizable propositions that have also been called principles.

104 As by Lord Mansfield in *Holman* v. *Johnson*, and *Randall* v. *Jones*, notes 1 and 6, above, and by Comyn, note 22, above.

7

Enforcement

'It is the general intention of the law', said Lord Atkinson in 1911, 'that, in giving damages for breach of contract, the party complaining should, so far as it can be done by money, be placed in the same position as he would have been in if the contract had been performed', adding confidently: 'That is a ruling principle. It is a just principle.'[1] This rule, or principle, was not new in 1911. It had been stated as a rule in 1848,[2] but it was not new even then, having been formulated only for the purpose of finding that an exception to it did not apply. Lord Atkinson's formulation was made not for the purpose of enlarging the damages available for breach of contract, but for the purpose of rejecting an excessive claim. It is significant that he said not only that it was a 'ruling principle', but also that it was a 'just principle', for general considerations of justice were prominent in the case. In rejecting the plaintiff's claim, Lord Atkinson said that 'one cannot but feel that the reasoning which leads to results so unjust and anomalous must be fallacious'.[3]

This rule, very often called a basic or fundamental principle, has been variously described as the 'normal' rule of contract damages, or the 'loss of bargain' measure of damages, or the 'expectation' measure. The relation between reliance and expectation in contract damages was discussed in an article by Fuller and Perdue, published in 1936, 'The reliance interest in contract damages'.[4] This much-cited article touched on a number of separate points. The authors distinguished among expectation, reliance and restitution interests in contract damages. They invited the reader to consider why the law should *ever* protect the expectation interest,

1 *Wertheim* v. *Chicoutimi Pulp Co.* [1911] AC 301, 307 (PC).
2 *Robinson* v. *Harman* (1848) 1 Ex 850, 855, not laying this down as a new rule, but affirming it as the general and long-established common law rule, to which a limited exception (made in 1776 by *Flureau* v. *Thornhill* 2 Bl W 1078) was held not to apply.
3 See note 1, above.
4 L. Fuller and W. Perdue, 'The Reliance Interest in Contract Damages' (1936) 46 *Yale Law Journal* 52, 373.

and offered as one possible explanation the suggestion that this was the most effective way, in the long run, of facilitating reliance on contracts, because, if adopted as a firm rule, it gave the promisee the strongest basis for confident action. The overall thrust of the article, when read as a whole (it was published in two parts), was in the direction of *enlarging* liability, by inviting the courts to protect reliance even where there was, or might be, no fully enforceable contract between the parties. The authors did not seriously pursue the suggestion that the law should, as a general rule, cease to protect the expectation interest where there *was* a contract, though it is true that they raised the possibility for the reader to contemplate.[5] Nevertheless, some have deduced from Fuller and Perdue's article that protection of reliance is the *only* proper function of the court. From this proposition it is possible to develop an argument for a *reduction* in liability for breach of contract, casting doubt on the 'normal' rule of expectation damages. If it is accepted as a starting point that protection of reliance is the sole proper objective, protection of the expectation interest (where there is no reliance) can be made to seem unprincipled.

One twentieth-century writer who pursued this line of thought was Patrick Atiyah. In several of his writings[6] Atiyah suggested that, in the absence of reliance, there was no strong reason to protect the expectation of the promisee, and in *The Rise and Fall of Freedom of Contract* (1979) he supported this view with an extended historical argument. Referring to the eighteenth century, he wrote:

> But my concern at present is not with modern theory but with that of the eighteenth century; and my suggestion is that at that time there was a much closer relationship between the nature of the liability sought to be imposed on a defendant, and the ground of the plaintiff's claim. In particular, if liability was sought to be imposed – as could quite typically be imposed in any contractual action today – for breach of a wholly executory and unrelied-upon promise, the reaction of the courts was still fundamentally hostile. The notion that a promisee was entitled to have his *expectations* protected, purely and simply as such, as a result of a promise and nothing else, was not generally accepted in eighteenth-century law.[7]

5 The article was concerned to a considerable extent with s. 90 of the Restatement of Contracts (promises without consideration enforceable by reason of subsequent reliance), where the First Restatement (1932) had made no provision for a limited measure of enforcement; the Second Restatement (1979), adopting Fuller and Perdue's views, provided that a limited measure of enforcement should, in that particular context, be available.

6 P.S. Atiyah, 'Contracts Promises and the Law of Obligations' (1978) 94 LQR 193, reprinted in Atiyah, *Essays on Contract*, 10; Atiyah, *Promises, Morals, and Law*.

7 Atiyah, *The Rise and Fall of Freedom of Contract*, 142 (emphasis in original).

Historical evidence suggests a more complex picture.[8] One source of evidence is Gilbert's work, written early in the eighteenth century, entitled *Of Contracts*, which has been discussed in an earlier chapter.[9] This manuscript work, not widely known or discussed in academic circles in 1979,[10] and still unpublished, offers very relevant evidence on the point now in issue, for it is clear that Gilbert assumed that contracts were fully enforceable. He did not directly address the question of the proper measure of damages for breach of contract, nor did he use the terms 'expectation' and 'reliance', but this strengthens the force of the conclusion that his assumptions corresponded with the general understanding of his time. That is, Gilbert did not address the question as one that was or might be controversial, or on which views plausibly held by others might require refutation; he simply assumed that contracts, when enforceable, were enforceable to the full extent of the value promised.

This assumption is inherent in his opening words: 'Contracts are 2-fold, Verbal & Solemn'. Gilbert here took as his conceptual starting point the law relating to formal promises, or covenants: promises made under seal ('solemn' contracts) were enforceable. He then went on to show that some informal promises ('verbal' contracts) were also enforceable (though not all, because consideration was required – a matter he discussed at great length). This way of approaching the subject assumes that both kinds of promise (formal and informal), when enforceable, were enforceable in the same way and to the same extent. No one has ever doubted that a formal contract (a covenant, deed, specialty or contract under seal), if enforceable, is enforceable to the full extent of the promise: enforceability in this context can scarcely have any other meaning. Gilbert evidently assumed that informal contracts, when enforceable (i.e. when there was consideration) had the same consequence.

In discussing the need for consideration, Gilbert raised the theoretical possibility that all promises, even if informal and without consideration, might be enforced, mentioning that some opinions favoured 'the

8 See J.H. Baker, 'Review: *The Rise and Fall of Freedom of Contract*' (1980) 43 *Modern Law Review* 467. The perceived need for the Statute of Frauds (1677) also suggests that the classes of contract listed there were fully enforceable. Marriage settlement contracts (one of the classes listed), for example, seem to have been fully enforced before and (where the statutory requirements were satisfied) after the statute. See *Gilmore* v. *Shuter* (1679) T Jones 108.
9 Gilbert, *Of Contracts*, f. 39. See Chapter 3, above, pp. 59–60.
10 A.W.B. Simpson referred to it briefly in 'Innovation in Nineteenth-Century Contract Law' (1975) 91 *Law Quarterly Review* 247, 266–6, reprinted in *Legal Theory and Legal History*, 190–1.

punctuall performance of every verbal promise'. That, however, was not Gilbert's own view, and he adduced quite vigorous arguments against it, as appears in the passages quoted in an earlier chapter, which tend to show that Gilbert assumed that, where enforceable, promises were enforceable to their full extent. The reference to the possibility of disposing of 'the fruits and effects of a long and painfull industry and all the certain advantages and conveniences of life by the meer breath of a word and the turn of an unwary expression', the reference to words that tend to a person's 'own destruction', and the reference to the danger of persons being obligated by 'random words' and 'ludicrous expressions' strongly suggest that, to Gilbert, enforceability meant full enforcement to the value of the promise. Another indication that tends in the same direction is Gilbert's view that the primary purpose of contracts was to transfer property. Starting with the second sentence of the treatise he defined his subject in these words: 'Now contract is the act of two or more persons concurring, the one in parting with, and the other in receiving some property right or benefit.'[11] This view of contract as primarily a means of tranferring property, a view taken also by Hale in the seventeenth century and by Blackstone in the later eighteenth century, necessarily implies enforcement to the full value of what is promised, for, if the only consequence of a contract were to protect the reliance (if any) of the promisee, contracts would not be an effective way of transferring property.

To these considerations may be added the significance of specific performance, also recognized in this context in the eighteenth century.[12] The Chancery court had power, where it judged it appropriate, to decree specific performance of contracts. This power was regularly used in land sale contracts, and, even if not frequently used elsewhere, its very existence necessarily implied that contractual obligations were, conceptually speaking, capable of full enforcement.

The topic of specific performance has been much debated by twentieth-century writers, different writers invoking the idea of 'principle' in support of opposite conclusions. Everything depends on what is taken by a writer to be 'the principle', or the conceptual starting point. If the principle is, as Atiyah suggested, that only reliance should be protected, specific performance would very rarely be available. On the other hand some have deduced from the proposition that damages are normally measured by the value of performance, a 'principle' that the object of the law is to put the claimant so far as possible in the position that he or she

11 Gilbert, *Of Contracts* f. 39, Chapter 3, above.   12 See Chapter 1, p. 15, above.

would have occupied if the contract had been performed, from which it is deduced that specific performance should always be available if the claimant chooses it.[13] Anglo-American law has not favoured either of these extreme views: the generally accepted approach has been that damages (on the expectation measure) are available as of right, but that specific performance is an exceptional remedy. It has been suggested that civil law systems accept a principle that gives an unfettered right to specific performance, but a ready comparison is difficult, because civil law systems may have general residual fetters on the exercise of rights, such as the doctrines of good faith and abuse of rights, and because most civil law systems do not enforce specific orders by contempt of court sanctions, which, in systems derived from English law, include instant imprisonment for disobedience.

Comparing common law and civilian systems, Anthony Ogus wrote, in an essay published in 1989, that:

> the latter [civilian systems] view the specific enforcement of agreements as a primary remedy, while the former accord it only secondary status, regarding it as appropriate only where the monetary equivalent of performance is 'inadequate'. At the same time, there is evidence that in practice the systems converge to some extent, that the types of contract which are specifically enforced in both systems share common characteristics.[14]

This view is confirmed by the *Draft Common Frame of Reference*, which proposes the following rule:

III – 3:302: Non-monetary obligations

(1) The creditor is entitled to enforce specific performance of an obligation other than one to pay money . . .

(3) Specific performance cannot, however, be enforced where:

(a) performance would be unlawful or impossible;
(b) performance would be unreasonably burdensome or expensive; or
(c) performance would be of such a personal character that it would be unreasonable to enforce it.

(4) The creditor loses the right to enforce specific performance if performance is not requested within a reasonable time after the creditor has

---

13 E.A. Farnsworth, 'Legal Remedies for Breach of Contract' (1970) 70 *Columbia Law Review* 1145; A. Schwartz, 'The Case for Specific Performance' (1979) 89 *Yale Law Journal* 271.
14 A. Ogus, 'Remedies 1: English Report' in Harris and Tallon (eds.), *Contract Law Today*, 243.

become, or could reasonably be expected to have become, aware of the non-performance.

> (5) The creditor cannot recover damages for loss or a stipulated payment for non-performance to the extent that the creditor has increased the loss or the amount of the payment by insisting unreasonably on specific performance in circumstances where the creditor could have made a reasonable substitute transaction without significant effort or expense.[15]

The conceptual starting point here is the civilian idea of a right to performance, but the open-ended nature of the exceptions is likely often to lead to results very similar to those reached in practice (though with an opposite conceptual starting point) by English law.

The comment to this article, having noted the opposite conceptual starting points, which might well be called opposite principles, adds that 'there is reason to believe, however, that results in practice are rather similar under both theories'.[16] As with the question of subjective intent, discussed earlier in Chapter 2, the wording ('there is reason to believe . . . that results in practice are rather similar') indicates an element of uncertainty or variation among the civilian jurisdictions referred to. Nevertheless, the comment is significant, as tending to exclude an easy supposition that specific performance is available as of right and without qualification in all civilian jurisdictions. That an apparent right to specific performance in civilian systems may be restrained by concepts such as good faith or abuse of rights is suggested by another comment headed 'Limitation on abuse of remedy',[17] referring to 'good faith and fair dealing', and to unreasonable insistence by a creditor on specific performance. Even where, as in civilian systems, a right to performance is taken as the conceptual starting point, there are many instances, as the exceptions included in the *Draft Common Frame of Reference* show, which cannot be precisely defined or enumerated, where specific performance would be inappropriate, unjust, and oppressive, particularly where enforced, as in Anglo-American systems, by the Draconian sanctions for contempt of court.

Conceptual approaches to questions of enforcement, or realization, of rights depend to a large extent on the degree to which right and remedy are viewed as interlinked. There has been much confusion of terminology and of thought on this issue. Browne-Wilkinson V-C said in 1986 that:

15 *Draft Common Frame of Reference.*   16 *Ibid.*, comment B, vol. 1, 829.
17 *Ibid.*, comment J, vol. 1, 833–4.

> In the pragmatic way in which English law has developed, a man's legal rights are in fact those which are protected by a cause of action. It is not in accordance, as I understand it, with the principles of English law to analyse rights as being something separate from the remedy given to the individual.[18]

This view suggests that right and remedy are, in one sense, inseparable, because the extent of a right cannot be determined without examining the remedy that the law gives, and as a matter of historical fact has given, to protect it. On the other hand, this approach has led some to perceive in English law a separation between right and remedy, in that the extent of the right does not itself necessarily determine the appropriate remedy, which appears to require a separate and distinct enquiry by the court, and a separate exercise of judgment, which has been called by some writers 'discretionary'.[19]

Professor Peter Birks took a sharply different view, writing that the obligation to pay compensatory damages is 'the same thing as the right, looked at from the other end',[20] and in several of his writings he objected to 'discretionary remedialism' as likely to be a source of unprincipled judicial activity.[21] This contrast of views has suggested that there are two conceptions of remedies, which have been called 'monism' and 'dualism'.[22] But a distinction along these lines is by no means easy to apply, either to the decisions of courts, or to the opinions of writers. In one sense every monist is a dualist, in that the right is initially defined without regard to the remedy, which is therefore conceptually separated from the definition of the right.[23] On the other hand, many 'dualists' would

18 *Kingdom of Spain* v. *Christie, Manson & Woods Ltd* [1986] 1 WLR 1120, 1129.
19 G. Hammond, 'The Place of Damages in the Scheme of Remedies', in Finn (ed.), *Essays on Damages*, 192, 228.
20 P. Birks, 'Definition and Division: A Meditation on *Institutes* 3:13' in Birks (ed.), *The Classification of Obligations*, 1 at 24.
21 P. Birks, 'Three Kinds of Objections to Discretionary Remedialism' (2000) 29 *Western Australia Law Review* 1; P. Birks, 'Rights, Wrongs, and Remedies' (2000) 20 *Oxford Journal of Legal Studies* 1; P. Birks, 'Book Review of *The Remedial Constructive Trust* by David Wright' (1999) 115 *Law Quarterly Review* 681.
22 G. Hammond, note 19, above, at 197; G. Hammond, 'Rethinking Remedies: the changing Conception of the Relationship between Legal and Equitable Remedies' in Berryman (ed.), *Remedies: Issues and Perspectives*, 87, at 90; M. Tilbury, 'Remedies and Classification of Obligations' in Robertson (ed.), *The Law of Obligations*, 11, at 17; E. Weinrib, 'Two Conceptions of Remedies', in Rickett (ed.), *Justifying Private Law Remedies*, 3.
23 Stephen Smith takes this approach in *Contract Theory*, 388: 'while remedial rules tell us important things about contractual obligations, they are separate from such obligations, strictly speaking . . . [C]ontract law, properly understood, is limited to the rules that govern the creation and content of contractual obligations.'

wish to say, with Browne-Wilkinson V-C, that right and remedy are interlinked: an obligation that is specifically enforceable differs from one that is not; an obligation that gives right to expectation damages differs from an obligation that is only enforceable to the extent of reliance; an obligation enforceable by an award of damages differs from one where the aggrieved party's remedy is only to rescind,[24] or to obtain restitution of an enrichment,[25] or to invoke penal or administrative sanctions,[26] or to demand an apology. On this view, no right can be fully understood without examining the extent of the remedy that the law gives for its infringement, and this brings the 'dualist' back to a kind of monism, though one with very different implications from the first kind. Professor Ernest Weinrib, in an article on this subject, while generally favouring the monist approach, also adopts the civilian concept of abuse of rights.[27] This is an important addition: the ideas that rights, as defined, are absolute and that remedies follow automatically take on a quite different colour if there is a general rule that rights must not be abused. Results that would be reached in one legal system through the concept of abuse of rights might, in another system, be reached by invoking a discretionary power to withhold an equitable remedy.

The word 'discretion', used with reference to judicial decision-making, is neither a simple nor a single concept,[28] and it is not, in all its senses, incompatible with principle. As often in the law, the same word has been used with different senses in various contexts. 'Discretion' is sometimes used to indicate that a legal rule has elements of uncertainty; sometimes it refers to a need for restrictions upon rights of appeal in the interests of expedition and finality; sometimes the word refers to a situation where the nature of the decision is such that the initial decision-maker is as likely as a reviewing court to reach a satisfactory conclusion, and sometimes it refers to situations where the initial decision-maker is thought to have a positive advantage in this respect. These concepts are different from each other, and have differing implications for the proper role of appellate tribunals. In many cases more than one concept is in play at the same time, with consequent confusion of ideas.

---

24 As under the former rule in *Bain* v. *Fothergill* (1874) LR 7 HL 158.
25 As in *Deglman* v. *Guaranty Trust Co. of Canada* [1954] SCR 725.
26 As in the case of an undertaking to the court, or by a solicitor to another solicitor.
27 Ernest Weinrib, note 22, above.
28 For a fuller discussion, see Waddams, 'Judicial Discretion' (2001) 1 *Oxford University Commonwealth Law Journal* 59. Many writers have identified a variety of meanings of the word, e.g., R. Pattenden, *The Judge, Discretion, and the Criminal Law*, 3–6, identifying six senses in the criminal law context.

All legal rules, as has always been recognized,[29] contain elements of uncertainty, because the circumstances in which the rules come to be applied cannot be precisely foreseen, nor can any rule, however detailed, describe in advance every possible future case. Many important and fundamental legal rules are necessarily very general, and are 'open-textured' in nature,[30] or allow for open-ended exceptions. It is sometimes said of rules of this kind that they are 'discretionary'.[31]

The word 'discretionary' is commonly so used of equitable remedies, because in English law and in systems derived from it orders of the court (injunctions and decrees of specific performance) have an immediate and drastic impact, demanding (as is not the case in many other legal systems) immediate obedience on pain of imprisonment for contempt of court. There are often good reasons for withholding or modifying such orders, but it is not possible to state all of these reasons fully and precisely in advance, and therefore the court retains a power to withhold its orders in appropriate circumstances. This feature of equitable remedies is usually summarized by saying that they are 'discretionary'.

It is not likely that usage in this respect will be altered, but it may be suggested that 'discretionary' would not, ideally, be the word of choice for this concept. What is meant is that it is not possible to define in advance the precise circumstances in which judicial orders will be made, but the use of the word 'discretionary' might be taken to imply, and has in other contexts been taken to imply, that some special deference is due by an appellate court to the judge of first instance. In *Elson* v. *Elson*, for example, dealing with a statutory provision for variation of division of spousal property where 'unfair', the Supreme Court of Canada said that 'Courts of Appeal should be highly reluctant to interfere with the exercise of a trial judge's discretion. It is he who has the advantage of hearing the parties and is in the best position to weigh the equities of a case.'[32] The reason given

---

29 Aristotle, *Nichomachaean Ethics*, V, 1137b, speaking of the need for flexibility in the application of legal rules, referred to a pliable leaden measuring stick used by masons at Lesbos to take impressions. The expression 'Lesbian Rule' was once in common English usage to mean a flexible legal rule (OED). Aristotle's analogy may also suggest the complex interaction between a rule and its application: a legal rule may take its form from what it regulates.

30 Hart, *The Concept of Law*, 121–32.

31 This is the meaning generally intended in discussions of judicial discretion, e.g., Dworkin, *Taking Rights Seriously*; K. Greenawalt, 'Discretion and Judicial Decisions: the Elusive Quest for the Fetters that Bind Judges' (1975) 75 *Columbia Law Review* 359; A. Barak, *Judicial Discretion*.

32 [1989] 1 SCR 1367, 1375.

here in the second sentence quoted applies, it is suggested, only where the 'advantage of hearing the parties' is really relevant. On some matters there is such an advantage.[33] However, the open-ended nature of a legal rule does not in itself present any particular reason to defer to a judge of first instance; on the contrary, the open-ended nature of a rule may be a very good reason for the appellate court to give guidance and to settle uncertainties.[34] This is true whether or not there is theoretically a 'correct' legal answer.[35] Thus, one favouring a broad power of relief from contractual liability on grounds of unfairness is not bound also to exclude the appellate courts from settling, defining, and developing the law, or from doing so on the basis of principle.

Generally, appellate courts have quite readily undertaken the review of final equitable orders, notwithstanding that they are called 'discretionary'. It has often been affirmed that a judge exercising discretionary powers is not thereby authorized to act on 'caprice',[36] or in a manner that is 'arbitrary or unregulated'.[37] The judge is obliged to apply the law, and it is ultimately for the appellate courts to say what the law is.[38] Moreover, it cannot be credibly maintained, simply because the judge has what is called 'discretion', that one decision is as good as another. In an English case, to be discussed more fully below, the question arose of whether a contractual obligation to conduct a business for a period of nineteen years into the future was specifically enforceable.[39] The judge of first instance refused a decree, the Court of Appeal, by a majority, decreed specific performance, and the House of Lords restored the judge's decision. The final disposition was the restoration of the judge's order, but not because special deference was due to the judge on this issue – still less because one decision on the question was thought to be as good as another. The question at stake was of enormous importance, both to the parties in the particular case and to contracting parties generally. Opinions in the legal profession and on the bench differed sharply, as is demonstrated by the

33 See Waddams, 'Judicial Discretion', note 28, above. It might also be possible in some cases to construe the legislation as actually restricting the right of appeal, but this seems implausible in *Elson* v. *Elson*.
34 Galligan, *Discretionary Powers*, 5–6, 25–6.
35 Dworkin, *Taking Rights Seriously*, 81, or Barak, *Judicial Discretion*, 16, 30.
36 *Beddow* v. *Beddow* (1878) 9 Ch D 89, 93.
37 *Harris* v. *Beauchamp Bros* [1894] 1 QB 801, 808; Barak, *Judicial Discretion*, 118.
38 R.J. Sharpe, 'The Application and Impact of Judicial Discretion in Commercial Litigation' (1998) 17 *Advocates Society Journal* 4.
39 *Cooperative Insurance Society Ltd* v. *Argyll Stores (Holdings) Ltd* [1998] AC 1 (HL). See below at notes 123–4.

division of opinion in the Court of Appeal, and between the majority in the Court of Appeal and the House of Lords. There was every reason for the appellate courts to entertain the question of what legal rule should govern such cases and to determine it.

Other decisions demonstrate the same point. In *Attorney-General* v. *Blake*,[40] also to be discussed below, the House of Lords asserted a power, in exceptional cases, to order an accounting of profits derived from breach of contract. Lord Nicholls said that 'when, exceptionally, a just response to a breach of contract so requires, the court should be able to grant the discretionary remedy of requiring the defendant to account to the plaintiff for the benefits he has received from his breach of contract'.[41] There are of course elements of uncertainty in such a principle, and Lord Nicholls was very careful not to lay down any precise rule. Some might criticize such a principle as too vague. Others will consider that a considerable element of flexibility is necessary or desirable, but those taking the latter view are not bound also to say that an appellate court should refrain from developing the law on a rational and consistent basis. In calling the remedy 'discretionary' Lord Nicholls evidently did not mean to imply that individual judges should be free to make contradictory decisions, and there was no suggestion that any special deference was due to the judge of first instance, who had refused to order an accounting of the profits. If the facts of the *Blake* case should recur, the result should be expected to be the same, irrespective of the predilections of the judge of first instance. Similarly on the question of proprietary estoppel, the legal principle is necessarily very flexible, but this does not mean that the decision of a trial judge is to be preferred to that of an appellate court,[42] nor that indistinguishable facts should lead to differing legal consequences according to the decision at first instance.

An opposite line of thought to Atiyah's has been that full enforcement (by specific performance or expectation damages) is required as a matter of principle, and that considerations relating to the usefulness of protecting reliance must be rigorously excluded as being matters of policy, unsuited to judicial contemplation. But historical evidence shows that, in this context, both kinds of consideration have been influential. Henry Sidgwick, writing in 1879, summarized the social benefits of contract law, stressing the protection of reliance:

---

40 [2001] 1 AC 268 (HL).   41 *Ibid.*, at 284–5.
42 See *Gillett* v. *Holt* [2000] 3 WLR 815, where the Court of Appeal reversed a trial judge who had refused to find a proprietary estoppel.

In a summary view of the civil order of society, as constituted in accordance with the individualistic ideal, performance of contract presents itself as the chief *positive* element, protection of life and property being the chief *negative* element. Withdraw contract – suppose that no one can count on the fulfilment of any engagement – and the members of the human community are atoms that cannot effectively combine; the complex co-operation and division of employments that are the essential characteristics of modern industry cannot be introduced among such beings. Suppose contracts freely made and effectively sanctioned, and the most elaborate social organization becomes possible, at least in a society of such human beings as the individualistic theory contemplates – gifted with mature reason and governed by enlightened self-interest. Of such being it is prima facie plausible to say that, when once their respective relations to the surrounding material world have been determined so as to prevent mutual encroachment and to secure to each the fruits of his industry, the remainder of their positive rights and obligations ought to depend entirely on that coincidence of their free choices, which we call contract.[43]

This kind of thinking was reflected in contemporary judicial comments. Sir George Jessel's remark, quoted in the previous chapter, illustrates the close association of principle and policy:

> If there is one thing which more than another public policy requires it is that men of full age and competent understanding shall have the utmost liberty of contracting and that their contracts when entered into freely and voluntarily shall be held sacred and shall be enforced by courts of justice.[44]

Right and remedy have been interlinked: the nature of the right determines the proper remedy, but the scope of the remedy defines the right.[45] It is true to say, as Fuller and Perdue did, that one of the beneficial effects often attributed to contract law is that it tends to facilitate reliance. But it does not follow that facilitation of reliance is the *sole* purpose of contract law. The promisee, as we have seen, can be said to have, in a real sense, a right to performance; but it does not follow that the right is an absolute or unfettered right, to be vindicated at the expense of all other values. In formulating what have been called principles, writers and judges, expressly or implicitly, have taken into account not only the interest of the promisee, but general considerations of justice to the promisor in particular disputes,

---

43 Sidgwick, *Elements of Politics*, 82. See also the views of Paley, Chapter 3, above, p. 63.
44 *Printing & Numerical Registering Co.* v. *Sampson* (1875) LR 9 Eq 462, 465 (Sir George Jessel, MR).
45 See note 18, above.

and to both parties in potential future disputes, matters that are not wholly separable from considerations of policy.

The principle, or purpose, of full compensation, 'if relentlessly pursued', as a twentieth-century judge said, would make the contract-breaker liable for all losses caused by the breach, 'however improbable, however unpredictable'.[46] The vivid image of 'relentless' pursuit indicates a perceived need to restrict the principle of full compensation by countervailing considerations, which may be summarized as fairness to the defendant, and commercial certainty and convenience for future contracting parties. The topic of remoteness of damages has, since 1854, been the subject of a continual search for principle. The question has also been described as a matter of policy, using 'policy' in the sense in which we have seen it elsewhere, of a residual sense of justice between the parties.[47] The leading case on the subject is the decision of the Exchequer Court in *Hadley* v. *Baxendale*.[48] The plaintiff, who operated a grist mill, agreed with the defendant, a nationwide carrier, to carry a broken mill shaft to serve as a pattern for the manufacture of a new shaft. The carrier's undue delay caused the mill to be stopped for longer than it would otherwise have been, and the mill-owner claimed compensation for the consequent loss of profits. The carrier was held not to be liable in the absence of knowledge of the probable consequences of the delay. In a well-known passage Baron Alderson said:

> Now we think the proper rule in such a case as the present is this: where two parties have made a contract which one of them has broken, the damages which the other party ought to receive in respect of such breach of contract should be such as may fairly and reasonably be considered either arising naturally, i.e., according to the usual course of things, from such breach of contract itself, or such as may reasonably be supposed to have been in the contemplation of both parties, at the time they made the contract, as the probable result of the breach of it.

But, he went on to say, if the damage arose from special circumstances not known to the contract-breaker, there should be no liability, and for this reason a new trial was ordered in *Hadley* v. *Baxendale*.

---

46 Asquith LJ, in *Victoria Laundry (Windsor) Ltd* v. *Newman Industries Ltd* [1949] 2 KB 528, 539 (CA).
47 *Kienzle* v. *Stringer* (1981) 130 DLR (3d) 272. This usage was pointed out by A. Robertson, 'Constraints on Policy-Based Reasoning in Private Law', in Robertson and Tang Hang Wu, *The Goals of Private Law*, 261, 265.
48 (1854) 9 Ex 341.

Alderson B referred to the propositions formulated by the court both as a 'rule', and as 'principles'. The need, as he perceived it, to formulate such a rule or principle sprang from general considerations of justice: 'if the jury are left without any definite rule to guide them, it will, in such cases as these, manifestly lead to the greatest injustice'. The underlying reason was that the extent of potential liability for breach of contract was relevant to other contractual terms, including price and agreed limitations on liability: 'for, had the special circumstances been known, the parties might have specially provided for the breach of contract by special terms as to damages in that case; and of this advantage it would be very unjust to deprive them'.

The tenor of the decision was very much in the direction of making the consequences of breach of contract predictable, as in another case decided two years later by the same court (including Alderson B). This was *Hamlin* v. *Great Northern Railway Co.*[49] where, a traveller having been stranded by the absence of a connecting train, the court laid down a rule (which stood for many years) excluding damages for mental distress for breach of contract. Pollock CB said:

> In actions for breaches of contract the damages must be such as are capable of being appreciated or estimated . . . [I]t may be laid down as a rule, that generally in actions upon contracts no damages can be given which cannot be stated specifically, and that the plaintiff is entitled to recover whatever damages naturally result from the breach of contract, but not damages for disappointment of mind occasioned by the breach of contract.[50]

The rule in *Hadley* v. *Baxendale* quickly proved to be incomplete. As early as 1860, Wilde B said, presciently:

> I think that, although an excellent attempt was made in *Hadley* v. *Baxendale* to lay down a rule on the subject, it will be found that the rule is not capable of meeting all cases; and when the matter comes to be further considered, it will probably turn out that there is no such thing as a rule as to the legal measure of damages applicable in all cases.[51]

In alluding to the wisdom of this forecast Lord du Parcq said, in 1949, that:

> It was necessary to lay down principles lest juries should be persuaded to do injustice by imposing an undue, or perhaps an inadequate, liability on a defendant. The court must be careful, however, to see that the principles

---

49 (1856) 1 H & N 408, 26 LJ Ex 20.   50 (1856) 1 H & N 408, 411.
51 *Gee* v. *Lancashire and Yorkshire Railway Co.* (1860) 6 H & N 211, 221.

laid down are never so narrowly interpreted as to prevent a jury, or judge
of fact, from doing justice between the parties. So to use them would be to
misuse them.[52]

Later cases have indeed imposed liability for losses that could not readily
have been foreseen, and have refused to impose liability for losses that
could quite easily have been foreseen.

A twenty-first century case of the latter kind is the decision of the
House of Lords in *Transfield Shipping Inc.* v. *Mercator Shipping Inc. (The
Achilleas).*[53] Here the charterer of a ship was nine days late in redelivering
the ship to the owner's disposition. The owner had meanwhile made a
very profitable contract to charter the ship to another charterer following
on at the end of the defendant's charter. The consequence of the defendant's delay under the first charter was that the second charterer became
entitled to cancel its contract because the ship could not be made available on the agreed date. A compromise settlement was made between the
owner and the second charterer, but, freight rates having declined in the
meantime, the owner lost a large part of the benefit of the very profitable
follow-on contract. The arbitrators, by a majority, held that the rule in
Hadley v. *Baxendale,* as interpreted in later cases,[54] entitled the owner to
compensation for this loss. The decision was upheld in the High Court
and in the Court of Appeal, but reversed in the House of Lords.

The reason for the conclusion in all the lower tribunals, imposing liability, was simply that it was readily foreseeable – indeed highly probable –
that the owner would enter into a follow-on contract, since owners do
not normally choose to keep their ships idle, and that such a contract
would be lost if the delivery date was missed.[55] Against this it was alleged
that there was a long-standing and general understanding in legal and
business shipping circles that charterers in such circumstances never had
paid, and were never expected to pay more than compensation measured
by market freight rates during the period of the delay. The majority arbitrators admitted that there was such a general understanding, but they
held it to be legally irrelevant.[56]

The law lords gave separate reasons, not entirely consistent with each
other. Lord Hoffmann, appealing to 'principle' said that 'all contractual

---

52 *Monarch SS Co. Ltd* v. *Karlshamns Oljefabriker (A/B)* [1949] 1 AC 196, 232.
53 [2009] 1 AC 61 (HL).   54 Particularly *Heron II* [1969] 1 AC 350 (HL).
55 It was conceded, perhaps unwisely, before the arbitrators by counsel for the charterer that
   these consequences were 'not unlikely'. See note 53, above, at para. 28.
56 *Ibid.,* at para. 7.

liability is voluntarily undertaken', concluding that 'it must be in principle wrong to hold someone liable for risks for which the people entering into such a contract in their particular market, would not reasonably be considered to have undertaken'.[57] The underlying reason for the conclusion was, as in *Hadley* v. *Baxendale* itself, the desire to make the probable cost of breach predictable at the time of contract formation, and for much the same reasons as given there. Lord Hoffmann said:

> The view which the parties take of the responsibilities and risks they are undertaking will determine the other terms of the contract and in particular the price paid. Anyone asked to assume a large and unpredictable risk will require some premium in exchange. A rule of law which imposes liability upon a party for a risk which he reasonably thought was excluded gives the other party something for nothing.[58]

Lord Hoffmann added that the risk sought to be imposed on the charterer 'would be completely unquantifiable, because, although the parties would regard it as likely that the owners would at some time during the currency of the charter enter into a forward fixture, they would have no idea when that would be done or what its length or other terms would be'.[59] These reasons, together with the differing reasons of the other members of the court, demonstrate the continuing difficulty of reducing the question to any simple principle.

As mentioned above, the case of *Hamlin* v. *Great Northern Railway* appeared to establish as a firm rule that damages for mental distress were not recoverable for breach of contract. This rule was affirmed by the House of Lords in *Addis* v. *Gramophone Co. Ltd*[60] and was sometimes referred to as a 'principle'.[61] It was, however, substantially modified by decisions of the English Court of Appeal in 1973,[62] and of the House of Lords in 2001.[63] In 2006, the Supreme Court of Canada abandoned the rule entirely, relying heavily on the concept of 'principle' (the word was used nineteen times within a few paragraphs), *Hadley* v. *Baxendale* being invoked in support of what was called 'the principle of reasonable expectation', not to restrict the defendant's liability, but to enlarge it.[64] The Supreme Court concluded that 'damages for mental distress for breach of contract may, in appropriate cases, be awarded as an application of

---

57 *Ibid.*, at para. 12.   58 *Ibid.*, para. 13.   59 *Ibid.*, [23].   60 [1909] AC 488.
61 *Farley* v. *Skinner* [2002] 2 AC 732, 757 (Lord Hutton); Treitel, *The Law of Contract*, 987–9.
62 *Jarvis* v. *Swans Tours Ltd* [1973] QB 233 (CA).
63 *Farley* v. *Skinner* [2002] 2 AC 732 (HL).
64 *Fidler* v. *Sun Life Assurance Co. of Canada* [2006] 2 SCR 3, para 29.

the principle in *Hadley* v. *Baxendale*',[65] and concluded that 'it follows that there is only one rule by which compensatory damages for breach of contract should be assessed: the rule in *Hadley* v. *Baxendale*'.[66] The radically differing judicial views on this question, as well as on the more general question of remoteness, demonstrate the difficulty of establishing and formulating enduring principles.

The rule that the claimant is to be put in the position, so far as money can do it, that she would have occupied if the contract had been performed has sometimes been invoked as a limiting principle, in order to preclude a larger recovery. In the *Golden Victory*[67] the question arose whether events occurring fifteen months after acceptance of breach should be taken into account to reduce damages for repudiation of a charterparty. The majority of the House of Lords, relying heavily on the concept of principle, held that the subsequent events should be taken into account in order to avoid overcompensation. But the dissenting judges also relied on the concept of principle, and on the need for commercial certainty, which appeared to the minority judges to favour a rule of early crystallization of damages. Lord Walker spoke of 'the principles of law applicable in this area, including the importance of certainty in commercial transactions',[68] and, as Lord Bingham pointed out, 'the importance of certainty and predictability in commercial transactions has been a constant theme of English commercial law at any rate since ... Lord Mansfield'.[69] But the majority described certainty as a mere 'desideratum [that] ... is not a principle, and must give way to principle',[70] a proposition that might have been formulated as an invitation, or framework, for the present study. From a historical perspective, as Lord Bingham's observation emphasizes, such a sharp dichotomy between principle and desideratum must be open to question. As we have seen, 'desiderata' (considerations of what is desired) have frequently been taken into account in the formulation of principles. In the *Golden Victory*, as in many other cases, the concept of principle was deployed by different judges in support of opposite conclusions.

Restitution of benefits conferred under a contract sometimes has the effect of putting the claimant in a better position than he or she would have occupied if the contract had been performed, and this result might

---

65 *Ibid.*, at para. 44.
66 *Ibid.*, at para. 54; paras 45–6 sound a rather more restrained note.
67 *Golden Strait Corp.* v. *Nissen Yusen Kubishika Kaisha (The Golden Victory)* [2007] 2 AC 353 (HL). See Chapter 8, below, pp. 228–9.
68 *Ibid.*, at para. 39.   69 *Ibid.*, at para. 23.   70 *Ibid.*, at para. 38.

ENFORCEMENT   189

also be said to offend a principle against overcompensation. Money payments made under a contract that is substantially broken by the other
party are usually recoverable; claims for the value of services are more
contentious.[71] This question has given rise to a vigorous and inconclusive
debate on whether a claim for restitution of benefits conferred under a
contract that has been substantially broken by the recipient, is a claim
based on contract or on unjust enrichment. The American Law Institute,
in the *Third Restatement of Restitution and Unjust Enrichment* has taken
the view that the claim must be purely contractual and must have nothing
to do with unjust enrichment.[72] Yet, historically, claims of this sort *have*
been linked with unjust enrichment. They are instances of 'money paid
upon a consideration which happens to fail',[73] and are closely analogous
to claims for repayment where the basis of payment fails but where the
defendant is not in breach of contract. There is a danger of setting up too
rigid a dichotomy in seeking to allocate this question exclusively either
to principles of contract or to principles of unjust enrichment. It is more
plausible to say that the claim has succeeded *both* because it supplies
a just remedy for breach of contract *and* because the defendant would
be unjustly enriched if the money were retained. The ideas are reciprocal: restitution has been perceived as an appropriate remedy for breach
of contract partly because otherwise the defendant would be unjustly
enriched, both by retaining money paid for a purpose that had failed, and
by making a profit from the breach of contract, and this enrichment is
perceived as unjust partly because restitution of the money is an appropriate response to the breach of contract, and the most effective and reliable
way of ensuring justice to the claimant.[74]

   Another aspect of the relation between principles of contract and those
of unjust enrichment is the vexed question of profit derived from breach of
contract, which also raises the issue of overcompensation. If it really were
an absolute, or ineluctable, principle that a person complaining of breach
of contract should never be put, by a judicial award, into a better position

---

71 In *Boomer* v. *Muir* 24 P. 2d 570 (Cal App, 1933) a builder recovered much more for partial
     performance than it would have recovered for full performance, but the decision is highly
     controversial, and is rejected in the *Third Restatement of Restitution.*
72 American Law Institute, *Third Restatement of Restitution, Working Draft,* (2010).
73 *Moses* v. *Macferlan* (1760) 2 Burr 1005, 1012.
74 See S.Waddams, 'Contract and Unjust Enrichment', in Rickett and Grantham (eds.),
     Structure and Justification in Private Law, 167, 181, where it is suggested that the result
     in *Boomer* v. *Muir* can be avoided without totally excluding the perspective of unjust
     enrichment.

than if the contract had been performed (as suggested by the majority in the *Golden Victory*) gain-based awards would necessarily be excluded. But the idea that a wrongdoer should not profit from the wrong, which may also be called a principle, appears to demand the opposite result.

The general topic of profits derived from wrongs was claimed as part of unjust enrichment (then called restitution) by the American Law Institute in 1937, and included in the subject by Goff and Jones (1966)[75] and by other leading writers. Professor Peter Birks included it in his *An Introduction to the Law of Restitution* (1985), while pointing out that it was distinctive, in that the claimant was not required to prove a loss corresponding with the defendant's gain. Later Birks called these cases 'remedial restitution' in contrast to 'substantive restitution',[76] but later still Birks, followed by other writers, seemed to deny altogether the link between the two topics. In an article published in 2001, Birks wrote that:

> The . . . categories are exclusive of one another . . . [I]t is no more possible for the selected causative event to be both an unjust enrichment and a tort than it is for an animal to be both an insect and a mammal . . . Wrongful enrichment belongs in the law of wrongs. The law of unjust enrichment is concerned solely with enrichments which are unjust independently of wrongs and contracts. To assert the contrary is to violate one of the basic principles of rationality, namely that a classified answer to a question must use categories which are perfectly distinct one from another.[77]

This is very forceful, but in his last book, *Unjust Enrichment* (2003), Birks modified his view on this question, as on other important questions of unjust enrichment, going so far as to say that 'almost everything of mine now needs calling back for burning'.[78] On the relation between unjust enrichment and profits derived from wrongs, he wrote that 'by assuming without proving, and in fact almost certainly incorrectly, that the claimant in unjust enrichment must have suffered a loss corresponding to the defendant's gain, I adopted a much too narrow view of the extent to which cases of restitution for wrongs are susceptible of alternative analysis in unjust enrichment'.[79] In the text of the book, Birks wrote:

> Suppose that when I am taking my summer holidays you use my bicycle for a month without my permission, then put it back in perfect condition; or that you stow away on my ship intending to take a free ride across

---

75 Goff and Jones, *The Law of Restitution.*   76 Birks, *Restitution – The Future*, 1, 10.
77 P. Birks, 'Unjust Enrichment and Wrongful Enrichment' (2001) 79 *Texas Law Review* 1769, 1781, 1794.
78 Birks, *Unjust Enrichment*, xiv.   79 *Ibid.*

the Atlantic. In these cases you have gained a valuable benefit but I have suffered no loss. I am no worse off. As long ago as 1776 in *Hambly* v. *Trott* Lord Mansfield indicated that a claim for the value of these benefits would lie. Such a claim might be explained as restitution for a wrong, but it is not obvious that it should be and it is very unlikely that Lord Mansfield was thinking on those lines. There is other evidence that a claimant in unjust enrichment need not have suffered a loss.[80]

In reference to the well-known Kentucky case of *Edwards* v. *Lee's Administrator*,[81] where the defendant profited by allowing access to a cave under Lee's land, but only accessible from the defendant's, Birks wrote: 'The result is easily explained as restitution for the trespass itself. In that light it is an instance of gain-based recovery for a wrong. Can it be understood, by alternative analysis, as restitution of unjust enrichment at [the claimant's] expense? The language used by the court is equivocal, but the answer must be yes.'[82]

This change of opinion was the subject of academic criticism at a conference held to discuss the book, and in the second edition (published posthumously, 2005) Birks acknowledged the criticism. He said, on this point, that the new edition 'now bears the marks of a near knock-out blow landed in defence of the view that the gain-based recovery of a claimant in unjust enrichment must be capped by the amount of his own loss', and he said that 'it is a difficult and doubtful question whether the claimant must have suffered a loss'.[83] But in his actual discussion of the question, he maintained, and indeed reinforced, the view expressed in the first edition.[84] In the second edition, words were added that had the effect of strengthening the conclusion, and emphasizing what Birks saw as a break with his own former thinking: 'once we break away from the requirement of corresponding loss the answer must be that it can [i.e. the Kentucky cave case can be understood as restitution of unjust enrichment at Lee's expense]. *Jones*[85] and *Foskett*[86] tell us that we have, unequivocally, made that break'.[87]

A first reaction to this sequence of opinions is admiration for Birks' intellectual courage and honesty. Few writers have ventured to say that 'almost everything of mine now needs calling back for burning', and

80 Birks, *Unjust Enrichment*, 1st edn, 64, 2nd edn, 79.　81 265 Ky 418 (1935).
82 Birks, *Unjust Enrichment*, 1st edn, 70, 2nd edn, 84 (words added strengthening the conclusion).
83 *Ibid.*, at 75.　84 *Ibid.*, at 79, 81–4.
85 *Jones Estate* v. *Jones* [1997] Ch 159.　86 *Foskett* v. *McKeown* [2001] AC 102 (HL).
87 Birks, *Unjust Enrichment*, 2nd edn, 84.

for a writer so eminent, prolific and successful as Birks to say so must be practically unique. There have been sharp differences of academic opinion on this point, both as among leading writers, and in the mind of individual writers over time. This strongly suggests that there is likely to be truth on both sides of this debate. Opinions in legal controversy that appear at first sight implacably opposed may often be reconciled by the consideration that each is describing a different dimension of a complex phenomenon, or by the consideration that each is addressing a slightly different question. Thus both, of seemingly opposite views, or several, of seemingly diverse views, may be correct. It is not possible to select one criterion exclusively as definitive: from a historical perspective the courts have been influenced by various factors.

In his article of 2001, Birks was addressing a conceptual question, and his conclusion necessarily followed from his premises (which were that every legal question must be assigned exclusively to a single distinct category, one of which was unjust enrichment defined so as expressly to exclude wrongs and contracts). The whole tone of the passage shows that this was a conceptual conclusion demanded by inexorable logic, not an invitation to join in a historical judgment. In his discussion of *Hambly* v. *Trott*,[88] by contrast, Birks was addressing a historical question, and he drew the conclusion that 'it was most unlikely that Lord Mansfield was thinking on those lines [i.e. that the claim might be explained as restitution for a wrong]', and therefore that the case was 'susceptible of alternative analysis in unjust enrichment'. As a matter of historical judgment this conclusion is entirely persuasive, because the question in issue in *Hambly* v. *Trott* was whether a claim for conversion survived against the estate of a deceased wrongdoer so as to enable the plaintiff to avoid the effect of the common law rule that a personal action dies with the person. The question was perceived as difficult, and after consideration the court held that, although a tort action was admittedly precluded by the common law rule, the plaintiff might nevertheless bring an action against the estate in assumpsit. Lord Mansfield's reasoning therefore depended entirely on the holding that the plaintiff was *not* compelled to categorize the claim as tortious.

The conclusion in *Hambly* v. *Trott* had much to do with unjust enrichment, in the general sense of that phrase: as many passages in the judgment make clear, the court considered it unjust that the estate should be enriched at the expense of the plaintiff. The case was not directly concerned with the measure of recovery for profits derived from wrongs,

88 (1776) 1 Cowp 371.

but, in the course of the judgment, Lord Mansfield used a hypothetical example that has often been quoted:

> if a man take a horse from another, and bring him back again; an action of trespass will not lie against the executor, though it would against him; but an action for the use and hire of the horse will lie against the executor.[89]

From this passage it has often been inferred that Lord Mansfield would, if the question had arisen, have permitted the plaintiff to recover against a living defendant an amount measured by the defendant's gain, even if this exceeded the plaintiff's loss. Birks said, in the passage quoted above from *Unjust Enrichment*, that Lord Mansfield 'indicated' that such a claim would lie. This conclusion is less compelling than the conclusion that Mansfield did not think that the plaintiff was compelled to categorize his claim as tortious, because the amount of the award was not in issue. The inference that, had the question been in issue, Lord Mansfield would have favoured a gain-based award against a living defendant has persuasive force, but the mode of persuasion is by invitation to join in a historical judgment, rather than by a peremptory demand to submit to inexorable logic. Strict logic might seem to demand, as Birks said in 2001, that the question be allocated exclusively to one only of two categories (wrongs or unjust enrichment), but, as his later writing shows, this conclusion must be accompanied by the observation that, in English law, *both* ideas have been influential. It is not a satisfactory account to say that the question has been classified exclusively as a matter of tort law and that therefore unjust enrichment is irrelevant, if the evidence shows that the idea of unjust enrichment has, in the past, been influential.

By a variety of means, and using a variety of concepts and terminology, courts have made money awards based, in whole or in part, on gains derived from wrongs. The means include, besides the so-called waiver of tort cases associated with *Hambly* v. *Trott*, the award of damages in substitution for an injunction, the award of exemplary damages, accounting of profits, and a group of cases, sometimes called the 'wayleave' cases, where the defendant has been required to pay a reasonable fee for the use of the plaintiff's rights. To these may be added various concepts that have enabled the court to allow a claimant to assert proprietary rights in assets held by the defendant and not obviously owned by the plaintiff, including tracing and constructive trust.

---

89 (1776) 1 Cowp 371, 375.

As we have seen, it is a controverted question whether these cases should or should not be classified as 'unjust enrichment cases'. But what is reasonably clear is that many cases of the kind just mentioned have been influenced by the general idea of unjust enrichment. Though the form of words differs widely, and while the phrase 'unjust enrichment' does not occur in most of these cases, the court usually indicates that it is conscious of taking special steps, going beyond the award of compensatory damages, in order to deprive the defendant of a gain that the defendant ought, on considerations of justice, to surrender to the claimant. Thus it may fairly be concluded that the idea of unjust enrichment, in the general sense of the phrase, has been influential. But it does not follow that the results can be explained *solely* in terms of unjust enrichment. The court has evidently been influenced also in many of the cases by considerations of wrongdoing, property and public policy. These considerations have not operated in isolation from each other. That is to say, justice requires the defendant to surrender the gain partly because the gain has been wrongfully acquired, and often it is adjudged to have been wrongfully acquired partly because it has been derived from the claimant's property; public policy in such cases requires surrender of the gain both because it has been wrongfully acquired and because it has been derived from something that, as between claimant and defendant, belongs to the claimant.

There are certain difficulties here of terminology and classification. One is that legal terms such as contract, tort, equity and property have both a general and a specifically legal meaning. Thus, while tort means wrong, it also means 'that conduct to which the law attaches liability'. The meanings are different, but, in an uncodified system they cannot be entirely dissociated, because, where a new question has arisen for decision, the perception of the defendant's conduct as wrong, though not legally conclusive, has been influential. The same is true of the term 'unjust enrichment'. The expression describes a branch of the law (sometimes called restitution), but, as new cases have arisen, the perception that it is unjust (in a general sense) for the defendant to retain the benefit in question has been influential. In his *An Introduction to the Law of Restitution* (1985) Birks suggested that the word phrase 'reversible enrichment' might preferably, or might just as well, be substituted for 'unjust enrichment'.[90] But in *Unjust Enrichment* (2003) he accepted that the words 'unjust' or 'unjustified' carry a general, as well as a purely technical meaning: 'The chosen adjective must serve as a peg on which to hang the reasons . . . why

90 Birks, *An Introduction to the Law of Restitution*, 19.

an enrichment should be given up, and it must be weakly normative.'[91] Like other legal terms, the phrase 'unjust enrichment' has had both a general and a technical sense.

Confusion is added by the variance in the meaning of the word 'restitution'. Sometimes (as mentioned) it means the branch of the law concerned with reversing unjust enrichment; sometimes it means a judicial award of money based on the defendant's gain; and sometimes the word means reversal of a transfer by the claimant to the defendant (as opposed to 'disgorgement' of gains derived by the defendant from other sources). The phrase 'restitutionary damages', though sometimes used as a synonym for money awards based on the defendant's gain, has not been universally accepted, and was rejected by Lord Nicholls in *Attorney General* v. *Blake*[92] as an 'unhappy expression'. The trouble with the phrase is that it is objectionable to different observers for different reasons: to some, gain-based awards are not 'restitutionary' because they are not based on unjust enrichment; to others they are not restitutionary because they involve a giving up rather than a giving back; and to others they are not properly called 'damages' because they do not constitute compensation for harm or loss.

Other difficulties are caused by the assertion that a claim in unjust enrichment cannot exceed the amount of the claimant's loss. The formulation that the defendant's gain must be 'at the expense of' the claimant is also sometimes taken to imply a loss on the claimant's side that corresponds precisely with the defendant's gain, but is sometimes understood in a more general sense as meaning that the defendant's gain is derived from something that belongs, in general terms, to the claimant. Again, it is not always clear whether a writer who asserts that there can be no claim in unjust enrichment exceeding the claimant's loss is addressing the question of what result justice requires between the parties, the question of how, accurately, to describe actual past decisions, or the question of how the issue, or how a legal result in favour of a claimant who has recovered an amount exceeding apparent loss, should be classified within a particular proposed scheme of classification. Some writers have emphasized the distinction between giving back (restitution) and giving up

91 Birks, *Unjust Enrichment*, 236. In the second edition (275) the words 'in order to encourage fine-tuning' are added, meaning, presumably, 'in order to deal with new cases as they arise'. See also 221 (2nd edn, 258): 'The law of unjust enrichment would itself be stultified if the criteria which normally identify an unjust enrichment were allowed in an exceptional case to compel restitution of one which was not unjust'. The last word in this sentence carries a general, not a technical sense.
92 [2001] 1 AC 268, 284.

(disgorgement). The idea that the claimant may suffer a loss of opportunity to bargain, discussed more fully below, tends to cut across all these lines of discussion, because it suggests that the courts have been influenced simultaneously, not only by considerations of compensation for loss, but also by considerations of avoidance of unjust enrichment, and also again by considerations of depriving the defendant of gains improperly acquired. This concurrence of reasons tends to disturb the neat dichotomies between compensation and restitution, between restitution and disgorgement and between wrong and unjust enrichment.

When we turn to gains derived from breach of contract, the element of unjust enrichment (in its general sense) is crucial, because retention of some gains derived from breach of contract has generally been perceived as permissible. In many of his writings, Birks divided the events that give rise to civil obligations into four categories, namely, consent, wrongs, unjust enrichment and other events. This scheme would appear to distribute contract law between two categories (consent and wrongs) and, as Professor Burrows has pointed out, this division would have some strange consequences. He wrote that 'while Birks' scheme may seem logically persuasive when one looks at unjust enrichment and restitution in isolation or along with only a part of private law, it causes difficulties when one widens the picture to include all private law. In other words, if one is following Birks' map, one may ultimately find oneself being led into strange places!'[93]

The idea of dividing primary contractual obligation from the obligation to pay compensation for breach of contract had been suggested by Anson in 1879 in the first edition of his book on contract (the other four of six categories being quasi contract, delict, judgments and miscellaneous)[94] but, though carried through seventeen editions over a period of fifty years,[95] Anson's scheme gained no following, partly for the reasons suggested by Burrows.

Birks did not develop in detail the consequences of his scheme for contract law, but one possible consequence would be that the wrong of breach of contract should be treated precisely like any other legal wrong, with precisely the same consequences. As a matter of past English law, this has not been the case. Non-contractual wrongs may often be restrained by judicial order (injunction); they may be abated where practicable by

---

93 A. Burrows, 'The New Birksian Approach to Unjust Enrichment' (2004) 26 *Restitution Law Review* 261.

94 Anson, *Principles*, 1st edn, 7–8.

95 Anson, *Principles*, J.C. Miles and L.J. Brierly (eds.), 17th edn, 7–8. See Chapter 2, pp. 54–5, above.

self-help; benefits derived from the threat of a wrong must be restored; persuading or assisting another to commit a wrong is itself a wrong; they may be punished by awards of exemplary damages; they generally attract moral disapprobation; and, most significantly for the present enquiry, gains derived from non-contractual wrongs must usually be given up.

The law (past and present) has not attached all these consequences to all breaches of contract, and few would argue that it should do so. Let us consider the case of a contract for routine personal services followed by a breach because the employee finds a more profitable use for her time (e.g. a contract by a student to paint a house during the whole of October, followed by breach because the student receives and accepts an unexpected opportunity to attend law school). The contract breaker is liable for damages, but if the houseowner can find a professional painter for the contract price or less there will be no substantial damages. It is plain that in this instance the houseowner is not (as a matter of past or present law) entitled to a decree of specific performance, nor to an injunction to prevent the student from attending law school, nor to punitive damages, nor (it is safe to say) to an account of the gains derived by the student from pursuing a legal career. The reasons for this set of interrelated conclusions may be summarized by saying that the houseowner is amply compensated by damages, has no special interest (more than an economic interest) in the actual personal services of the student, ought not to have anything like a proprietary interest in the student or in her services, and that there is a public as well as a private interest in freedom of action on the part of the defendant, and on the part of potential defendants. The student is enriched in this example by the breach of contract, but by no means is the enrichment unjust, nor is it made 'at the expense of' the houseowner. On the contrary, if the law should compel the student to pay over to the houseowner the full present value of her future legal career most observers would say that the law would have exacted an unjust confiscation and would have conferred an undeserved windfall on the houseowner. Another way of putting the matter would be to say that the houseowner has no legitimate interest in recovering more than the extra cost (if any) of doing the work.

As the example just discussed shows – and many others could readily be given[96] – there are circumstances in which all may find themselves from

96 Daniel Friedmann, 'Economic Aspects of Damages and Specific Performance Compared', in Saidov and Cunnington (eds.), *Contract Damages*, 65, at 74–82, gives examples of losing contracts and wasteful performance, usefully suggesting the term 'tolerated' (rather than 'efficient') breach to signify the law's unwillingness to award more than compensatory damages.

time to time where it is reasonable to break a contract on payment of compensatory damages to the other party. The situation just discussed is where a more profitable opportunity arises for the plaintiff's time or other resources. Another common situation is where the cost of performance greatly exceeds the economic benefit of it, as in the case of a promise to restore damaged land, where the cost of restoration may greatly exceed the economic benefit of doing the work.[97] In these cases, unless the plaintiff has a not unreasonable non-economic interest, and is likely actually to carry out the work, the courts have refused damages based on the cost of performance. These also are cases in which the defendant is permitted to benefit from the breach, because the defendant saves the cost of actual performance on payment of a lesser sum of compensatory damages. Another very simple and everyday example would be cancellation of a hotel or restaurant reservation because of the customer's change of plans. The customer might (perhaps, and at the most) be liable for the hotel or restaurant's loss of profit, but no one would seriously contemplate specific performance to compel the customer to stay at the hotel or to dine at the restaurant, or an injunction to prevent the change of plans, or exemplary damages, or requiring the giving up of gains made through the change of plans.

It may seem an advance in elegance, logic and simplicity to treat breaches of contracts in the same way as torts, but though there are close analogies between contractual and non-contractual obligations, there are also important differences.[98] Contractual obligations are defined by the parties with practically no restrictions. Thus, a contractual obligation may turn out to be extremely onerous, even ruinous, to the promisor, and performance of contractual obligations may have the effect of very greatly enriching the promisee. The exchange of a few words, casually spoken or written, may easily create an obligation that exceeds the defendant's total wealth. These features are absent from most non-contractual obligations, where the burden on the defendant is defined and limited by the general law. The reasonable person may usually avoid committing torts without suffering very heavy burdens, and the failure to commit torts does not usually in itself enrich others. Tort liability often requires proof of fault, whereas liability for breach of contract is strict, and a contract

---

97 *Peevyhouse* v. *Garland Coal & Mining Co.* 382 P2d 109 (Okla. SC, 1962); *Tito* v. *Waddell* [1977] Ch 106; *Ruxley Electronics and Construction Ltd v. Forsyth* [1996] 1 AC 344 (HL).
98 See S. Waddams, 'Breach of Contract and the Concept of Wrongdoing', (2000) 12 *Supreme Court Law Review (Second series)* 1.

may be made and broken entirely without blame. No moral opprobrium therefore attaches to a breach of contract in itself. Breach of contract is often tolerated, both as a matter of business morality and in law, and has been said by many commentators, and by some courts, sometimes to be 'efficient'.[99] As we have seen, the law does not always attach the same consequences to a breach of contract as to a tort. Thus a court will not usually order specific performance of contracts, or issue an injunction to restrain breach. Neither punitive damages nor profits derived from breach are usually available for breach of contract. Threatening to break a contract is not in itself wrongful. Another aspect of the matter is that there is usually an independent public interest in encouraging observance of tort law, but the acts or omissions that constitute breaches of contract are not in themselves inherently objectionable: usually they are, considered simply as actions or omissions, harmless, being wrongful only in the sense that a private agreement has made them so. A further important consideration is that the anticipated cost of breach affects the contract price. It is often in the interest of both parties to limit liability for breach of contract in exchange for a reduced price, and it may often be in the interest of consumers generally for the liability of those supplying goods or services useful to the community to be limited in exchange for a low price. These considerations lie behind the widespread use of limitation of liability clauses, and statutory restrictions on liability of carriers and warehousers. Insurance is also an important factor: it is often more beneficial for both parties for the owner of property to insure against loss, than for a carrier or warehouser to insure against liability while adding the cost of insurance to the contract price. Cumulatively these are cogent reasons for making a distinction between contractual and non-contractual obligations. The law may be said to treat the contractual promisee quite generously in allowing the full measure of expectation damages, as Fuller and Perdue suggested in their article; it is not very surprising that, where the claimant's interest is only economic, this has usually been the limit of the defendant's obligation.

The economic idea of 'efficient breach', or 'tolerated breach' as Daniel Friedmann has usefully called it,[100] is relevant in this context. Economists have pointed out that, where the defendant finds a more remunerative

---

99 *Bank of America Canada* v. *Mutual Trust Co.* [2002] 2 SCR 601; *Hillspring Farms Ltd* v. *Walton (Leland) & Sons Ltd* (2007) 312 NBR (2d) 109 (CA); *Delphinium Ltee* v. *512842 N.B. Inc.* (2008) 296 DLR (4th) 770 at [51].
100 See note 96, above.

use of her resources, as in the house painting example just discussed, it may enhance the welfare of the two contracting parties jointly for the contract to be broken on payment of damages: the promisee is no worse off (on receipt of full expectation damages), and the promisor, who puts her resources to better use, is better off. This is a useful insight that may be welcomed by lawyers, but it does not follow that all breaches of contract are efficient, or that the law has been or should be governed by economics. The idea of efficient breach may be described as a parallel insight, that tends to support the legal conclusion, and which probably rests on similar underlying values, including the avoidance of an unjust windfall to the claimant, and reasonable freedom of action on the part of the defendant. But the acceptance of such a parallel insight does not mean that the law has deferred, or should defer to economics. If an ethicist, or a philosopher, or a civil lawyer, should say that certain conclusions of English law had often conformed to principles of ethics, or to certain systems of philosophy, or to certain civil law systems, these comments would probably be welcomed by lawyers (as tending in a general way to increase confidence in the legal conclusions) without however implying that ethics, or any particular system of philosophy, or any particular system of civil law, had in itself been, or should in the future become, the single, overriding, or dominant reason for the legal conclusions.

It may seem, at first sight, that the concept of efficient or tolerated breach is one that tends to benefit the contract-breaker, but this is by no means self-evident. The contract-breaker remains liable for full money compensation (on the expectation measure) no matter how reasonable the decision to break the contract – even if breach was in effect compelled by circumstances. The liability to pay damages is strict. A legal system that failed to recognize the concept of tolerated breach might well, in practice, afford a complete defence, based on impossibility or impracticablity, to one compelled by circumstances to break a contract. The intermediate position of Anglo-American law (no specific performance but full expectation damages) enables a firm economic guarantee of performance to be given, received and safely relied on, no matter how reasonable may be the other party's excuse for a subsequent breach.

The idea of efficient breach, though it may be said to correspond to the approach of the law in many cases, is not in itself a binding legal principle or rule. There are cases in which supra-compensatory remedies have been available. These are cases, also, in which the claimant has had more than a purely economic interest in performance, where the breach deprives the claimant of an opportunity to bargain, where compensatory

damages have been perceived as inadequate, where the claimant has something like a proprietary interest, where it is not in the public interest for
the contract to be broken, and where the defendant would be unjustly
enriched by gains derived from the breach. It is in these cases that specific
performance is often available, where an injunction is often available to
restrain breach, where exemplary damages might be appropriate (if they
are appropriate anywhere), where breach of the contract is perceived as
morally reprehensible, and where the defendant is required to account
for gains. The various considerations are interlinked: it is in just the kind
of case where there is a right to specific enforcement that the claimant
is perceived to have a proprietary right, or something like one, and it is
in just such a case that the defendant is likely to be thought to be acting
reprehensibly by taking something that belongs not to him, but to the
claimant, and where retention of a gain so made is perceived as an unjust
enrichment. *Attorney-General v. Blake*[101] (publication of memoirs by former secret service agent) may be given as an instance where an accounting
was required. The reasons that tended to support the result in that case are
cumulative: the government had more than a purely economic interest in
preventing the publication; the information, in a sense, belonged to the
government; publication of it was closely akin to a breach of fiduciary
duty; an injunction might have been obtained to restrain publication at
an earlier date when the information was still confidential; the government had a legitimate interest in preventing publication of such memoirs
independent of its interest in receiving Blake's services; Blake's conduct
was reprehensible, and contrary to the public interest.

The features just mentioned do not accompany every contract, but
they do, in whole or in part, accompany some contracts. Therefore, no
simple rule is available that treats all breaches of contract alike, and the
search for a simple or single rule on the point, so far from representing an
advance in clarity or precision, is likely to obscure important distinctions
that are necessary to the attainment of justice and to the articulation of
sustainable principles.

Several possible principles have been suggested to govern the question
of gains derived from breach of contract. The simplest, impliedly suggested by some writers though usually not made fully explicit, is that the
plaintiff should have an unfettered right to recover all such gains from
the contract-breaker. The instances of the student painter and the case
where the cost of performance is extravagant in relation to the economic

---

101 [2001] 1 AC 268 (HL).

benefit show that no such principle has been acceptable. The opposite view, that a contract-breaker is never accountable for gains made from breach of contract, is also unacceptable, and does not correspond, as we have seen, with past law. Therefore some additional factor, other than breach of contract, must be required. It has been suggested that recovery of gains should be available where there is an 'abuse of contract'[102] or a 'cynical'[103] or 'opportunistic'[104] breach, or where performance is 'skimped',[105] or where the gain is derived from doing what the defendant promised not to do.[106] All these raise difficulties, and none was accepted as a principle by the House of Lords in the *Blake* case. Lord Nicholls reaffirmed that the general rule was not to require an accounting of gains made by breach of contract, but he accepted that in exceptional circumstances an accounting would be appropriate. He was, in view of earlier unsuccessful attempts including those of the Court of Appeal in the *Blake* case itself, understandably reluctant to lay down a precise rule as to what those exceptional circumstances were, suggesting 'as a useful general guide, although not exhaustive' the test of 'whether the plaintiff had a legitimate interest in preventing the defendant's profit-making activity and, hence, in depriving him of his profit', adding immediately that 'it would be difficult and unwise to attempt to be more specific'.[107]

This test has attracted some criticism on the ground that it lacks substance, and leaves the matter too much in the discretion of the court. Lord Hobhouse, dissenting, and making a sharp distinction between principle and policy, considered that there was no principled basis for a decision in favour of the Attorney-General and that the majority had wrongly allowed policy considerations to displace principle:

> The policy which is being enforced is that which requires Blake to be punished by depriving him of any benefit from anything connected with his past deplorable criminal conduct. Your lordships consider that this policy can be given effect to without a departure from principle. I must venture to disagree.[108]

102 E.A. Farnsworth, 'Your Loss or My Gain? The Dilemma of the Disgorgement Principle in Breach of Contract' (1985) 94 *Yale Law Journal* 1339.
103 P. Birks, 'Restitutionary Damages for Breach of Contract: *Snepp* and the Fusion of Law and Equity' (1987) *Lloyd's Maritime and Commercial Law Quarterly* 421; see also Birks, *An Introduction to the Law of Restitution*, 334–5 (favouring recovery in case of deliberate exploitation). For a fuller discussion see Waddams, 'Profits Derived from Breach of Contract: Damages or Restitution?' (1997) 11 *Journal of Contract Law* 115.
104 *Restatement (Third) of Restitution and Unjust Enrichment*, Tentative Draft No. 4, s. 39.
105 *Attorney General v. Blake* [1998] Ch 439, 458 (CA).   106 *Ibid.*
107 *Attorney General v. Blake* [2001] 1 AC 268, 285 (HL).   108 *Ibid.*, at 299.

In defence of the majority decision it may be suggested that principle need not exclude all elements of uncertainty and that there are dangers in attempting to be over-precise, as the earlier unsuccessful attempts to formulate a principle on this question have shown. The concept of 'legitimate interest in preventing the defendant's profit-making activity' signifies activities likely to cause damage to the government (memoir-writing, for example) independent of what would have been caused by simple neglect of contractual duties (unauthorized absences to pursue landscape painting, for example). Such independent damage is likely to occur in precisely those cases where the plaintiff suffers a loss of opportunity to bargain, where damages measured by the plaintiff's loss will seem inadequate, where the obligation is likely to be, or to have been at some point in time, specifically enforceable,[109] where the defendant can be said to have infringed a proprietary or quasi-proprietary interest, where the defendant is unjustly enriched and where there is a public policy in preventing the breach. Not all these factors have been present in every case, nor can they be considered in isolation from each other, for they tend to be mutually interdependent.

One dimension of the question is the argument that in many of the cases the claimant has suffered a real loss, though one that is difficult to quantify, by being deprived of an opportunity to bargain with the wrongdoer for a rent, licence charge or fee.[110] This consideration might in some cases, though not in all, support a substantial award on purely compensatory principles. But, even where it does not, it has not been wholly irrelevant because, as Sir Thomas Bingham put it, of 'the obvious relationship between the profits earned by the defendants and the sum which the defendants would reasonably have been willing to pay to secure release from the covenant'.[111] This is not an *alternative* analysis that seeks to displace ideas of property, wrongdoing and unjust enrichment. On the contrary, it is another way of looking at the same question that *incorporates* those ideas and supplies an additional reason in many cases (not in all) in support of a substantial money award. Compensation cannot supply the *sole* explanation of the cases, but neither has the idea of compensation

---

109 The American Law Institute comments that 'the fact that a promisee might have obtained a remedy by injunction or specific performance is . . . a significant indication of the propriety of disgorgement': *Restatement (Third) of Restitution and Unjust Enrichment,* Tentative Draft No. 4, s. 9.

110 R.J. Sharpe and S.M. Waddams, 'Damages for Lost Opportunity to Bargain' (1982) 2 *Oxford Journal of Legal Studies* 290.

111 *Jaggard v. Sawyer* [1995] 1 WLR 269, 282.

been wholly irrelevant. To put the point at its lowest, the idea that the claimant has suffered an actual loss, though one that is difficult to quantify, has tended to strengthen the claim to a substantial money award, and, together with other considerations, has been influential in supporting awards based in some degree on gains derived by the defendant. Lord Lloyd said that 'the principle [supporting a substantial award] need not be characterized as exclusively compensatory, or exclusively restitutionary; it combines elements of both'.[112]

Not all breaches of contract involve a loss of bargaining power, because, where the claimant has no property interest that the court will protect in advance, and where the contract is not specifically enforceable (as in the example of the student painter) the claimant never had effective power to prevent the breach of contract in the first place. Thus, if the student painter announced in advance her intention to break the contract in order to attend law school, the houseowner would not have been in any stronger position: the most he could effectively have said would have been that he would hold the defendant responsible for payment of any damages. No injunction or decree of specific performance would have been available. But where the contract-breaker infringes a property right, or a quasi-proprietary right that the court would have protected, or defeats a right to specific performance or an injunction, the claimant does suffer a real loss, and the defendant, in a real sense, has taken something of value that belonged to the claimant. This is not a fiction: a person deprived of an opportunity to prevent a wrong, or to withhold or to demand terms for the grant of a valuable licence, may realistically be said to have lost something of value, even if in fact she would never herself have exploited the opportunity for money gain.

Measuring the value of what the defendant has taken is not an easy task where, as is usual in such cases, no market price can be ascertained. Some cases have given an accounting of profits, and some have awarded the amount of the reasonable licence fee that the plaintiff might have demanded. These measures, though sometimes contrasted,[113] are closely linked 'because of the obvious relationship between the profits earned by the defendants and the sum which the defendants

---

112 *Inverugie Investments Ltd* v. *Hackett* [1995] 1 WLR 713, 718 (PC). Lord Denning spoke to the same effect in *Strand Electric Engineering Co. Ltd* v. *Brisford Entertainments Ltd* [1952] 2 QB 246, 255 (CA).
113 Lord Nicholls in *Blake*, note 107, above, at 280.

would reasonably have been willing to pay to secure release from the covenant'.[114] The full amount of the profit derived from the breach is the maximum that the defendant, foreseeing the future, would have paid. If the defendant does not accurately foresee the future the plaintiff may recover more than the actual profit,[115] a result that can be supported on a principle of compensation for loss of bargaining power, but not on the principles either of unjust enrichment or of gain-based damages. In most cases[116] we cannot know the minimum that the claimant might have accepted, but that is because of the defendant's wrong, and it is not unusual, in the law of damages, for presumptions to operate against a wrongdoer where the wrong itself impedes precise evaluation.[117] It may be said that there is an element of artificiality involved, but this is no greater than that involved in the valuation of a unique chattel wrongfully taken by the defendant which the claimant would never in fact have sold. There is nothing fictitious in the observation that the net profit to be derived from doing something is closely related to, and often identical with, the price that a reasonable person would pay for permission to do it. The assessment of a reasonable licence fee, and the accounting of profits are not therefore unrelated: they are alternative ways of doing justice between the parties by setting a value on what the defendant has taken. Sometimes the one method, and sometimes the other, will be the more convenient. In the *Wrotham Park* case[118] the court awarded only 5 per cent of the sum calculated to be the defendant's total anticipated profit. However, Brightman J stressed that there were peculiar factors including delay on the part of the plaintiff that justified 'great moderation'. Where these factors are absent, and where the accounting process gives full credit for

---

114 See note 111, above, and *Experience Hendrix LLC* v. *PPX Enterprises Inc.* [2003] EWCA Civ 323 (CA); *WWF – World Wide Fund for Nature* v. *World Wrestling Federation Entertainment Inc.* [2007] EWCA Civ 286 (CA); Waddams, 'Gains Derived from Breach of Contract', in Saidov and Cunnington (eds.), *Contract Damages: Domestic and International Perspectives*, 187, 202–4.

115 *Pell Frischmann Engineering Ltd* v. *Bow Valley Iron Ltd* [2009] UKPC 45 (Jersey).

116 But in *Star Energy Weald Basin Ltd* v. *Bocardo SA* [2010] UKSC 35, where the claimant had statutory powers of expropriation, the probable compensation that would have been payable under the statute was taken into account to reduce the claimant's recovery. In this situation the claimant, at the time of the wrong, had a diminished bargaining power, with, of course, no right to a permanent injunction.

117 *Armorie* v. *Delamirie* (1722) 1 Str 505.

118 *Wrotham Park Estate Co. Ltd* v. *Parkside Homes Ltd* [1974] 1 WLR 798 (Ch).

all factors favourable to the defendant (deduction of all expenses including overheads, and insistence on proven causal link between wrongdoing
and profit, with due allowance for the defendant's time and skill),[119] it
is likely that in many cases the measures will converge. A conscientious
accounting is often complex, and frequently less beneficial to a claimant
than at first appears likely. It is perfectly legitimate for a court, in seeking
to minimize the expense of litigation and to do practical justice to both
parties, to adopt a somewhat rough and ready assessment of what, in
the circumstances, would have been a reasonable licence fee, in order to
avoid a lengthy, expensive and possibly inconclusive accounting. As Dr
Lushington said in another context:

> The true principle is, not to adopt that system which, in special cases, may
> best arrive at the truth, regardless of delay and expense, but to choose that
> course which, on the whole, will best administer justice with a due regard
> to the means of those who seek it.[120]

Awards of gain-based damages have been linked by some writers with
punitive and deterrent considerations. It is true that, in some cases, such
as *Blake*, considerations of public policy have been prominent. But it
should be remembered that breach of contract, infringement of property
rights and unjust enrichment may all occur without any fault on the part
of the defendant. It is not desirable, therefore, to subordinate gain-based
awards to punitive considerations, as the reference in the last paragraph
to credit for items favourable to the defendant was intended to suggest.[121]
It is understandable that, in a case like *Blake*, the court was not inclined to
be very diligent, in the process of accounting, to seek out items to enter to
the credit of the defendant. But in many other cases the breach of contract,
together with the concomitant infringement of proprietary right and the
unjust enrichment, will be entirely or largely without fault, and in such
cases the defendant is in justice entitled to insist on satisfactory proof of
the amount of the profit alleged to have been derived from the wrong.

The *Draft Common Frame of Reference* omits any provision for gain-
based awards, and the drafters' brief note shows that the omission was
deliberate:

---

119 See *Boardman* v. *Phipps* [1967] 2 AC 46 (HL).
120 *The Resultatet* (1853) 17 Jur 353, 354.
121 Ralph Cunnington has convincingly pointed out the danger of confusing exemplary with
     compensatory damages: 'The Border between Compensation, Restitution and Punish-
     ment' (2006) 122 *Law Quarterly Review* 382, commenting on *Borders (UK) Ltd* v. *Com-
     missioner of Police of the Metropolis* [2005] EWCA Civ 197.

> The legal systems seem to agree that damages are not awarded if there has
> been a gain for the defaulting debtor but no loss to the creditor.[122]

English law is noted as exceptional on this point. The absence from civilian systems of any principle supporting the recovery of gain-based damages for breach of contract lends support to Lord Nicholls' cautious approach to the formulation of a principle in the *Blake* case.

It is common in judicial reasoning for a matter to be determined by a number of factors, all relevant, but none on its own conclusive. An example, very closely related to gain-based awards, is the power of the court to decree specific performance of contracts. In *Co-operative Insurance Society Ltd* v. *Argyll Stores (Holdings) Ltd*, Lord Hoffmann, having mentioned various factors that tended to make courts reluctant to decree specific performance, said:

> The cumulative effect of these various reasons, *none of which would neces-
> sarily be sufficient on its own*, seems to me to show that the settled practice
> [i.e. of refusing specific performance] is based upon sound sense.[123]

One of the main reasons given by Lord Hoffmann for refusing specific performance in that case was that a decree would give the claimant power to extract from the defendant the gains to be derived from breach, in other words to obtain the equivalent of a gain-based award.[124] It was, in large part, because Lord Hoffmann judged that result to be unjust that he refused specific performance. The ideas are interrelated and interdependent: where specific performance is appropriate, a gain-based award is likely also to be appropriate; looking at the matter from the other direction, if it is first judged that a gain-based award would *not* be appropriate, this is itself a reason for *refusing* specific performance. This line of thinking shows also the significance in this context of the idea of lost opportunity to bargain: where specific enforcement is available the claimant has a very valuable bargaining power, and suffers a real loss if deprived of it, but where specific enforcement would never have been contemplated (as in a routine contract for personal services), the claimant had no bargaining power, and has no legitimate claim to profits made by the defendant. The availability of specific performance and the recovery of profits made in breach of contract are closely connected because the availability of specific performance is interrelated with the question of whether the defendant has infringed a proprietary right, and this in turn is interrelated with the

---

122 *Draft Common Frame of Reference*, III – 3:702, Note 3, vol. 1, 927.
123 [1998] AC 1, 16 (emphasis added).   124 [1998] AC 1, 15.

question of whether the defendant's gain has been made at the claimant's expense. As Lord Hoffmann's comment shows, the availability of specific performance itself depends on multiple cumulative factors, and many of the same factors, particularly those just mentioned in the last paragraph, are likely to be relevant also to the determination of when a gain-based award is appropriate.

The questions discussed in this chapter have usually been allocated in Anglo-American law to the topic of 'remedies'. As we have seen, many propositions called principles, not all mutually consistent, have been deployed. Often the judicial response to the non-performance of a contractual obligation has been determined by a general judgment resting on multiple considerations. The courts have taken account of whether the claimant has had a legitimate interest, in all the circumstances, in imposing on the defendant the consequences that, in practice as well as in theory, will ensue on the making of the judicial order that is sought. The application of these considerations necessarily involves some uncertainty, but they are not for that reason to be rejected as unprincipled. Principle need not exclude a general judgment resting on multiple considerations:[125] on the contrary, too great an insistence on formulating a single precise rule, or on allocating an issue to a single category has sometimes led to the assertion of propositions that have proved to be over-simplified, unsustainable and therefore ultimately self-defeating. Precision, simplicity and elegance, though good in themselves when attainable, are not overriding objectives and have yielded, here as elsewhere, where they have come into conflict with the court's perception of policy, with general considerations of justice, and with considerations of practical convenience in administering it.

---

125 But whether this should be called 'discretion' is another question. See discussion at notes 28–9, above.

8

Conclusion: joint dominion of principle and policy

Comparisons have been made by English commentators at various times between English law and the systems based on Roman law, usually to the advantage of the civil law, which has often appeared to its English admirers to be better ordered, more elegant and more principled than English law. Such comparison was familiar in the seventeenth century, as appears from Sir Matthew Hale's preface to Rolle's *Abridgment* (1668).[1] Hale defended English law against other systems on the ground of the greater precision of the former:

> The Common-laws of *England* are more particular than other laws, and this, though it render them more numerous, less methodical, and takes up longer time for their study, yet it recompenseth with greater advantages, namely, it prevents arbitrariness in the Judge, and makes the law more certain . . . It hath therefore always been the wisdome and happiness of the *English* Government, not to rest in Generals, but to prevent arbitrariness and uncertainty by particular Laws, fitted almost to all particular occasions.[2]

Critics of English law, Hale continued, objected to its lack of ordered classification, saying:

> that it wants method, order, and apt distributions, and this hath bred some prejudice against it, not only in men much addicted to subtil learning, but also in the Professors of the Civil Law, who think that Law much more methodicall and orderly than the Common-law.[3]

After a discussion of methods of resolving moral questions, Hale remarked, in defence of English law, 'yet it were a vain thing to conclude it is irrational, because not to be demonstrated or deduced by Syllogismes'.[4]

---

1 Rolle, *Un abridgement*, Preface. See Alan Cromartie, *Sir Matthew Hale, 1606–1676*, 119.
2 Rolle, *Un abridgement*, Preface (n.p: third page; emphasis in original).
3 *Ibid.*, sixth page.   4 *Ibid.*, seventh page.

In his posthumously published *Analysis of the Law* he suggested that, after all, 'it is not altogether impossible, by much Attention and Labour, to reduce the law of *England* at least into a tolerable *Method* and *Distribution*'.[5]

As we have seen, many nineteenth-century writers on English contract law expressed admiration for the apparent elegance, system, logic, principle, order and science of the civil law. Some judges followed this line of thinking, but Pothier's logical but inconvenient view of revocation of offers was decisively rejected by several nineteenth-century English writers, and by two judges in 1880.[6] At the beginning of the following century Lord Halsbury said, in declining to extend the doctrine of ratification in the law of agency to the case of an undisclosed principal:

> [T]he contract was made and the parties to it ascertained, and I am of opinion that upon no principle known to the law could the present appellants be made parties to that contract. They could, of course, make another contract in the same terms if they pleased, but it would not be this contract. It is suggested by the judgment of the Court of Appeal as possible, that what is described as ratification might, if the parties had so pleased, make the contract, which was one made between A. and B., to include C. as one of the contracting parties. I think such a suggestion is contrary to all principle, and for it there is no decision which calls for your Lordships to override it, though I confess I should have no hesitation in doing so if there were.[7]

He was pressed with an argument based on logical coherence with other aspects of agency law, but he did not hesitate to reject the argument: 'If it is said it is an anomaly, it certainly is not the only one in our law, and if it were sought to make our laws harmonious by deciding that any proposition which our laws establish involves as a necessary consequence the establishment of everything that is analogous to it, the result would be very perplexing indeed.'[8] The concept of principle was applied here to constrain the apparent effect of logic and coherence. Shortly afterwards, in another case, he said that 'every lawyer must acknowledge that the law is not always logical at all'.[9] Many other judges have declined to follow the apparent demands of logic where it has appeared to lead to results

---

5 Hale, *The Analysis of the Law*, Preface, second page (emphasis in original).
6 See Chapter 2, above.   7 *Keighley Maxted & Co.* v. *Durant* [1901] AC 240, 243–4.
8 *Ibid.*, at 244.   9 *Quinn* v. *Leathem* [1901] AC 495, 506 (HL).

thought to be 'unjust and anomalous',[10] or contrary to 'common sense and practical necessity',[11] or 'inconvenient in practice'.[12]

Logic alone has not been a sufficient justification for imposing results judged, on general grounds, to be unacceptable. On the other hand, mere pragmatism alone has also been insufficient. Anglo-American law has sometimes seemed to take a kind of satisfaction in a pragmatism that rejects or even defies logic, as in Hale's disparaging reference to syllogisms, quoted above. Oliver Wendell Holmes asserted in 1881 that 'the life of the law has not been logic, it has been experience', but this much-quoted sentence has usually been cited out of context. The immediately preceding words were 'it is something to show that the consistency of a system requires a particular result, but it is not all'.[13] A mere opinion that a particular result would have desirable consequences has not, unless supported by principle, been sufficient justification either for imposing or for restricting a contractual obligation. The concept of principle, though imprecise, has constrained the arbitrary effects of pure pragmatism or consequentialism, requiring a degree of coherence with the past, neither entirely subordinated to logic nor excluding prudential considerations. Principle might be said to have clothed judicial decisions with legal form.

As we have seen, English treatises in the nineteenth century were strongly influenced by a search for order, method and science. Leake wrote in his preface that he had:

> endeavoured to collect the general rules and principles of the law of con-tracts . . . [and] to divide and arrange the work methodically, according to the logical order of the subject, in order that a proper place may be readily found for every rule and principle; and to carry it out with such a degree of completeness that, it is hoped, some notice of every point of importance may be found in its proper place.[14]

Anson, too, sought this kind of precision, but found difficulty in attaining it. In a letter presenting a copy of his book to Lord Justice Thesiger he said that:

---

10 *Wertheim* v. *Chicoutimi Pulp Co.* [1911] AC 301, 307.
11 *ITO* v. *Miida Electronics Inc.* [1986] 1 SCR 752 (McIntyre J), approved in *Homburg Houtimport BV* v. *Agrosin Private Ltd* [2004] 1 AC 715, 749–50 (HL) (Lord Steyn).
12 *Sudbrook Trading Estate Ltd* v. *Eggleton* [1983] 1 AC 444, 483 (Lord Fraser of Tullybelton).
13 Holmes, *The Common Law*, 1.
14 Leake, *The Elements of the Law of Contracts*, Preface. Catharine MacMillan describes Leake as 'the first scientific treatise writer of contract law', *Mistakes in Contract Law*, 112.

writing as I have done for students and beginners I have ventured on a definiteness of statement as to the results of the cases which would have been presumptuous in a book of practice. I took a good deal of trouble to arrange the various parts of the subject in due proportion & order, but it wasn't till I began to fill in my outline that I realized how much labour was needed & how much more learning than I possessed. Some parts of the subject are very interesting, and here and there it seems, though I may be wrong, that the law is still unsettled even on rudimentary points, and in such matters one feels the excitement of an explorer. I can only hope that I have not done discredit to your chambers.[15]

This letter is revealing in a number of ways. It reflects the deference, in part assumed but in part real, that English academic writers of the period paid to judges as to the only authoritative sources of legal principles. It shows that Anson was conscious of having over-simplified his account of the law, and that he had found it difficult to match a logical outline of the subject with the mass of English law as he found it. He acknowledged in his published preface that 'I . . . have often run the risk of seeming to dogmatise'.[16] It is significant that Anson found the law 'still unsettled even on rudimentary points', a phrase that implies recognition both of need for change and of confidence in future progress. He likened himself to an explorer, but the image suggested is not only of one who maps pre-existing territory, but also of one who assists in bringing about improvements: colonizer as well as surveyor.

Admiration of the civil law, as we have seen, was common in the nineteenth century when Pothier and Savigny were, for a time, treated by some writers and judges almost as sources of a universal contract law, and, therefore, of English law. References to civilian writers as sources of English contract law declined in the twentieth century. But at the beginning of the twenty-first century the relationship of the common law to the civil law again commanded wide attention as various projects were in progress designed to harmonize English and Irish law with the law of other European jurisdictions. The most prominent of these was the *Draft Common Frame of Reference*, published in 2009,[17] which discussed the relation of principle and policy at some length. In a paragraph headed 'Meaning of "principles"' the authors wrote that 'the word is susceptible to different interpretations. It is sometimes used, in the present context, as a synonym for rules which do not have the force of law . . . Alternatively,

---

15 Anson to Lord Justice Thesiger, 20 March 1879, slipped into (and now bound into) copy of first edition at the library of the Institute of Advanced Legal Studies in London.
16 Anson, *Principles*, 1st edn, vii.   17 *Draft Common Frame of Reference*, Full Edition.

the word "principles" might be reserved for those rules which are of a more general nature, such as those on freedom of contract or good faith. However, in the following paragraphs we explore a third meaning.'[18] The document then discussed 'fundamental principles', mentioning that, in an earlier interim document no fewer than fifteen items had been listed as fundamental principles, including justice, freedom, protection of human rights, economic welfare, solidarity and social responsibility, establishing an area of freedom, security and justice, promotion of the internal market (of the European Union), protection of consumers and others in need of protection, preservation of cultural and linguistic plurality, rationality, legal certainty, predictability, efficiency, protection of reasonable reliance and the proper allocation of responsibility for the creation of risks.[19] Any of these fundamental principles could quite well be described as policies.

This miscellaneous collection of objectives seemed too varied and multifarious to be a satisfactory list of 'fundamental principles', and in the later version the document distinguished between 'underlying principles', which were reduced to four (freedom, security, justice and efficiency) and 'overriding principles', described as matters of 'a high political nature' such as protection of human rights, the promotion of solidarity and social responsibility, the preservation of cultural and linguistic diversity, the protection and promotion of welfare and the promotion of the internal market.[20] In a later section headed 'Principles', the document discussed the four 'underlying' principles (freedom, security, justice and efficiency), pointing out that 'it is characteristic of principles such as those discussed here that they conflict with each other',[21] and that 'the principles also overlap'.[22] It is no criticism of this useful and influential document to observe that a civilian perspective does not necessarily produce a simple definition or understanding of the concept of principle, or a sharp distinction between principle and policy.

The concept of good faith, though not itself described as an underlying principle, is discussed in the *Draft Common Frame of Reference* as part of the underlying principle of justice, with the subheadings 'Not allowing people to rely on their own unlawful, dishonest or unreasonable conduct', 'No taking of undue advantage' and 'No grossly excessive demands'.[23] These subheadings indicate that considerations of policy, in the sense

18 *Ibid.*, Introduction, para. 10, vol. 1, 4–5.
19 *Ibid.*, Introduction, paras 11–12, vol. 1, 5, referring to Interim Outline Edition (2008).
20 *Ibid.*, Introduction, paras 15–16, vol. 1, 7–8.
21 *Ibid.*, Principles, para. 1, vol. 1, 37.   22 *Ibid.*, Principles, para. 1, vol. 1, 38.
23 *Ibid.*, Principles, paras 42–4, vol. 1, 54–5.

of what were thought to be desirable standards of behaviour, were not
absent from the minds of the drafters. English law, while not recognizing
a general duty of good faith, has often reached results similar to those
suggested by these subheadings by employing the technique of implied
terms,[24] by using a discretion to withhold equitable remedies, and by
other methods.

The *Draft Common Frame of Reference* includes a duty of good faith,
and in a note to the relevant article the drafters comment that, although
England and Ireland do not recognize a general obligation to conform to
good faith and fair dealing:

> many of the results which in other legal systems are achieved by requiring
> good faith have been reached in England and Ireland by more specific
> rules ... Thus to some extent the present Article merely articulates trends
> already present in English law. But the English approach based on con-
> struction of the agreement is a weak one as it cannot prevail against clear
> contrary provisions in the agreement ... Thus the Article represents an
> advance on English and Irish law.[25]

This passage, it may be observed, shows some indications of committee
drafting, and of wishful thinking. Inconsistent lines of thought can be
discerned: this Article will make no substantial difference to English law;
or not very much; in any event the *trends* are in this direction; at least
they *should be* in this direction if English law is to *advance*.

The object of this observation is not to criticize the drafters. From
their point of view harmonization was, understandably, an overriding
objective, and this could not have been achieved without including a duty
of good faith because all European countries except England and Ireland
recognized some version of it.[26] But the Notes point out that there is a
wide variation among the civil law jurisdictions as to the meaning and
significance of good faith, and to the prominence of its role.[27] It is likely,
therefore, that, if the *Draft Common Frame of Reference* were adopted in
English law, or in systems derived from English law, substantially different
meanings of 'good faith' would emerge in different contexts.[28]

Good faith is a concept that has been used in different senses to address
several distinct questions in contract law. These questions include, among
others, whether pre-contractual negotiations can be broken off, whether

---

24 See Chapter 2, above.   25 *DCFR*, Note 7 to III – I:103, Full Edition, vol. 1, 681.
26 *DCFR*, Notes 1 and 2 to III – I:103, Full Edition, vol 1, 679–80.   27 *Ibid.*
28 On American law, see Victor Goldberg, 'Discretion in Long-Term Open Quantity Contracts: Reining in Good Faith', in Goldberg, *Framing Contract Law*, 101.

material facts known to one party must be disclosed to the other in pre-contractual negotiations, whether contracts are enforceable if induced by misrepresentation or mistake, whether and to what extent the courts should imply terms into contracts, whether terms that are very unfair can be enforced, whether non-performance by one party excuses the other, whether deliberate breaches of contract justify punitive damages, whether the exercise of contractual rights may in some circumstances be restrained or precluded, and whether and when the interests of a person who acquires property from a non-owner should be protected. The concept of good faith, as applied to these various problems, necessarily varies substantially in meaning and significance, and for that reason it is not possible to assign a single meaning to the concept, nor is it plausible to call 'good faith', when applied to such disparate questions, a single principle. The phrase itself suggests a condemnation of selfish motives, but selfish motives could not, in all contractual disputes, be conclusive against a party entertaining them; nor could pure unselfish motives in themselves enlarge contractual rights, or excuse a party who was actually in breach of a contractual obligation.[29] Neither could the motives of either party be conclusive on the question of whether contractual terms were unfair. It may seem attractive, or innocuous, to embrace an overriding principle of good faith, but the effect of doing so on the scope of contractual rights and obligations would be far from clear: a contractual right that could only be exercised for unselfish reasons would, to the extent that it could not be exercised, lack the usual characteristics of a 'right'.

It would, indeed, be possible to conceive of the whole of contract law as the embodiment of the idea of good faith. Frederick Pollock wrote in his third edition in 1881 and repeated in subsequent editions that 'the law of Contract is in truth nothing else than the endeavour of the sovereign power, a more or less imperfect one by the nature of the case, to establish a positive sanction for the expectation of good faith which has grown up in the mutual dealings of men of average right-mindedness'.[30] Evidently Pollock was thinking of good faith primarily as supplying a reason for *enforcement* of promises, not as a limit on enforcement. He meant that the rules of contract law, taken as a whole, themselves reflected the community's sense of what good faith required – an idea that Pollock associated with protection of reasonable expectations – not that good faith should be deployed to modify or displace the actual rules of English

29 See Chapter 2, p. 48, above.
30 Pollock, *Principles of Contract*, 3rd edn, xx. See Chapter 2, p. 51, above.

contract law: a contracting party must defer to the other party's interests insofar, but only insofar, as the contract, properly interpreted and applied in accordance with the law, requires such deference. Good faith in this sense has nothing to do with the state of mind of a party seeking to exercise a contractual right. Whether as a reason for enforcement or as a limit on enforcement, the adoption of good faith as a general principle could not eliminate the need for particular rules in the various contexts in which it has been invoked, and, as suggested, it seems probable that such particular rules would develop in English law if the *Draft Common Frame of Reference* were adopted, or if a general concept of good faith were adopted from another source.[31]

Pollock showed, in the sentence quoted in the last paragraph, that he thought that the principles of contract law (the title of his book), taken as a whole, gave effect to sound policy. Principle, as we have seen, has been used in many different senses by writers on English contract law, almost always as a word of approbation. Principle has usually signified a proposition that is perceived at the time it is adopted or approved to supply a stable link between present and past and between present and future. It explains past cases thought to have been rightly decided; it resolves the current case in a satisfactory manner; and it seems likely to resolve all those future cases that can then be envisaged in a manner that is adjudged to be desirable. Principle always appears to be stable at the time it is approved or adopted, as it must appear for it to be called principle, but the infinite variety of the circumstances of human interaction, combined with the inherent flexibility of an uncodified system of law, mean that, from a historical perspective, principle has been constantly in flux as it is adapted and reformulated to meet unforeseen instances.

Policy, as applied to judicial decision-making in English law, has some-times been a word of approbation, signifying that which it is desirable for judges to do, as, for example in the eighteenth-century case of *Omychund* v. *Barker*, where the future Lord Mansfield argued that the inherent flex-ibility of the common law gave it a superiority over the legislature as a rule-maker, but sometimes it has signified the opposite, as in the opinion of the nine judges in *Egerton* v. *Brownlow*, where policy considerations were supposed by those judges to be excluded from the proper judicial sphere.[32] A similar view has been expressed by some modern writers.[33]

31 See also Waddams, 'Good Faith, Unconscionability, and Reasonable Expectations' (1995) 9 *Journal of Contract Law* 1.
32 See the discussion of these cases in Chapter 6, above.
33 See discussion in Chapter 1, p. 20, above.

Discussion of these matters, as frequently in legal discourse, is complicated by linguistic questions. A writer may use the word policy to mean 'such matters as are inappropriate for judicial consideration'. A writer is, of course, entitled to use the word in that sense, if it is explained to the reader. The conclusion, that judges ought not to consider policy, is then true by definition, but it is true *only* by definition. Unless independent content is given to 'policy', the proposition tells the reader nothing about what matters judges have considered in the past, or about what matters they ought to consider in the future. The tendency of this kind of argument might be that judges ought to exclude what may be called prudential considerations; but, on the other hand, it might just as well be that judges should include them, but that they ought not to be called policy.

In the past, as we have seen, judges have given attention to a wide variety of prudential considerations. In an uncodified system, where the courts have a rule-making function, it is inevitable that, to some degree, they should give attention to whether the rule they propose to adopt or approve is likely in the future to have desirable results. Courts, in adjudicating private disputes, have a dual role: they determine the rights of the parties in particular disputes, and they also (especially at the appellate level) establish legal principles and rules 'not only to rule the particular case then under consideration, but to serve as a guide for the future'.[34] In performing their rule-making task the courts have, in the past, often taken account of social, economic and political considerations. It is not necessary to call such considerations, taken collectively, 'policy', but it would not be a misuse of language to do so. Professor Peter Cane has written that, in a sense, 'all rules and principles that state individuals' legal rights and obligations are underpinned by policy arguments because policy arguments are arguments about what individuals' legal rights and obligations ought to be',[35] and Professor Ernest Weinrib has pointed out, with cogency, that private law has a public aspect, because the court, in performing its rule-making function, 'extends the significance of its decision beyond the specific dispute, making it a norm for all members of the state'.[36]

---

34 Chapter 1, p. 6, above.
35 P. Cane, 'Another Failed Sterilisation' (2004) 120 *Law Quarterly Review* 189, 192.
36 E Weinrib, 'Private Law and Public Right' (2011) 61 *University of Toronto Law Journal* 191, 196.

On the other hand, as Weinrib has also cogently argued,[37] private law cannot be subordinated to any particular policy external to the law itself. The force of this argument as it relates to contract law might be illustrated in many ways. The example chosen for discussion here is associated with economics, but the choice of example is made in order to test the limits of policy as a source of contractual obligation, not for the purpose of criticizing economic analysis of law.

Analysis of the actual probable social and economic consequences of legal rules is understandably of value, and becomes an essential part of legal discourse when the courts recognize that they have a rule-making function, and seek guidance in exercising it. Those writers who would wish to exclude social, political and economic considerations altogether from private law cannot derive support for their views from the past. But it does not follow that economic considerations have been or are the *only* relevant considerations, or that they have had, or should have overriding force. An economic analysis of the exchange between buyer and seller of conflicting printed forms (the 'battle of the forms') might suggest that the court should adopt the 'better' of the two forms, or should simply impose economically efficient terms, taking into account the merits of the business practices of each party in drafting forms for use in other transactions where they occupy the opposite position from that occupied in the current dispute, and taking account of incentives to efficient behaviour.[38] The difficulty with such a proposal is that the court would impose on a party an obligation to which that party had clearly not assented (on either a subjective or objective test), and on grounds that had nothing to do with the relationship between the parties to the particular dispute. The effect would be to cut the obligation loose from any recognized or recognizable principle of contract law, and to weaken the ties of economic analysis of contract law with its own roots, which lie in the notion of voluntary agreement. An obligation would be imposed not because the parties had agreed to it, or appeared to a reasonable person in the position of the promisee to have agreed to it, but because, in the opinion of the decision-maker, considerations of fairness, of efficiency and of appropriate incentives justified that result. Standing alone, reasons of this sort have not been sufficient to justify the imposition of contractual obligations. On a theoretical level, the proposal does not

---

37 Weinrib, *The Idea of Private Law*.
38 A somewhat similar (not identical) suggestion is discussed in S. Waddams, 'The Economics of Contract Law' (2007) 45 *Canadian Business Law Journal* 305, 307–10.

reflect the parties' actual or apparent agreement. On a practical level, such a rule would open the door to numerous disputable questions about the morality of the parties' general business practices, and about what factors should be taken into account in identifying the 'better' form, and in judging what incentives were appropriate.

Another difficulty with such a proposal is that it is by no means clear what incentives it would in fact create. If the rule were that any form proposed by one party could be imposed on the other, if judged subsequently by the court to have been the 'better' form, and if this result could not be avoided even by strenuous protest that the other party did *not* assent to the form, the incentive would quite probably be for the party with stronger bargaining power to refuse to deal at all with any party that used such a form. This might in turn lead to the demise of the use of printed forms, except by parties in strong bargaining positions. Whether or not this would in fact occur, and whether or not, if it did, it would be a net social benefit are highly contentious and debatable questions on which social consensus is lacking.

Sellers usually desire to restrict liability for consequential damages, but if no such restriction is agreed upon, the seller would be exposed to potentially very large liability. A large seller, advised that restriction of consequential damages could not be guaranteed if the buyer used any kind of printed form, might well refuse to sell to any buyer using such a form, and would probably insist on the buyer's signature to the seller's terms. Some might argue that this would be a desirable result, but if the creation of appropriate incentives were really to be a determining consideration, there would be almost unlimited scope, varying with the social and economic circumstances of the particular parties in each case, for debate on what would in fact probably happen if a particular rule were adopted, and whether, on balance, such results would be socially beneficial. Policy considerations often tend in opposite directions, and, where social consensus is lacking, there is very good reason for the courts to rest their conclusions on generally acceptable propositions cast in the form of legal principles.

The Uniform Commercial Code provision on the battle of the forms (2–207) turned out to be one of the least successful of the Code provisions. It went through a succession of drafts, as representatives of buyers' and sellers' interests successively influenced the drafting process. In the end the provision lost its internal coherence, and, so far from putting an end to the battle of the forms, the section intensified it, as parties sought to redraft their forms to take account of the Code provisions. The official text was revised in 2003, but not all states have adopted the change. A case can certainly be made for reform of this section, but in that event would it not be a simpler solution to restore the pre-Code common law? It was always open, under the pre-Code American common law, and still is open to buyer or seller to insist on the other party's signature to a contractual document. Where business persons choose not to do so, and pin their hopes on the chance of enforcing a printed form not signed by the opposite party, they knowingly take a business and legal risk. Of course they are entitled to do so, and, from a business point of view, the risk might be fully justified. The chance of a dispute might be small, and the business value of the transaction might quite legitimately be thought to outweigh the chance of liability. But the person who acts in this way has no valid complaint against the law, or against legal principles, if the risk materializes and the person's own form is found to be ineffective. From the point of view of efficiency and incentives, the pre-Code common law might be said to have been quite efficient in that it created a moderate incentive to the parties to clarify their intentions by agreeing to and signing a single document, while leaving them free not to do so if they wished to take the associated business and legal risks. But that would be to offer a *commentary* from an economic perspective on a rule that existed for independent reasons based on a legal principle (assent), not a reason for *overriding* that principle.

I have chosen this example, not because the subject is itself of great importance, but because it supplies an illustration, more vivid than is usually available, of the constraining role of the concept of principle. It is one thing to say that, in the past, judicial decisions have been influenced by economic or other policy considerations. As a matter of history this proposition is demonstrably true, and pointing it out when it is in danger of being forgotten is very useful. But it is altogether another thing to say that economic or other policy considerations have had or ought to have overriding force, or that, standing alone and detached from legal principle, they can themselves justify the imposition of contractual obligations. The dissenting judgment of Bramwell LJ in *Parker* v. *South Eastern Railway Co.* will be recalled from Chapter 2. Bramwell was ready to impose upon travellers terms that he thought reasonable, no doubt in part for reasons that might be expressed in economic terms, but the majority of the court insisted on maintaining a link with the principle of assent, attenuated though it was by the objective approach.[39]

39 See Chapter 2, pp. 38–9, above.

The foregoing discussion of 'the battle of the forms' prompts the wider question of whether the principles of contract law have been governed by any non-legal system of thought – economic, social, religious, ethical, political or philosophical. If the question is whether the principles of English contract law have, in the past, been influenced by non-legal systems of thought the answer must be yes. If the question is whether the principles of contract law have coincided with those of non-legal systems, the answer must be that often (though not always) they have done so, and that both lawyers and adherents to other systems of thought have noted such coincidences, each from his or her own point of view, often with satisfaction. But the influences and coincidences have been so numerous and so varied that no system could plausibly be selected as having been the single source of legal principles. Moreover, if any single non-legal system of thought were to be determined to have been authoritative, the principles of contract law would be perceived not to be legal principles at all, but to be practical applications of the precepts of the prevalent non-legal system. Thus an attempt to explain contract law in non-legal terms would dissolve the phenomenon sought to be explained. A polity might be imagined in which legal rules depended entirely on the application of the precepts of some non-legal system of thought – several experiments of this sort have been tried – but this has not been the history of Anglo-American contract law. Many extra-legal considerations have been influential, as this study has shown, but no single system could be said to have fully understood, explained, governed, dominated, embraced, included or overcome – in a word, comprehended – contract law, and none could claim to have been the exclusive source of its principles. For this reason, and no doubt for others also, the study of contract law has not been absorbed into the study of economics, sociology, ethics, religion, politics or philosophy, though it has been influenced by all of them. The concept of principle, while it has not excluded the influence of non-legal ideas, has tended to discourage an unmediated appeal to any of them as an authoritative or overriding justification for legal results.

An instance of a concept that was, in the past, proposed by judges to exclude contractual liability, but which failed to qualify as a principle, is the proposition, discussed in Chapter 6, above, that judges should exercise a discretionary power to decline to try cases of bets and wagers. The proposition that judges might exercise a discretion to refuse to try cases that they considered to be 'frivolous or improper', or 'trifling, ridiculous, or contemptible', could not rank as a principle. It lacked reasoned support, it would have left individual judges without precise guidance, and it would have been likely to affect all kinds of contracts in wholly unpredictable ways. Moreover a simple discretionary refusal to try an action would have been potentially unjust to claimants because it would have prevented any opportunity to adduce argument that the case should be heard, or that the transaction was not a wager at all, or to know the reasons why the judge had rejected the claim, or to appeal from such a rejection.

The judges were rescued from their difficulties on this particular point by the statute of 1845 which made all bets and wagers void. But a judicial rule to the same effect had been established in Scots law[40] (also an uncodified system) and, in the opinion of at least one English judge in 1790,[41] might well have been adopted in England. A rule that wagers, or 'idle' wagers, were unenforceable, supported by such reasons as those given by Buller J in *Good* v. *Elliott,* and echoed by other eighteenth-century commentators,[42] might, as suggested in an earlier chapter,[43] if supported by a sufficient social consensus, have been recognized as a principle and defended on a mixture of private and public considerations. The considerations include fairness to the individual parties and the avoidance of unjust enrichment, but include also consistency with the past both in theory and in practice (taking account of the effect of statutes as well as of judicial decisions), the appropriate use of judicial resources, the predictability and stability of the proposed rule, the fitness and qualification of judges to apply it and the effect that such a rule would have on the future behaviour of others.

The questions addressed here have sometimes been posed in terms of a contrast between 'internal' and 'external' considerations. This distinction is difficult to apply to contract law, viewed as a historical phenomenon, because considerations that have effectively influenced the law have, by that very fact, been internalized. Thus, the avoidance of unjust enrichment (in its general sense), the facilitation of commerce, the maintenance of public policy and the encouragement of good faith have all been, to some degree, internalized by the rules of contract law itself. The suggestion that these objectives are external or alien to contract law could only

---

40 Buller J, dissenting, in *Good* v. *Elliott* (1790) 3 TR 693; *Report from Select Committee on Gaming,* Appendix; and Walker, *The Law of Contracts and Related Obligations in Scotland,* 12.11 ('since the end of the seventeenth century . . . accepted doctrine') citing *Roberton* v. *Balfour* 1938 SC 207, 211, and Kames, *Principles of Equity,* 22.

41 Buller J dissenting in *Good* v. *Elliott* (1790) 3 TR 693, 697.

42 E.g., Blackstone, *Commentaries on the Laws of England,* vol. 4, 171–4, in support of the gaming statutes.

43 See Chapter 6, above.

be maintained by assuming that contract law must be so defined as to exclude them, as, for example, by defining contract law exclusively in terms of consent, a definition that could not be supported by historical evidence.

It may seem that courts must choose between, on the one hand, adhering to a rigorous application of stable, ordered and coherent principles, and, on the other hand, opening the door to unconstrained and unpredictable appeals to each judge's view of what might constitute desirable policy. From a historical point of view this choice presents too stark a dichotomy. English contract law has not, during the past 250 years, been perfectly ordered, stable and coherent; but neither has it been wholly chaotic and unpredictable. The concept of principle has enabled courts to accommodate legal change and to give effect to general ideas of common sense, convenience and justice, while at the same time imposing restraint, in practice, on the unmediated invocation of policy.

The word 'principle' has been used in many different senses, and, from one perspective, this may seem regrettable: from an analytical point of view uncertainties and ambiguities in the use of language often appear as deficiencies. But from a historical perspective it may be observed that it is the very malleability of the concept of principle that has enabled an uncodified system of contract law to hold the mean between rigorous formalism on the one hand and unpredictable applications of ever-changing policies on the other.

The application of pure principles without any attention to their practical consequences would bear little resemblance to contract law as it has been. Neither, looking at the matter from the opposite end, could policy, standing alone, be accepted as a sufficient reason for imposing or for denying contractual obligations, as the earlier discussions of the battle of the forms and of wagers, and the discussion in Chapter 4 of redistribution of wealth as a reason for setting aside disadvantageous contracts, were intended to show. But policy considerations, when they can be incorporated in a rule that corresponds with past practice, that is likely to be fair to individual parties, that is judged to be likely to have beneficial effects in the future, that can be articulated in a form that is likely to be stable and that is suitable to be applied by judges are apt to be called principles. Thus policy may take the form of principle. Policy itself has often been called a principle, and public policy, as administered by courts, has been said itself to be governed by principles.

That contracts should be enforced has, as we saw in Chapter 6, been called a principle; it has also been called a policy: 'if there is one thing more than another that public policy requires it is that contracts should be held sacred'.[44] On the other hand, the *limits* to enforcement of contracts, for reasons of mistake, or inequality of exchange or undue influence, have also sometimes been described as policy. The doctrine of undue influence is an important part of the law protecting weaker parties and preventing unjust enrichment, and would rightly be regarded as primarily concerned with justice between the individual parties.[45] But it has had a public aspect also. In 1887, Cotton LJ said that when a presumption of undue influence arises 'the court interferes, not on the ground that any wrongful act has in fact been committed by the donee, but *on the ground of public policy* and to prevent the relationship which existed between the parties . . . being abused'.[46] Approaching the question from the other side, restraint of trade is an aspect of public policy, and would rightly be regarded as concerned mainly with the public interest, but it has also played a part in securing justice between individual parties. In a case in the House of Lords in 1974, Lord Diplock, in striking down a contractual clause in favour of a music publisher, pointed out that the doctrine of restraint of trade had been concerned not only with the public interest, but also with justice between individual parties:

> [W]hat your lordships have in fact been doing has been to assess the relative bargaining power of the publisher and the song writer at the time the contract was made and to decide whether the publisher had used his superior bargaining power to extract from the song writer promises that were unfairly onerous to him . . . Under the influence of Bentham and of laissez-faire the courts in the 19th century abandoned the practice of applying public policy against unconscionable bargains to contracts generally, as they had formerly done to any contract considered to be usurious, but the policy survived in the application to penalty clauses and to relief against forfeiture and also to the special category of contracts in restraint of trade. If one looks at the reasoning of 19th-century judges in cases about contracts in restraint of trade one finds lip service paid to current economic theories, but if one looks at what they said in the light of what they did, one finds that they struck down a bargain if they thought it was unconscionable as between the parties to it, and upheld it if they thought it was not. So I would hold that the question to be answered . . . is: 'Was the bargain fair?'[47]

44 See Chapter 6, p. 161, above.   45 See Chapter 4, above.
46 *Allcard* v. *Skinner* (1887) 36 Ch D 145, 171 (emphasis added), and see Chapter 4, p. 116, above.
47 *A. Schroeder Music Publishing Co. Ltd* v. *Macaulay* [1974] 1 WLR 1308, 1314–15 (HL).

Public policy and the concept of justice between individual parties have thus not been entirely dissociated.

The concept of principle is itself a policy, because it has been thought to be in the public interest that private disputes should be settled according to clear and predictable standards, knowable in advance, fairly applied by impartial judges and testable for these qualities by neutral observers and by appellate courts. In refusing to extend the concept of proprietary estoppel to a case where both parties knew that they had no enforceable agreement Lord Scott said:

> Proprietary estoppel requires, in my opinion, clarity as to what it is that the object of the estoppel is to be estopped from denying, or asserting, and clarity as to the interest in the property in question that that denial, or assertion, would otherwise defeat. If these requirements are not recognised, proprietary estoppel will lose contact with its roots, and risk becoming unprincipled and therefore unpredictable, if it has not already done so.[48]

The links made here between principle, clarity, and predictability demonstrate Lord Scott's fear that the doctrine of proprietary estoppel might become a device for enabling judges to impose contractual obligations in circumstances where there was admittedly no contract without articulating satisfactory reasons for their conclusions.

Every reference to principle incorporates a reference, express or implied, to the past, as in the passage just quoted, where Lord Scott referred to the danger that proprietary estoppel 'will lose contact with its roots'. The concept of principle links the present with the past, but, as we have seen in many instances, the judge who formulates or reformulates the principle also formulates a view of the past with which the principle appears to conform. This view of the past may not, regarded as history of the earlier period, be accurate, for advocates and judges are not always good legal historians, and in their role as advocates or judges they are not primarily concerned to understand the past. The common law, even when consciously making new law, has sought to anchor every innovation in the past, 'the principle upon which our decision is founded being universally admitted in all the cases', as Buller J said in *Goodison* v. *Nunn* in effectively approving a new legal rule.[49] This process rarely constitutes good history of the earlier period, but it is of interest to legal historians studying the later period: the use made in the past of references to the

---

48 *Cobbe* v. *Yeoman's Row Management Ltd* [2008] 1 WLR 1752, para. 28 (HL).
49 See Chapter 1, above.

more remote past is itself a part of legal history, whether the references to the more remote past are or are not accurate. Opinions held in the nineteenth century about the eighteenth century are part of the history of nineteenth-century ideas, and do not cease to be so because they were inaccurate; indeed they may be of particular interest and significance precisely because they *were* inaccurate. The role of the legal historian differs from that of the advocate, from that of the judge, from that of the treatise-writer and from that of the philosopher, but it is not opposed to any of them. Good advocacy, good judgment, good writing and good theory are assisted rather than impaired by a better understanding of the past. The corollary is that, insofar as advocates, judges and writers make references (express or implied) to the past, they ought to take account of the best historical evidence available to them.

'Principle' means beginning (*principium*), but it is evident that this is not a point in historical time: it is more akin to a conceptual or notional origin, root or source. From this it follows that principles are liable to vary according to the concepts or notions of the speaker or writer who uses the word, and that they are liable to be reformulated according to the perspective of each writer, or the perspective of the same writer on different occasions. The search for principle in law is not a purely historical inquiry – historical research, however diligent, could not discover a set of original principles of contract law – but it has historical dimensions, and the past perceptions and meanings of principle are part of legal history. Addison said that contract law was founded on principles that were immutable, eternal and universal, but the present inquiry suggests that it has not been possible to formulate principles that have been stable even over a short period of time in the history of one part of a single legal system. 'Principle' has, to say the least, been a very versatile concept, changing its shape to suit diverse purposes: on the question of third-party beneficiaries, in the hands of Viscount Simonds, principle prohibited reform; in the hands of Crompton J at an earlier period, and of Lord Denning at a later period, principle demanded reform – but in entirely opposite directions.[50] Denning's ultimately unsuccessful attempt will be recalled to formulate a principle to explain and govern the legal concept of estoppel.[51] Lord Denning did not ignore the past, but his successive formulations were not the fruits of historical research. It is evident that he was motivated primarily by a desire to formulate a legal rule that would be

---

50 See Chapter 3, above.   51 *Ibid.*, pp. 71–3.

acceptable to his contemporaries and that would be just and convenient
in its future operation.

From a historical perspective, contract law cannot be reduced to any
single or simple explanatory idea, internal or external. The interdependence of principle and policy is part of the reason for this conclusion:
every principle, since it incorporates prudential considerations, has operated in tension with countervailing considerations which themselves can
be, and often have been, formulated as principles. It does not follow that
the concept of principle has been useless or unimportant; on the contrary, the constant appeal by courts and writers to principle suggests that
the *concept* of principle, though not the formulation of any particular
proposition, has been perceived as an essential aspect of legal reasoning.
It has sometimes been suggested that, without stable principles, the law
would lapse into chaos, but, from a historical perspective, this suggestion
presents too sharp a dichotomy: principles have indeed changed, but no
one has plausibly suggested, as a matter of historical judgment, that chaos
is an apt word to describe nineteenth- and twentieth-century English
contract law.[52]

As with other complex social institutions, opposite ideas have been
entertained simultaneously and held in tension: sanctity of contract,
avoidance of unjust enrichment (in its general sense) and maintenance
of public policy have not always been mutually compatible in their application to particular cases. The concept of principle has not supplied any
simple resolution to such tensions, nor has it excluded general considerations of convenience, justice and common sense. The frequent appeal to
principle by writers and judges suggests that it has played a very important
role in enabling contract law to accommodate such general considerations
and to avoid undue rigidity, while yet preserving (not only in appearance
but also in reality) a substantial measure of predictability and stability and
guaranteeing the efficacy of reasoned argument. General considerations
of common sense, convenience, policy and justice have usually,[53] as we
have seen, been reflected in and incorporated into principle. But it does
not follow that the concept of principle could have been dispensed with,
or that the law could have been or could be – still less that it should be –
restated in purely policy terms. Common sense, convenience, policy and

---

52 van de Kherchove and Ost, *Legal System Between Order and Disorder*, 172–3, have
   described the work of the judge as a 'constant arbitration between order and disorder'.
53 The treatment of third party beneficiaries discussed in Chapter 3, above, is an instance
   where such considerations were, for a period, excluded.

justice, as free-standing ideas, have not been sufficiently stable or precise to support legal conclusions: principle has been an essential component of legal decision-making and at the same time an essential restraint on it, and an important part of what has made legal reasoning distinctively legal. Andrew Robertson has written that 'formal legal values operate to constrain the operation of non-formal policy arguments'.[54]

The questions addressed in this study continue to resonate in the twenty-first century, with practical as well as theoretical consequences, as was shown by the case of the *Golden Victory*, mentioned in the previous chapter.[55] The issue in the case was whether damages for repudiation of a charterparty should be reduced by reference to events occurring fifteen months after acceptance of the repudiation. The majority held that damages should be reduced, giving priority to the principle that the claimant should not be put into a better position than it would have occupied if the contract had been performed. Lord Scott of Foscote, for the majority, spoke in very forceful, indeed almost in peremptory, terms:

> The arguments of the owners offend the compensatory principle . . . The argued justification for thus offending the compensatory principle is that priority should be given to the principle of certainty. My lords, there is, in my opinion, no such principle. Certainty is a desideratum and a very important one, particularly in commercial contracts. But it is not a principle and must give way to principle. Otherwise incoherence of principle is the likely result.[56]

But the dissenting judges also relied on a principle, namely, that the claimant should be compensated for the full value of what it had lost at the time of the breach of contract, a rule that also might be presented as giving effect to the compensatory principle, and which the dissenting judges thought conducive to certainty, stability and predictability. Historically, as Lord Bingham of Cornhill said, 'the importance of certainty and predictability has been a constant theme of English commercial law at any rate since the judgment of Lord Mansfield [in 1774]'. Lord Bingham used the word 'principle' as a heading to four crucial paragraphs in his opinion, and said that the majority view 'involves an unfortunate departure from principle'.[57] Lord Walker of Gestingthorpe, who agreed

---

54 A. Robertson, 'Constraints on Policy-Based Reasoning in Private Law', in Robertson and Tang Hang Wu (eds.), *The Goals of Private Law*, 261, 265.
55 *Golden Strait Corp.* v. *Nissen Yusen Kubishika Kaisha (The Golden Victory)* [2007] 2 AC 353 (HL). See Chapter 7, p. 188, above.
56 *Ibid.*, at para. 38.   57 *Ibid.*, at para. 1.

with Lord Bingham, said that 'his opinion clearly sets out the principles of law applicable in this area, including the importance of certainty in commercial transactions'.[58]

The sharp distinction drawn by Lord Scott between principle on the one hand and mere 'desideratum' on the other, is, as Lord Bingham pointed out, difficult to sustain as a matter of history. The formulation of principles has often, as we have seen, been influenced by considerations of what general rule has been thought to be desirable, or advantageous. The dissenting opinions in the *Golden Victory* illustrate another common feature of debates about principle, which is that countervailing considerations to an asserted principle can themselves almost always be formulated as principles. Success then goes to the argument that can more effectively invoke in its own support the concept of principle: the *Golden Victory* might well, in a differently constituted panel, have been decided in accordance with the views of the minority.

Over a period of about two-and-a-half centuries, since the time of Blackstone and Mansfield, advocates, judges and writers have sought to establish principles of contract law. Each, in pursuit of persuasive argument, right judgment, accurate description or wise prescription has formulated and asserted propositions that have been called principles. These propositions have appeared stable and permanent at the time of their assertion, as they must have done in order plausibly to be called principles. Yet, from a historical perspective, it can be seen that principles confidently asserted at one time have subsequently been reformulated, modified or discarded. The familiar phrase 'it is now settled that...' has been so often used of points of contract law, and so often used with conviction and success, that one might suppose that every point must long ago have been determined. But the phrase has not been effective to prevent the point in issue from being subsequently unsettled, sometimes very soon afterwards. Advocates, judges and writers have been constantly in search of settled principles – and rightly so, for the search is a part of their duties – yet the permanence and stability they have supposed to be attainable has remained always just out of reach. 'The principles are perfectly clear', or its near equivalent, is a phrase that occurs hundreds of times in the law reports, only to be followed by dissenting judgments, reversals and overrulings.[59] It is possible that at some future time the

---

58 *Ibid.*, at para. 39.
59 A striking twentieth-century example is the rule that damages could not be awarded in foreign currency, very forcefully affirmed in *Re United Railways of Havana and Regla*

principles of contract law might be so clearly and finally established that they will exclude any resort to considerations of policy; it is also possible, on the other hand, that a version of policy might come to achieve such ascendancy that every question of contract law could be resolved by a direct appeal to policy, unmediated by principle. Neither possibility can derive support from historical evidence.

Paradoxically, the concept of principle has prevailed only by appearing to be what it is not: while ostensibly precluding legal change, the concept of principle has, in practice, facilitated change by permitting innovations to be formulated in terms of restoration of temporarily lost original authority.[60] Though it has not suppressed policy considerations, it has served to constrain and channel them, and to direct them into legal forms. Principle has played an important role – perhaps an essential role in an uncodified system – but that role is not better understood by concealing its complexity.

Warehouses Ltd [1961] AC 1007 (HL), but rejected in *Miliangos* v. *George Frank Textiles Ltd* [1976] AC 443 (HL).
60 See the discussion of *Goodisson* v. *Nunn* in Chapter 1, pp. 1–6, above.

SELECT BIBLIOGRAPHY

Addison, C., *A Treatise on the Law of Contracts and Rights and Liabilities Ex Contractu* (London: W. Benning, 1847)

American Law Institute, *Second Restatement of Contracts* (St Paul: American Law Institute Publishers, 1979)

American Law Institute, *Third Restatement of Restitution and Unjust Enrichment* (St Paul: American Law Institute Publishers, 2011)

Anson, W., *Principles of the English Law of Contract*, 1st edn (Oxford: Clarendon Press, 1879)

Anson, W., *Principles of the English Law of Contract and of Agency in its Relation to Contract*, 5th edn (Oxford: Clarendon Press, 1888)

Anson, W., *Principles of the English Law of Contract and of Agency in its Relation to Contract*, 6th edn (Oxford: Clarendon Press, 1891)

Anson, W., *Principles of the English Law of Contract and of Agency in its Relation to Contract*, J.C. Miles and J.L. Brierly (eds.), 17th edn (Oxford: Clarendon Press, 1929)

Aristotle, *The Nichomachean Ethics of Aristotle*, translated by Sir David Ross (Oxford University Press, 1954)

Atiyah, P.S., *Essays on Contract* (Oxford: Clarendon Press, 1986)

Atiyah, P.S., *Promises, Morals, and Law* (Oxford: Clarendon Press, 1981)

Atiyah, P.S., *The Rise and Fall of Freedom of Contract* (Oxford: Clarendon Press, 1979)

Ball, W.E., *Principles of Torts and Contracts* (London: Stevens, 1880)

Ballow, H., *A Treatise of Equity* (London: printed by E. and R. Nutt and R. Gosling (assigns of Edward Sayer, Esq.) for D. Browne and J. Shuckburgh, 1737)

Bant, E. and Harding, M. (eds.), *Exploring Private Law* (Cambridge University Press, 2010)

Barak, A., *Judicial Discretion*, translated by Yadin Kaufmann (New Haven, CT: Yale University Press, 1989)

Beatson, J., *Anson's Law of Contract*, 27th edn (Oxford University Press, 1998)

Bell, J., *Policy Arguments in Judicial Decisions* (Oxford University Press, 1983)

Benjamin, J.P., *A Treatise on the Law of Sale of Personal Property; With References to the American Decisions and to the French Code and Civil Law*, 1st edn (London: H. Sweet, 1868)

Benjamin, J.P., *A Treatise on the Law of Sale of Personal Property; With References to the American Decisions and to the French Code and Civil Law*, 2nd edn (London: H. Sweet, 1873)

Benjamin, J.P., *A Treatise on the Law of Sale of Personal Property; With References to the American Decisions and to the French Code and Civil Law*, W.C.A. Ker and A.R. Butterworth (eds.), 5th edn (London: Sweet and Maxwell, 1906)

Benjamin, J.P., *A Treatise on the Law of Sale of Personal Property; With References to the American Decisions and to the French Code and Civil Law*, W.C.A. Ker (ed.), 6th edn (London: Sweet and Maxwell, 1920)

Benson, P., *The Theory of Contract Law* (Cambridge University Press, 2001)

Berryman, J. (ed.), *Remedies: Issues and Perspectives* (Scarborough, Ontario: Carswell, 1991)

Birks, P., *An Introduction to the Law of Restitution* (Oxford: Clarendon Press, 1985)

Birks, P., *Restitution – The Future* (Annandale, NSW: Federation Press, 1992)

Birks, P. (ed.), *The Classification of Obligations* (Oxford: Clarendon Press, 1997)

Birks, P., *Unjust Enrichment* (Oxford University Press, 2003)

Birks, P., *Unjust Enrichment*, 2nd edn (Oxford University Press, 2005)

Blackstone, W., *Commentaries on the Laws of England*, 1st edn, 4 vols. (Oxford: Clarendon Press, 1765–69)

Blackstone, W., *Commentaries on the Laws of England*, 15th edn, 4 vols. (London: A. Strahan, 1809)

Brownsword, R., Howells, G. and Wilhelmsson, T. (eds.), *Welfarism in Contract Law* (Aldershot: Dartmouth Publishing Co., 1994)

Burns, R., *The Justice of the Peace and Parish Officer*, 18th edn, 4 vols. (London: T. Strahen and Z. Woodfall for B. Cadell, 1793)

Burrows, A., *The Law of Restitution* (London: Butterworths, 1993)

Burrows, A. and Lord Rodger of Earlsferry (eds.), *Mapping the Law: Essays in Memory of Peter Birks* (Oxford University Press, 2006)

Celebration Legal Essays: to Mark the 25ᵗʰ Year of Service of John H. Wigmore as Professor of Law in Northwestern University (Chicago, IL: Northwestern University Press, 1919)

Cheshire, G.C. and Fifoot, C.H.S., *The Law of Contract*, 6th edn (London: Butterworths, 1964)

Chitty, J., *A Practical Treatise on the Law of Contracts not under Seal: and upon the Usual Defences to Actions Thereon*, 1st edn (London: S. Sweet, 1826)

Chitty, J., *A Practical Treatise on the Law of Contracts not under Seal: and upon the Usual Defences to Actions Thereon*, 2nd edn (London: S. Sweet, 1834)

Chitty, J., *A Practical Treatise on the Law of Contracts not under Seal: and upon the Usual Defences to Actions Thereon*, 3rd edn (by Tompson Chitty) (London: S. Sweet, 1841)

Chitty, J., *A Treatise on the Law of Contracts*, 13th edn (London: Sweet & Maxwell, 1896)

Chitty, J., *A Treatise on the Law of Contracts: and upon the Defences to Actions Thereon*, 12th edn (London: Sweet & Maxwell, 1890)

Chitty, J. (the elder) (ed.), *Commentaries on the Laws of England by the late Sir W. Blackstone, a New Edition with Practical Notes*, 4 vols. (London: William Walker, 1826)

Colebrooke, H.T., *Treatise on Obligations and Contracts* (London: printed for the author, 1818)

Colebrooke, T.E., *Miscellaneous Essays [of H.T. Colebrooke], With the Life of the Author by His Son, Sir T.E. Colebrooke* (London: Trübner, 1873)

Comyn, S., *A Treatise of the Law Relative to Contracts and Agreements not under Seal: with Cases and Decisions Thereon in the Action of Assumpsit* (London: J. Butterworth, 1807)

Coote, R.H., *A Treatise on the Law of Mortgage* (London: J. Butterworth, 1821)

Corbin, A.L., *Corbin on Contracts: a Comprehensive Treatise on the Working Rules of Contract Law*, 12 vols. (St. Paul, MN: West Publishing Co., 1950–63)

Cromartie, A., *Sir Matthew Hale, 1606–1676: Law, Religion and Natural Philosophy* (Cambridge University Press, 1995)

Daniell, E.R., *The Practice of the Chancery Division of the High Court of Justice, and on Appeal Therefrom: Being the Sixth Edition of Daniell's Chancery Practice with Alterations and Additions, and References to a Companion Volume of Forms*, 6th edn (London: Stevens and Sons, 1882–84)

Degeling, S. and Edelman, J. (eds.), *Unjust Enrichment in Commercial Law* (Sydney: Law Book Co., 2008)

Denning, A.T., *The Discipline of Law* (London: Butterworths, 1979)

Dictionary of National Biography, edited by Leslie Stephen (London: Smith, Elder, 1885–1900)

Draft Common Frame of Reference. See *Principles Definitions and Model Rules of European Private Law*

Duxbury, N., *Frederick Pollock and the English Juristic Tradition* (Oxford University Press, 2004)

Duxbury, N., *Patterns of American Jurisprudence* (Oxford: Clarendon Press, 1995)

Dworkin, R., *Justice in Robes* (Cambridge, MA: Belknap Press of Harvard University, 2006)

Dworkin, R., *Taking Rights Seriously* (Cambridge, MA: Harvard University Press, 1977)

Encyclopaedia Britannica, 11th edn, 29 vols. (Cambridge University Press, 1910), vol. 7

Evans, W., *An Essay on the Action for Money Had and Received* (Liverpool: Merritt and Wright, 1802), reprinted in *Restitution Law Review*, 25 (1998), 1–33

Farnsworth, E.A., *Contracts* (Boston, MA: Little, Brown, 1982)

Finn, P.D. (ed.), *Essays on Damages* (Sydney: Law Book Co., 1992)

Foulkes, W., *A Generation of Judges, by their Reporter* (London: Sampson, Low, Marston, Searle, and Rivington, 1886)

Fry, E., *A Treatise on the Specific Performance of Contracts*, 3rd edn (London: Stevens, 1892)

Galligan, D.J., *Discretionary Powers* (Oxford: Clarendon Press, 1986)

Gilbert, J., *Of Contracts* (manuscript: British Library, Hargrave, 265, about 1710)

Goff, R. and Jones, G.H., *The Law of Restitution* (London: Sweet & Maxwell, 1966)

Goldberg, V., *Framing Contract Law: An Economic Perspective* (Cambridge, MA: Harvard University Press, 2006)

Gordley, J., *The Philosophical Origins of Modern Contract Doctrine* (Oxford: Clarendon Press, 1991)

Grantham, R. and Rickett, C. (eds.), *Structure and Justification in Private Law: Essays for Peter Birks* (Oxford: Hart Publishing, 2008)

Hale, M., *The Analysis of the Law Being a Scheme, or Abstract, of the Several Parts of the Law of England, Digested into Method*, (London: printed for John Nott, 1703)

Halsbury, Earl of, *The Laws of England*, 28 vols. (London, Butterworth & Co., 1907–15)

Hardcastle, The Hon Mrs (ed.), *Life of John, Lord Campbell, Lord High Chancellor of Great Britain: Consisting of a Selection from his Autobiography, Diary, and Letters*, 2nd edn, 2 vols. (London: J. Murray, 1881)

Hargrave, F., *Collectanea Juridica, Consisting of Tracts Relative to the Law and Constitution of England* (London: printed for E. and R. Brooke, 1791)

Harris, D. and Tallon, D. (eds.), *Contract Law Today: Anglo-French Comparisons* (Oxford: Clarendon Press, 1989)

Hart, H.L.A., *The Concept of Law* (Oxford: Clarendon Press, 1961)

Hart, H.L.A., *The Concept of Law*, 2nd edn (Oxford: Clarendon Press, 1994)

Hobbes, T., *Leviathan* (London: A. Crooke, 1651)

Holmes, O.W., *The Common Law* (Boston, MA: Little, Brown, and Co., 1881)

Holmes-Pollock Letters: the Correspondence of Mr. Justice Holmes and Sir Frederick Pollock, 1874–1932, M. Howe (ed.), 2 vols. (Cambridge, MA: Harvard University Press, 1941)

Hume, D., *A Treatise of Human Nature*, 3 vols. (London: 1839–40)

Johnston, D. and Zimmermann, R. (eds.), *Unjustified Enrichment: Key Issues in Comparative Perspective* (Cambridge University Press, 2002)

Jones, W., *An Essay on the Law of Bailments* (London: printed by J. Nichols for Charles Dilly, 1781)

Jones, W., *An Essay on the Law of Bailments*, D. Ibbetson (ed.) (Bangor: The Welsh Legal History Society, 2007)

Kames, H.H., *Principles of Equity* (Edinburgh: 1760)

Kenny, M., Devenney, J. and Fox O'Mahoney, J. (eds.), *Unconscionability in European Private Financial Transactions: Protecting the Vulnerable* (Cambridge University Press, 2010)

Leake, S.M., *An Elementary Digest of the Law of Contracts* (London: Stevens and Sons, 1878)

Leake, S.M., *The Elements of the Law of Contracts* (London: Stevens and Sons, 1867)

Lewis, A., Brand, P. and Mitchell, P. (eds.) *Law in the City: Proceedings of the Seventeenth British Legal History Conference, London, 2005* (Dublin: Four Courts Press, 2007)

MacCormick, N., *Legal Reasoning and Legal Theory* (Oxford University Press, 1978)

MacMillan, C., *Mistakes in Contract Law* (Oxford: Hart, 2010)

Maddaugh, P. and McCamus, J., *The Law of Restitution* (Aurora, Ontario: Canada Law Book, 1990, and looseleaf)

Maine, H.S., *Ancient Law: its Connection with the Early History of Society, and its Relation to Modern Ideas [1861]*, 1st American from 2nd London edn (New York: Scribner, 1864)

Maine, H.S. (with introduction and notes by Sir Frederick Pollock), *Ancient Law: its Connection with the Early History of Society, and its Relation to Modern Ideas* (London: Murray, 1906)

Megarry, R., *A Second Miscellany-at-law: a Further Diversion for Lawyers and Others* (London: Stevens, 1973)

Mitchell, C. and Mitchell, P. (eds.), *Landmark Cases in the Law of Contract* (Oxford: Hart, 2008)

Mitchell, C. and Mitchell, P. (eds.) *Landmark Cases in the Law of Restitution* (Oxford: Hart, 2006)

Neyers, J., Bronaugh, R. and Pitel, S. (eds.), *Exploring Contract Law* (Oxford: Hart Publishing, 2009)

Paley, W., *The Principles of Moral and Political Philosophy* (London: printed for R. Faulder, 1785)

Palmer, G., *Mistake and Unjust Enrichment* (Columbus, OH: Ohio State University Press, 1962)

Pattenden, R., *The Judge, Discretion, and the Criminal Law* (Oxford: Clarendon Press, 1982)

Pollock, F., *Introduction and Notes to Sir Henry Maine's "Ancient Law"*, 2nd edn (London: Murray, 1925)

Pollock, F., *Principles of Contract at Law and in Equity: Being a Treatise on the General Principles Concerning the Validity of Agreements, With a Special View to the Comparison of Law and Equity, and with References to the Indian Contract*

Act, and Occasionally to Roman, American, and Continental Law, 1st edn
(London: Stevens and Sons, 1876)

Pollock, F., *Principles of Contract at Law and in Equity: Being a Treatise on the General Principles Concerning the Validity of Agreements, With a Special View to the Comparison of Law and Equity, and with References to the Indian Contract Act, and Occasionally to Roman, American, and Continental Law*, 2nd edn
(London: Stevens and Sons, 1878)

Pollock, F., *Principles of Contract: a Treatise on the General Principles Concerning the Validity of Agreements in the Law of England*, 3rd edn (London: Stevens and Sons, 1881)

Pollock, F., *Principles of Contract: a Treatise on the General Principles Concerning the Validity of Agreements in the Law of England*, 4th edn (London: Stevens and Sons, 1885)

Pollock, F., *Principles of Contract: a Treatise on the General Principles Concerning the Validity of Agreements in the Law of England*, 5th edn (London: Stevens and Sons, 1889)

Pollock, F., *Principles of Contract: a Treatise on the General Principles Concerning the Validity of Agreements in the Law of England*, 6th edn (London: Stevens and Sons, 1894)

Pollock, F., *Principles of Contract: a Treatise on the General Principles Concerning the Validity of Agreements in the Law of England*, 7th edn (London: Stevens and Sons, 1902)

Pollock, F., *Principles of Contract: a Treatise on the General Principles Concerning the Validity of Agreements in the Law of England*, 8th edn (London: Stevens and Sons, 1911)

Pollock, F., *Principles of Contract: a Treatise on the General Principles Concerning the Validity of Agreements in the Law of England*, 9th edn (London: Stevens and Sons, 1921)

Pollock, F., *Principles of Contract: a Treatise on the General Principles Concerning the Validity of Agreements in the Law of England*, 10th edn (London: Stevens and Sons, 1936)

Pothier, R.J., *A Treatise on Obligations Considered in a Moral and Legal View, Translated from the French of Pothier*, translated by F-X Martin (Newburn NC: Martin & Ogden, 1802)

Pothier, R.J., *A Treatise on the Law of Obligations, or* Contracts, translated by W.D. Evans, 2 vols. (London: printed by A. Strahan for J. Butterworth, 1806)

Pothier, R.J., *Treatise on the Contract of Sale [1817]*, translated by L.S. Cushing (Boston: C.C. Little and J. Brown, 1839)

Powell, J.J., *Essay Upon the Law of Contracts and Agreements*, 2 vols. (London: printed for J. Johnson and T. Whieldon, 1790)

Principles, Definitions and Model Rules of European Private Law: Draft Common Frame of Reference (DCFR), prepared by the Study Group on a European

Civil Code and the Research Group on EC Private Law (Acquis Group), C. von Bar *et al.* (eds.), Interim Outline Edition (Munich: Sellier, European Law Publishers, 2008)

Principles, Definitions and Model Rules of European Private Law: Draft Common Frame of Reference (DCFR), C. von Bar *et al.* (eds.), 6 vols. (Munich: Sellier, European Law Publishers, 2009)

Reports from the Select Committee of the House of Lords Appointed to Inquire into the Laws Respecting Gaming; and a Report Thereon to the House; with the Minutes of Evidence Taken before the Committee, and an Index Thereto (London: ordered to be printed 26 April, 22 July and 5 August 1844)

Restatement of the Law of Contracts, 2 vols. (St Paul, MN: American Law Institute, 1932)

Restatement (Second) of the Law of Contracts, 12 vols. (St Paul, MN: American Law Institute, 1979)

Restatement (Third) of Restitution and Unjust Enrichment, Tentative Draft No. 3 (Philadelphia, PA: American Law Institute, 2004)

Restatement (Third) of Restitution and Unjust Enrichment, Tentative Draft No. 4 (Philadelphia, PA: American Law Institute, 2005)

Rickett, C.E.F. (ed.), *Justifying Private Law Remedies* (Oxford: Hart, 2008)

Rickett, C.E.F. and Grantham, R. (eds.), *Structure and Justification in Private Law* (Oxford: Hart, 2008)

Robertson, A. (ed.), *The Law of Obligations: Connections and Boundaries* (London: University College London Press, 2004)

Robertson. A. and Tang Hang Wu (eds.), *The Goals of Private Law* (Oxford: Hart, 2009)

Rolle, H., *Un abridgement des plusieurs cases et resolutions del Common ley, alphabet-icalment digest besouth severall titles, ovesque un table des general titles contenus en ceo*, 2 vols. (London: Crooke, 1668), preface ['Lord Hale's Preface to Rolle's Abridgement'] reprinted in Francis Hargrave, *Collectanea Juridica. Consisting of tracts relative to the law and constitution of England* (London: printed for E. and R. Brooke, 1791), 263–82

Rose, F. (ed.), *Restitution and Banking Law* (Oxford: Mansfield Press, 1988)

Saidov, D. and Cunnington, R. (eds.), *Contract Damages: Domestic and International Perspectives* (Oxford: Hart Publishing, 2008)

Sharpe, R.J., *Injunctions and Specific Performance*, 2nd edn (Aurora, Ontario: Canada Law Book, 1992)

Sheridan, L.A., *Fraud in Equity: A Study in English and Irish Law* (London: Pitman & Sons, 1957)

Sidgwick, H., *Elements of Politics*, 2nd edn (London: MacMillan, 1879)

Simpson, A.W.B., *Leading Cases in the Common Law* (Oxford: Clarendon Press, 1995)

Simpson, A.W.B., *Legal Theory and Legal History* (London: Hambledon Press, 1987)

Smith, S.A., *Contract Theory* (Oxford University Press, 2004)

Spence, M., *Protecting Reliance: the Emergent Doctrine of Equitable Estoppel* (Oxford: Hart, 1999)

Spry, I.C.F., *The Principles of Equitable Remedies: Injunctions, Specific Performance and Equitable Damages*, 2nd edn (London: Sweet & Maxwell, 1980)

Stebbings, C. (ed.), *Law Reporting in Britain* (London: Hambledon Press, 1995)

Story, J., *Commentaries on Equity Jurisprudence, as Administered in England and America* (Boston, MA: Hillard, Gray & Co., 1836)

Story, J., *Commentaries on Equity Jurisprudence, as Administered in England and America*, 13th edn, 2 vols. (Boston, MA: Little, Brown, 1886)

Tamanaha, B.Z., *Beyond the Formalist-Realist Divide: the Role of Politics in Judging* (Princeton University Press, 2010)

Trebilcock, M.J., *The Common Law of Restraint of Trade: A Legal and Economic Analysis* (Toronto: Carswell, 1986)

Trebilcock, M.J., *The Limits of Freedom of Contract* (Cambridge, MA: Harvard University Press, 1993)

Treitel, G.H., *The Law of Contract*, 11th edn (London: Sweet & Maxwell, 2003)

van de Kherchove, M. and Ost, F., *Legal System Between Order and Disorder* (Oxford University Press, 1994)

Waddams, S.M., *Dimensions of Private Law: Categories and Concepts in Anglo-American Legal Reasoning*, (Cambridge University Press, 2003)

Walker, D.M., *The Law of Contracts and Related Obligations in Scotland* (London: Butterworth, 1979)

Weinrib, E., *The Idea of Private Law* (Cambridge, MA: Harvard University Press, 1995)

Whewell, W., *Lectures on the History of Moral Philosophy in England*, new edn (Cambridge: Deighton Bell, 1862)

Wright, R.A., Lord Wright of Durley, *Legal Essays and Addresses* (Cambridge University Press, 1939)

INDEX